NAKED IN
DA NANG

NAKED IN DA NANG

A FORWARD AIR CONTROLLER IN VIETNAM

MIKE JACKSON AND TARA DIXON-ENGEL
FOREWORD BY FRANK BORMAN

ZENITH
PRESS

First published in 2004 by Zenith Press, an
imprint of MBI Publishing Company, Galtier
Plaza, Suite 200, 380 Jackson Street, St. Paul, MN
55101-3885 USA

ISBN 0-7603-2076-4

Printed in the United States of America

CONTENTS

To all those who serve in the
United States military with courage and
conviction— past, present, and future.

FOREWORD

BY FRANK BORMAN

AMERICA and the world underwent a dramatic transformation between 1965 and 1973. At Christmastime 1968, the crew of Apollo 8—Jim Lovell, Bill Anders, and I—became the first humans in history to gaze on the far side of the moon. We stood in mute wonder as we witnessed the spectacle of "earthrise."

Even now, from the vantage point of more than three decades, it is difficult to fully convey the range of emotions that crowded our minds as we watched our brilliant blue planet slowly ascend between the ragged peaks and valleys of the moon. Floating there in the cold, hostile blackness of space, that planet seemed like a tiny oasis of beauty and peace. Yet we knew that all was not peaceful down among the green hills of Earth.

By December 1968, Bobby Kennedy was dead, Martin Luther King was dead, the nation was polarized, college campuses were in flames, and American boys were dying at a rate of dozens per day in a faraway place called Vietnam.

Although almost thirty years have passed since the fall of Saigon, Americans continue to fight the Vietnam War—on television, in the movies, in the political arena, and over the radio airwaves. And the brave soldiers, sailors, and airmen who put their lives on the line in Southeast Asia continue to be casualties in one form or another.

Popular culture has often painted Vietnam veterans as unstable, unreliable, and downright antisocial. Only recently have Americans begun to revisit the soldiers of Vietnam, acknowledging them not as society's castoffs but as fathers, sons, husbands, and friends.

The time has come to stop viewing Southeast Asia through a political prism, but to examine it through the passion and energy of the human experience, with all its joy, regret, fear, love, and laughter.

Colonel Mike Jackson's *Naked in Da Nang* is a rare breed among Vietnam memoirs; it emphasizes the humanity we all share, and it reminds us that, even in a war zone, humanity endures.

As one of the northernmost forward air controllers in South Vietnam, Mike "enjoyed" a front row seat to the Easter Offensive of 1972, the fall of Quang Tri, the Vietnamization of the war effort, and the general lack of clarity that seemed to define the entire conflict. Like Mike himself, the stories in this book are lively, compelling, offbeat, and frequently laugh-out-loud funny.

He does not attempt to argue that Vietnam didn't change him; he freely acknowledges that it changed an entire generation. What he does say, with alternating humor and eloquence, is that it didn't ruin him. It didn't ruin America either. It *could* have, and maybe, according to the law of averages, it *should* have. But it didn't. *Naked in Da Nang* is, as much as anything, a story of endurance and triumph. It is the story of one man's journey from small-town America to war and back again. It is a coming of age tale to which anyone born between 1945 and 1965 should be able to relate. And, as with everything else in his life, Colonel Jackson tells it from his own unique, irrepressible perspective.

PREFACE

A CHARMED LIFE

MINE is the story of a charmed life. Not a perfect one, but one that seems destined to work out, not necessarily because of my actions but often in spite of them.

When all is said and done, it boils down to a question of perspective. Some other guy might live my life and argue that it's been nothing but a series of bad breaks. He'd be wrong. When I revisit the past fifty-seven years, I see a string of events that gave my life depth and color and meaning. Nothing was easy, at least nothing that was worthwhile. Then again, I don't ever remember wishing for easy. I am much happier, much more content with "interesting." For me, hell on Earth wouldn't be strange encounters, unusual people, and unpredictable events. It would be boredom, pure and simple.

It has been my great fortune to gravitate toward people and circumstances that don't necessarily fall into the realm of "normal." There have been times when I've questioned my own sanity for deliberately seeking situations that many would find ridiculously complex or stressful. But when the dust clears, things always seem to work out for me. Call it dumb luck, kismet, or destiny, I've managed to live through a lot of weirdness and inconsistency and come out the other side with a wealth of offbeat stories and unconventional friends—and I wouldn't have it any other way.

For years I'd jotted down vignettes and memories from my typi-cally unorthodox military career, specifically the year I spent in a place called Vietnam. When I finally tried to string them all together, I had no idea what I hoped to accomplish. I'd tell people, only half joking, that I was writing a book about "funny things that happened to me in Vietnam," and they'd look at me as though I was nuts. It didn't espe-cially bother me; I tend to seize any and all opportunities to confound people. But I wrestled with whether I could actually stay focused on the writing process and had anything of value to say.

Let's face it, for years the Vietnam War has been dissected, inter-preted, and painfully revisited. But until recently no one has really gotten it right, at least not from the perspective of the average Joe who fought—and all too often died—over there. The guys who went to Vietnam were no different—no better, no worse—from those who did likewise in World War II, Korea, or the Gulf, or those who are risking their lives in the war on terror. We were as different from and as similar to any young man who ever put on his country's uniform and fought to defend an ideal, a way of life, or a patch of ground.

But I never saw that commonality, that humanity, reflected in anything filmed or written or spoken about the Vietnam era. By and large, Vietnam vets were and are portrayed as society's castoffs: flash-back-addled has-beens who weren't sane to begin with and were even less so after their tour in-country. Judging by the movies, books, and "expert" analyses, the guys who did the fighting and dying in Vietnam were drug-numbed, robotic killing machines.

I think it's easier for people who have never been in combat to believe that those who have been aren't fully formed human beings, that somehow, if you are willing to kill—or be killed—you must be hovering down there a rung too low on the evolutionary ladder. As a result, the maniacal painted warrior as portrayed by Marlon Brando in *Apocalypse Now* becomes more believable, more comforting even than Mel Gibson kneeling at bedside, praying with his children in *We Were Soldiers*. Some part of us needs to believe that only crazy people fight wars, especially wars such as Vietnam, where there are no clear objectives and no definitive divisions between "good" and "evil."

One thing I can tell you with certainty is that every war ever fought takes an emotional toll on those who served. Combat is never clean or neat or absent confusion, indecision, and unspeakable acts of cruelty. Yet it is equally true that warriors are still human beings, still fully capable of embracing fear, joy, anger, clarity, and laughter.

Somehow, people managed to find humor in the Korean conflict, thanks to the movie *M*A*S*H*. But even *M*A*S*H* made a point of perpetuating the idea that only the civilians thrust into a war zone (in this case, doctors) were capable of humanity, compassion, and laughter. By and large, those representing professional soldiers were portrayed as insane or stupid.

In reality, the military is a microcosm of humanity; there are no more and no fewer dipshits and losers than in the whole of society. If this book conveys anything, I hope it reflects my pride in having worn the uniform of the United States Air Force for twenty-three years. Make no mistake about that. Any misgivings I have (and there are plenty) about the way our government prosecuted the war in Vietnam do not diminish my pride in having served my country.

So the mission of this book is simply to confirm that human beings bring to war exactly what they bring to life—humanity, in all its many tones and hues. That humanity, in order to be genuine, must include laughter. It's what keeps us sane when nothing else makes sense.

The title *Naked in Da Nang* refers to one of many funny things that happened to me in Vietnam. On a larger level, it probably also defines the way we each arrived in-country—pretty much as infants— uncertain, helpless, and lacking the proper emotional attire for the hectic new life that greeted us. A sign at the airfield in Da Nang hailed new arrivals with "Welcome to Da Nang. You'll love it here!"

Well, I definitely *didn't* love it. But it was part of my life, part of what made me who I am today. And I'm pretty happy with that person, all things considered.

The Vietnam War itself was a political mess, a waste of promising young lives. It shouldn't have happened, at least not the way it did. But it's part of our history now, and, like all history, it will never be completely, accurately revisited. It can only be remembered and interpreted.

I was one of the lucky ones. I lived through it. And while I am still young enough to do so, I offer this record—a personal odyssey—of what Vietnam was like for me, one little guy from Tipp City, Ohio, who remembers Southeast Asia with a range of emotions, including, always, laughter.

CHAPTER ONE

THE FACS
OF LIFE

I SHIFTED my weight from cheek to cheek and tried to count the American flags jutting across the angled aisles of Veterans Hall in Columbus, Ohio. As the unofficial poster child for attention deficit disorder, I have little patience with pomp and ceremony; in fact, I have little patience for much of anything. It's a character trait that served me well in the military and above the jungles of Southeast Asia. But in the more relaxed setting of the real world, I often find myself stepping to the rhythm of a snare drum while everyone else marches to a more dignified bass beat.

Okay, Jackson, unclench your jaw, relax your neck, and chill. This shindig is partly to honor you, after all. The least you could do is try not to look like someone's giving you an enema.

I heaved an inaudible sigh and peered past the edge of the stage, where my family and friends sat listening for my name and military history. Their cameras were poised in preparation for the moment when I would leave my orange plastic chair and collect the plaque, medal, and handshake that formalized my induction into the Ohio Veterans Hall of Fame.

I shifted again. Sitting still has never been one of my strong suits, and it is complicated by the enduring pain of getting bounced on my head during a rocket attack in 1972. But today's discomfort was only partly physical; something larger gnawed at my psyche. I was not at all comfortable with the event unfolding around me. I like to think I've got a pretty firm grasp on who I am and where I fall in the grand scheme of things, and I was certainly honored to be sitting on this stage, proud to be considered one of Ohio's exemplary veterans.

But my mental hobgoblins were relentless in their quest for emotional integrity. *How the heck does a regular guy from Tipp City, Ohio, end up being honored alongside soldiers who survived the Bataan Death March and earned the Medal of Honor?* As proud as I am of my tenure as a United States Air Force officer, and my subsequent volunteer work with veterans, I wasn't certain that any aspect of my career quite compared to the sacrifices and contributions of the men who surrounded me.

Then again, it wasn't like me to step shyly away from the spotlight.

Sit back and enjoy yourself. You were nominated and selected; apparently someone has a more enlightened view of your accomplishments than you do. And this isn't exactly the time or place to debate the issue.

Twenty-three years of military service had instilled a measure of discipline in my body, but my mind raced merrily along its own peculiar path. Impatience and energy were the hallmarks of my life. Certainly they had come in handy in my previous life as a forward air controller (FAC) in Vietnam. In fact, it was one of the few vocations I could think of where attention deficit disorder not only wasn't a disadvantage, it was absolutely essential.

FACing was not a job for the faint of heart or the slow of wit or, in my case, the sound of mind. Wrapped in a sluggish, marginally militarized civilian aircraft, FACs hugged the Earth, plodding along at ridiculously low levels to direct air strikes, observe troop movements, gather intelligence, and/or choreograph search-and-rescue missions.

The FAC had to be a master of multitasking long before computers popularized the term. We were the traffic cops of Southeast Asia, telling everyone where to go, when to go, how to get there, and what to do once they were there. We were everybody's eyes and ears, everybody's link to one another.

We called the shots, literally, but even we had a higher power that scripted our movements. In any encounter with the enemy, our bible was a kaleidoscope of insanely complex Rules of Engagement, or ROEs. A contemporary version might be titled "The Idiot's Guide to Combat." It was apparent to everyone in-country that two different wars were being waged: the one we lived with twenty-four hours a day, and the one that somebody behind a desk in the capital had dreamed up after a few too many boilermakers at some Washington pub.

The ROEs were modified monthly, sometimes weekly. They reeked of political engineering, with little or no semblance of military strategy. But as FACs, we had to know them inside and out. We had no choice in the matter; we were tested on every nuance, on each fresh layer of political bullshit. *If the sun is shining on the west side of a VC weapons cache at 17 minutes past noon on the third Buddhist holiday of the calendar year, no FAC may call in an air strike on that cache, unless it is covered by green burlap and lies within 20 meters of the DMZ.*

If it wasn't always quite that bad, it came *too* close *too* often.

The ROEs tied our hands at every turn while simultaneously placing us in charge of practically everything that happened in the air or on the ground. For all intents and purposes, FACs owned the world, or at least the spit of land that hugged Laos and Cambodia on the west and spilled into the South China Sea on the east. Ours was not, however, an enviable position, for with ownership came responsibility.

On any given mission, we could be scanning the terrain for troop movements, orchestrating a search-and-rescue mission, or coordinating interaction between troops-in-contact and vital air support. A-rated FACs were fighter trained, the luck of the draw (or lack thereof) having separated us from our high and fast brethren. Because we understood fighter pilot hows and whys, we were the only guys allowed to play with firepower around American troops. We'd been schooled in air-to-ground operations, jungle survival, and ground combat procedures. When we were knee-deep in a mission, our focus ricocheted between four radios, target coordinates, fighter activity, the location of friendlies on the ground, and—oh yeah—guarding our own young asses against enemy fire, not to mention bombs or napalm dropping from the very fighters we were directing. Once the dust settled and the fighters headed home, we got to hang around and play cleanup, evaluating the extent of the damage and the success of the strike. If there was fuel left in our tanks and time left on the clock, we'd head off to the next target and do it all over again, no matter how badly our bodies longed for a hot shower, a warm meal, or a stiff drink.

For friendlies on the ground, a skilled FAC was a guardian angel with metal wings. A lousy FAC might as well have enlisted in the Army of North Vietnam; the end result was the same. We all knew the worst-case scenario. It was the stuff of nightmares, more potent, even, than those sweat-soaked dreams about our own body bags. These nightmares involved doing something stupid that got an American soldier, or a whole bunch of them, killed. We called such tragedies "short-round" incidents. The American public came to know these lethal screw-ups by the ridiculously inappropriate label "friendly fire."

No FAC could afford to be too cautious, but neither could he take hotshot risks that would place ground troops and fighters in peril. We walked a tenuous and solitary tightrope over the jungles of Southeast Asia. Our jobs as FACs, as soldiers—as Americans—always seemed strangely at odds with the ROEs and the convoluted grand plan that somebody, somewhere thought would win the war. It was the most irritating of many inconsistencies that governed my daily life from 1971 to 1972.

Suddenly aware that the induction ceremony was proceeding in my "absence," I shook off the impromptu trip down memory lane and attempted to refocus my attention on the parade of speakers. My thoughts never returned to Vietnam without uncorking a jumble of emotions and memories. I had found a lot of humor there, sometimes laughing at things that were genuinely funny, sometimes laughing because it was the only way to keep from crying. I had also found fear, stupidity, anger, and waste.

But I wasn't one to squander mental energy revisiting the past. The thought of re-fighting the war in my head smacked of both self-indulgence and self-defeat. Plus, I figured it would be as much an exercise in futility now as it had been the first time around. On the rare occasions when I permitted myself to resurrect detailed memories of Southeast Asia, it always left me feeling perplexed, disheartened, and thoroughly disgusted. Even now, perched on a stage surrounded by people, my stomach twisted into a queasy knot and my jaw grew tight and rigid. Startled by my physical response to these thoughts, I took a breath and brought my muscles back to parade rest. Too much reflection.

Someone at the podium was rattling brief biographies of each inductee into the Ohio Veterans Hall of Fame class of 1997. We sounded like quite an impressive group—loyal, trustworthy, brave, and reverent. I smiled to myself. I hope I am any or all of those things when the situation warrants it. But none of those qualities paints an accurate or complete picture of me. I suspected the same was true of everyone else on that stage. We all sat straight and stone-faced in our stiff orange chairs. Model citizens. Model soldiers. "The best Ohio has to offer," the speaker solemnly declared. I knew better. We weren't the best, or the worst, or any other fancy adjectives. We were just a bunch of guys shifting uneasily under the weight of praise. Each of us had distinctly personal combat and military experiences. Each of us had endured, survived, and moved forward with a unique blend of strengths and weaknesses. And sometimes it was hard to distinguish a strength from a weakness. They trade places from time to time, depending on the circumstances. That's what makes people interesting, and why every individual reacts differently to combat and other absurdities.

I knew that others on the stage had war stories and recollections vastly different from mine. Some of these guys had genuinely lived through hell on Earth. My 210 combat missions didn't leave me horribly scarred, either mentally or physically. Admittedly, I don't care to relive them, especially now that I have grown accustomed to the finer things in life—such as hot and cold running water, cars with leather seats and shock absorbers, sheeted beds with comfort-built mattresses, clothing that isn't being consumed by some strange jungle rot, and functional television sets (or, for that matter, television programs; there were nights in Da Nang when a rerun of *Gilligan's Island* in Burmese would have been a rare treat).

All of these thoughts crowded my mind as the color guards' heels clacked across the stage with crisp precision. The speaker traded places with the presenter, and the event shifted from a celebration of Ohio's knack for breeding warriors to the gentle rhythm of your garden-variety awards ceremony.

As the first inductee was lauded, I pondered the irony that although combat itself could drag on forever, those same battlefield encounters could be summarized in a few brief words. Was it really that simple? Could an entire year of my life—a year unique in its extremes—be summed up in less than one sentence?

Once again my mind wandered backward. Despite my best efforts to remain in the here and now, the years fell away as I stood face-to-face with that awkward all-American kid who stepped off an airliner at Cam Ranh Bay into a world unlike anything he'd ever known. I winced as my youthful apprehension flooded back. There I was—naive, still sporting pimples and peach fuzz, looking like a troubled tourist in desperate need of a refund. I recalled my mute discomfort as I watched an elderly Vietnamese woman squat down in the airport terminal and pee right in front of everyone. Culture shock didn't even begin to describe it.

Two weeks later that same green kid climbed into his twin-engine O-2, pushed up the throttles, and coolly initiated a takeoff roll that would place him directly over some of the most heavily defended turf in the history of warfare.

Cripes, Jackson, what kind of mental calisthenics did it take to turn a naive little altar boy into someone who could casually count the number of legs scattered on the ground below, divide by two, and call in a bomb damage assessment?

Every so often, almost as a passing thought, I wonder who I would have become had Vietnam not intervened. It's not something I dwell on, because I try to avoid pondering impossible questions. Still, my world was never quite as simple after a year in Southeast Asia, and the same could be said for my psyche. I'm not sure all the changes were bad, nor do I know how many were natural byproducts of maturity (though many people would argue that I managed to grow up without ever quite making the leap into maturity). It could have been an intriguing (and lengthy) personal dissection, if it didn't violate my prohibition against overanalyzing the past.

I renewed my focus on the ceremony—or tried to—but this time the past would not be denied. The induction process had flipped a switch. I gave up and handed the controls back to that awkward twenty-four-year-old lieutenant: cocky on the outside, clueless on the inside. I could smell the aviation fuel and feel the throttles in my hand as I shoved them forward and barreled down the runway and into a gray morning sky.

CHAPTER TWO

TROOPS IN CONTACT

I NUDGED my O-2 off the runway, easing back the yoke as the engines slipped out of sync and groaned the familiar *wah-wah-wah* that told me all was well, or at least normal. Eventually I'd get around to tweaking them back into sync—probably the only miracle that I could hope for under the circumstances.

Enjoy the rhythm, Scoop. It's the closest thing to pleasure you're gonna feel for a long, long time.

I grinned at my own dark humor and pointed my plane's nose toward the distant mountains. I was headed deep into my area of operations (AO), which cut from Da Nang west and up the A Shau Valley, hugging the demilitarized zone (DMZ) all the way back to the South China Sea. A lovely little piece of real estate, carpeted with dense jungle, periodic thickets of scarred and matted trees, a patchwork pattern of bomb craters, and an assortment of indigenous peoples—who were armed to the teeth and wanted to kill me.

I gently rolled my airplane to the north, peering across the empty right seat for a better view of the tangled terrain below. Then I rocked to the south and stared at the same green and brown landscape on my left. My O-2 training had taught me that low-level combat flight demanded frequent altitude changes and perpetual jinking to evade the enemy, or maybe just make him dizzy. I decided early on that dancing all over the sky just distracted me from my work; plus I figured I'd be just as likely to dance *into* enemy fire as away from it. Anyway, my speed was such that I couldn't have been moving more than a couple of feet from side to side— hardly enough to avoid any serious assault on my person. So I just held the airplane steady and maintained a series of gentle turns that let me eyeball the land below without craning my neck too far.

Among FACs, the O-2 was affectionately dubbed the Oscar Duck, Oscar Deuce, or the flying speed brake. I sometimes referred to her as the sky pig or the subsonic savior of Southeast Asia, which, depending on the day's events and my mood at the time, might be uttered with heartfelt sincerity or bitter irony. In coarser moments, she was simply known as Suck and Blow, a testament to her push-me, pull-you engine configuration.

Some of the nicknames may have seemed a bit harsh for a perfectly decent flying machine, but they reflected our hard-won knowledge that, in combat, good was not necessarily good enough. Away from a war zone, the O-2 was better known as the Cessna 337 Skymaster, a twin-boom, twin-engine little number whose designers had probably viewed her as the Nash Rambler of airplanes, something sturdy and efficient that you could pile into with the wife and kids and go for a happy little sightseeing tour. I'm pretty sure that tracers, .50-caliber anti-aircraft fire, and surface-to-air missiles were never serious considerations during the design phase.

Although the O-2 was a darned site better than its predecessor, the O-1 (which was little more than a Piper Cub on steroids), it was nothing like what it should have been. Then again, that could be said of pretty much everything in Southeast Asia.

As I guided my airplane westward, it occurred to me that the odd-looking little Cessna was a metaphor for the entire Vietnam mess, well-intentioned but missing most of the essential pieces necessary to get the job done. Not being a metaphorical kind of guy by nature, I quickly discarded the thought in favor of something more tangible.

War metaphor, hell. This airplane is just like everyone else over here. It got yanked out of civilian life and outfitted for battle, but no one really bothered to give it the right tools for the job.

The development of the OV-10 Bronco (kind of an O-2 on steroids) corrected some of those omissions by adding some armor, ejection seats, and genuine offensive capabilities. But for those of us still flying O-2s, the increasingly sophisticated enemy missiles made "low and slow" a dicey proposition.

On the plus side, flying any airplane, especially this one, was almost second nature to me these days. I had one year in a stateside FAC unit under my belt and almost a full year as an O-2 pilot in combat. The checklists and procedures had been seared into my brain. Some guys bragged that their airplane was like an extension of their body. I'm not sure I'd have gone that far, but I understood the machine and knew how to make it perform under pressure. There was much comfort in that knowledge. And with comfort came confidence. I didn't exactly look forward to my missions, but I wasn't filled with perpetual dread either. I had a job to do, and I was reasonably sure I had the skill to get it done right—and come back in one piece.

Today was no different, except that the weather was lousy as I lifted off at Da Nang. Dark, ragged clouds closed in around me, and my windscreen misted over in a matter of seconds.

What a crummy day for a war. Tell ya what, guys, let's call it on account of rain, throw a tarp over this whole stupid place, and show that on the evening news for a change.

I grinned at the idea of everyone giving up, going home, and hunkering down until clear skies prevailed. Maybe a little sunshine would take the fight out of everybody. *Yeah, right.* I knew better than that; I'd spent too many bright, beautiful days dodging enemy ground fire. Regardless of the weather, everyone over here stayed pissed off most of the time.

These days, they were more pissed off than ever. Late in the winter of 1971, our clumsy dance with the North Vietnamese changed rhythms; *they* started leading. We kept up as best we could, not certain at first how things had changed but knowing for sure that something was up. The dinks weren't just wandering south, then skittering back to their own turf. Instead they'd become like bad relatives who show up uninvited and refuse to leave. Wave after wave of men and equipment poured across the DMZ in what would eventually be known as the Easter Offensive. It was an accurate name for the invasion: They definitely managed to screw up Easter, and I, for one, was plenty offended.

It began with a buildup of supplies, followed by the disconcerting arrival of surface-to-air missiles—SAMs—big, ugly suckers that had previously dogged F-105s and F-4s over North Vietnam. All of a sudden, little guys like me got to play tag with missiles the size of telephone poles. The whole thing struck me as ludicrous, and I made my feelings known on more than one occasion. In fact, I was particularly vehement after getting sideswiped by one of them near the DMZ and almost losing my airplane, not to mention a variety of valuable (at least to me) body parts.

"This is nuts," I vented bitterly to my hooch mate, Ed O'Connor. "My airplane cost about fifty thousand dollars. These SAMs are worth something like a couple million each. If the frigging North Vietnamese will agree to mail me a check for the difference, I'll blow up my own stupid O-2, pay the government, keep the change, and make everyone happy. Charlie won't waste his precious missiles, and I won't have to spend so much time staring down my own mortality."

I never got around to proposing my fiscally enlightened warfare strategy to the enemy, although it seemed to make as much sense as anything else in this godforsaken country.

By the spring of 1972, a new supply route was weaving its way from the western corner of the DMZ into Laos and through the A Shau Valley. We called it the Green Alpine Highway, a damned lyrical name for a dirt road whose sole purpose was to funnel enough men and arms into South Vietnam to topple the government and kill or repel every American over there.

Charlie was up to something. *We* knew it. And, more important, he *knew* we knew it. But by this time, it just didn't matter anymore. The North Vietnamese Army (NVA) had long ago learned that even the world's most sophisticated weapons are no match for an endless tidal wave of men and machines. When one North Vietnamese soldier fell, two more stepped in and took his place. And unlike the climate back home in America, nobody in Hanoi was counting body bags, staging sit-ins, or tucking daisies into rifle barrels.

Today had started out reasonably quiet. It was May 15, 1972, and I'd had precious few quiet days since the NVA started its southward push on March 30. I knew that the silence was at best a momentary lull and at worst a calculated attempt to catch me with my pants down.

I leveled off around 2,500 feet above the ground and continued rolling through the shallow banks that gave me my best view. I knew the terrain of my AO the way I knew the streets of my Tipp City neighborhood. Tipp was small-town USA, and nothing ever happened or changed that didn't become common knowledge in an instant. The A Shau Valley was a long way from Ohio, but the principle was the same. Every day I leaned out over the sprawling "back fence" and soaked in the news from the night before. Charlie wasn't as talkative as our neighbors in Tipp, but he told his story in other ways, and over the months and miles I'd become an attentive listener.

I scanned the valley floor, taking in everything at once, then breaking it down piece by piece: the trees, the patches of elephant grass plastered against bare earth, the skeletal remains of trucks and airplanes from this war and the endless turf battles preceding it. My observational skills had matured over eleven months, and I no longer mistook cemetery plots for bomb craters. That, however, was an honest mistake; the Vietnamese buried their dead in raised, round barrows, which gave the landscape a strange, pockmarked look, eerily similar to the grotesque scars from a generation of bomb drops. In the air you could barely tell the difference. It occurred to me, with no small measure of irony, that on most days my objective was to see to it that bomb craters did, indeed, do double duty as gravesites.

Morning sunlight filtered through the heavy cloud bank that hugged the coastal side of the mountains. The bright rays leaked across the valley floor and puddled between shadows, emphasizing a harsh and unforgiving terrain. The A Shau was a ragged gash more than twenty-five miles long that ran north-south along the Laotian border. Its dense underbrush, towering elephant grasses, and triple canopy jungle provided ideal camouflage for the Communist troops that poured into South Vietnam from the west and north. Friendly forces had long since abandoned the valley, turning it into a free fire zone—loose translation: if it moves, shoot it; if it doesn't move, blow it up.

The A Shau was a dangerous place to be in the event of engine trouble or a severe case of "lead poisoning." Still, I liked being the first guy on the scene each morning. The air at dawn was clearer and more defined than the sweltering afternoon haze that dulled details, senses, and ambition, particularly among those of us unaccustomed to living inside a Turkish bathhouse. But clarity was not the only advantage to early morning missions: The North Vietnamese were cagey and used the cover of darkness as prime time for reinforcing manpower and weaponry, so first light often yielded a target-rich environment, thanks to the previous night's activity.

"Morning guys, it's your old buddy, Scoop," I muttered, using the nickname my pilot training buddies had bestowed on me, courtesy of long-time Washington state senator Henry "Scoop" Jackson. In the beginning, I wasn't convinced I was exactly a "Scoop," (not that I knew what one was) but the months and the miles had given the name a certain resonance and comfort. It fit now. It suited me.

I snaked my way down the valley, keeping the O-2 in lazy banks. Sometimes, when the land looked deserted and the minutes lumbered into hours, I had to remind myself that there were people down there who wanted to kill me. Most of the time, I didn't even know when I was being shot at, unless I got hit. My flight helmet and the engine hum muffled most of the noise from below, and it was only occasionally that I noticed the flash from a muzzle or the red streak of a tracer whizzing past. By and large I was blissfully ignorant and pretty content with it. I wasn't at all sure I wanted to see the one that got me, especially if I saw it too late to take corrective action. I'd enjoyed my life up till now, but I didn't relish the idea of watching it flash before my eyes in the split second preceding impact.

I flew on, half bored, trying to detect some new variation in the same old shapes and colors that hugged the earth beneath me. My UHF radio crackled to life, and for an instant I felt my heart rate jump and my gut twist. Fortunately, I had learned over the long months that any physical reactions would, temporarily at least, be overcome by events.

"Bilk Two Four, this is Covey Control. We've got a troops-in-contact situation about twenty miles west of Hue. An ARVN [Army of the Republic of Vietnam] unit is pinned down and taking heavy fire from a company of NVA regulars. They've requested close air support. Contact them at FM frequency 68.5. We've got two F-4s being diverted; you should have them on UHF 321.0 in about ten minutes."

I yanked a grease pencil from my flight suit and scribbled coordinates and frequencies on the side window of my O-2. It was an unorthodox method of preserving information; but as events spiraled into overdrive, a FAC couldn't afford to waste precious seconds scrambling for scraps of paper. By and large the window stayed put; if it didn't, I had bigger problems than tracking down missing coordinates. You never had to ask a FAC whether he'd had an eventful mission. If his windscreen looked like an elementary school chalkboard, it was a cinch that things had gotten pretty hairy up there.

"Roger, Covey Control. I'm on my way."

I made a slight course correction, heading away from the A Shau Valley, as I pulled out my maps and tried to zero in on the location. My penchant for microorganization came in handy at times like this. I had made certain that each map—there were about twenty-five of them—was carefully divided, labeled, and coded to the corresponding map the next size down. An outsider might have called me obsessive, but an outsider wouldn't have understood that flying an airplane into combat was a whole lot easier when you knew where the good guys were, where the bad guys were, and where you were.

Once I'd located the coordinates on my 1:50,000 map, I headed east-northeast, climbing steadily to avoid a wall of mountains that rose well over 5,000 feet. In a matter of seconds, the world around me disappeared, replaced by a sea of dense gray mist that shrouded the mountain peaks. It was a claustrophobic's worst nightmare—no discernible shapes or familiar terrain, no point of reference whatsoever. If you let your imagination stray too far, you could almost see the renegade peak that pierced the haze and waited for its chance to swat your airplane out of the sky and smash it against some desolate stack of rocks here at the edge of nowhere.

This kind of flying bore absolutely no resemblance to my carefully structured instrument flight instruction. I had no controllers, no navigational aids, and no instrument flight rules (IFR) clearances to keep the law of averages delicately balanced in my favor. All I had at this moment was a mission that required me to proceed from point A to point B, and a cloud barrier blocking the shortest distance between those two points.

Contrary to all previous training, not to mention my natural instinct for self-preservation, I simply pressed ahead and hoped that some other guy wasn't on the opposite side of the cloud bank making the same decision. The whole idea of facing combat every day, only to meet my maker by smashing into another O-2 or into the side of a mountain, irritated me far more than it scared me. I had enough real stuff to worry about; I refused to let a bunch of clouds unravel my judgment. Eyeing the instruments carefully, I held my airplane steady until the cloud bank loosened its grip, as it always did once the terrain began to unbuckle and level out.

Edging toward Hue city, I trimmed the plane for straight and level flight, then began looking for the spot where the Song Ho river split into three muddy little tributaries that meandered north, south, and west. According to my coordinates, the friendlies were holed up some two-and-a-half miles up the branch of the northernmost stream, with their backs pressed against a 3,200-foot mountain. I lost some altitude and flew into the river valley, waiting for the Song Ho to cut sharply to the northwest just before splitting off.

Bingo, there it is. Now follow it down a little. Yep, three of 'em, just where they're supposed to be.

A twisting snarl of tiny waterways veered in opposing directions. Satisfied that I was in the vicinity, I rolled into a circle about five miles wide, tuned my FM radio, and called for the friendlies in trouble. My call was quickly answered.

A panicked Vietnamese voice hissed a plea for air support.

"Bilk Two Four, this is Delta Two Eight. We have many NVA troops all along north bank of Rao Trana—small river off Song Ho. Much weapon fire close in. Don't know how many out there, but beaucoup."

The ARVN officer mumbled something else in a hushed voice. I couldn't tell whether he was still talking to me or was issuing troop commands without releasing his mic button. Under the best of circumstances, it was tough to decipher the thick Vietnamese dialects; the added elements of fear and urgency made me feel as though I was watching a foreign film with no subtitles.

"Roger, Delta Two Eight. Slow down a little and take it easy. I have fighters on the way, but I need to know exactly where you are and how many men you have. If you can pop smoke on my command, that'll help."

"Roger, Bilk. I have about twenty-five men, eight seriously wounded. We located, ah, on south side of river. We all on south side. Enemy troops on north side. Very many. All along north side. Need immediate air support. You ready for smoke?"

His voice cracked and wavered, and I could almost feel the dryness in his mouth and the tightening of his throat. His words were punctuated by bursts of gunfire and the sharp crack of incoming mortar rounds. The sound effects painted a vivid mental picture of soldiers pressed belly down in the elephant grass and mud, stoked on adrenaline, frantically trying to set up a defense without giving away their positions to the enemy. As much as I hated flying into the eye of the storm, the NVA could fire every SAM ever built at me and I still wouldn't trade places with those guys on the ground.

"Affirmative, Delta. Pop smoke."

Okay, Scoop, sharpen those eyes. Where is it? Where is it? Stupid jungle canopy. I'm lucky if I can see the ground let alone a little puff of nothing that may or may not make it through the leaves. Geeze. C'mon guys, where the hell are you?

I banked the sky pig and strained to catch any wisp of smoke. My peripheral vision picked up an odd series of sparkles in the darkness that spilled across a green tangle of foliage north of the river. At first glance I was reminded of the way that Fourth of July fireworks fizzle and fade in the nighttime sky. In almost the same instant, I realized that those dazzling glitters were pouring from the tip of a machine gun.

Shit.

This was one of those times when it wasn't any fun to be a FAC. Charlie had nothing to lose right now. He knew I was aware of his presence. He knew I was calling in fighters. And he knew that the only thing that would keep those fighters at bay was the absence of a FAC to direct the strike. Stop the FAC and stop the air strike.

For the moment, I could separate myself from the immediate threat, but once I rolled in to mark the target, it would be open season on the Scoop. Survival depended on never forgetting that reality but never letting it overwhelm you, either—easier said than done.

I banked the O-2 back to the south just in time to catch a puff of orange smoke filtering through the trees to the east.

"Delta Two Eight, I see smoke. What color did you pop?"

"Roger, Bilk. We pop orange, maybe twenty-five meters from river?"

"Roger, Delta Two Eight. I have orange smoke. Hold tight, guys. Help is on the way."

As if on cue, the next sequence of events began to unfold.

"Gunfighter Three Six, flight check-in."

"Two." My fighters were saying howdy on the assigned UHF radio frequency.

"Bilk Two Four, Gunfighter Three Six flight is with you at twenty-four thousand feet, feet wet [over the water, in this case the South China Sea], about fifteen miles southeast of Hue city."

"Roger, Gunfighter. Bilk Two Four's on the Da Nang three three five radial at twenty-seven miles, thirty-five hundred feet. Do you know where Firebase Bastogne is?"

"Negative, Bilk."

"Okay, then, once you get to Hue, take a heading of approximately two three zero degrees for about fifteen miles. The weather's not great, but I think we can work you through the breaks in the overcast. It's about three-quarters broken to overcast. Once you get into the area, give me a call and I'll brief you after I talk to the guys on the ground."

"Roger, Bilk. Gunfighter Three Six."

Okay, hold tight, guys. The cavalry's on its way.

"Delta Two Eight, this is Bilk Two Four. You guys holding up okay?"

The ARVN commander's voice crackled back at me, distant and weak. I wasn't sure whether it was poor radio quality or the hollow sound of hope fading.

"We okay right now. Much shooting, much mortar rounds. We alive for now, but if we to stay that way, we need air strike bad."

"Sit tight for just a couple more minutes. We'll get you all the firepower you need. It's going to be fine. Just a minute and things will look a lot better."

Maybe.

I didn't always believe it when I said it. But it was important to give them something to cling to. At this point, hope was all I could offer, but that was about to change.

I headed north again and dipped my nose a bit, angling west of where my buddy the machine gunner had been holed up. I figured the NVA guys were somewhere around 100 to 150 meters past the north riverbank. If everyone stayed on his own side of the river, we'd be fine.

Yeah, right, Jackson. If the dinks had a habit of staying put, your sorry ass would be back in "the world" pondering weighty problems like whether to order a second piece of lemon meringue pie.

"Gunfighter Three Six, Bilk Two Four's ready for your line-up."

"Bilk, Gunfighter Three Six is a flight of two Fox-4s, mission number Two Four Alpha. We each have six Mk-82 high drags, four cans of nape, and twelve hundred rounds of 20 mike-mike. We're turning to the southwest over Hue city at this time and should be almost over your position. We have about ten minutes time on target."

Another series of scrawls and numbers made their way to my windscreen. The rapid-fire thoughts kicked into high gear.

Okay, think this through, Scoop. You don't dare try to bring them in on a north–south run-in. If a bomb drops short, you push the NVA right into the friendlies. If it drops long, you kill the guys you're trying to save. ". . . and today we'd like to present Captain Jackson with a Communist Flying Cross and the enduring gratitude of the People's Republic of North Vietnam." Yikes.

As always, my tendency to think beyond the moment came in handy in these situations.

Okay, we've got twenty-five ARVN guys pinned down. We've got NVA troops dug in all along the river, creek—whatever the hell it is. And I know they've got at least one machine gun, probably a lot more than that.

A dull red tracer sliced the air to the northeast of me.

Oops, steady. That's it, Jackson. Keep your nose pointed south, away from the pretty sparkles. So, what do I know right now? Well, I know the bad guys are on the north side of the river, somewhere north of the orange smoke. If I can put in the strike right about there—I eyed a rocky outcropping that wound its way up from the river and melted into the shadows of the tree line—*then I've got a shot at taking out the guys in front and pushing the survivors back to the north and west. If I try to drop anything much farther north, I risk sending the bad guys right into the arms of my ARVN buddies. Any farther south, and there won't be any ARVN buddies to worry about.*

I clenched my jaw and exhaled sharply. I didn't enjoy playing God. Being in control was one thing, but wielding the power of life and death was altogether out of my league. No matter what action I took or didn't take, someone was going to die today; it was my job to make sure that when everything was over, all the dead guys were on the north side of the river.

I referenced the side window, where I'd scrawled the fighters' ordnance. First, I'd level the landscape with the high drags and get a clear view of who was where. Next we'd hit them with napalm, which would lay out a nice flaming buffer zone between their troops and ours. If necessary, the 20 millimeter could clean up those guys stupid enough to hang around till the bitter end.

"Roger, Gunfighter. Bilk Two Four copies all. Do you see the river coming southwest to the north of Hue?"

"Roger."

"Can you see where that river splits off into three branches?"

"Looking, Bilk. Tallyho!"

"The FAC is about three miles to the west of where the river splits."

"Tally on the FAC. Gunfighter has you in a left turn."

"Roger, Gunfighter. Bilk Two Four is in a left turn, going right, and now left again. Do you have me in sight?"

"Roger, Bilk. Gunfighter has you in sight and we are in your nine o'clock position high."

"Bilk has you in sight."

Hey! Nice work, guys. We actually found each other! This beats the hell out of futzing around for thirty minutes just trying to figure out who's where. That happened far more often than anyone cared to admit.

"Your target is enemy troops engaged in a firefight with a unit of ARVN. The northernmost river branch cuts through a small valley, where we've got good guys on the south side and NVA to the north. The target elevation is five hundred feet with low hills to the north and a thirty-two-hundred-foot hill just south of the river. Weatherwise, you're looking at four thousand feet, broken to overcast. Shouldn't be a problem if you stay north of that mountain. Judging by the ARVN smoke, you've got light winds at zero nine zero degrees."

I took a quick breath. This was where the rubber met the road. Everything I said in the next two minutes would influence the air strike's outcome, for better or worse. This was the point where perfection ceased to be an ideal and became a necessity.

"The friendlies are sitting on the south side of the river. Bad guys to the north. There's moderate gunfire with at least one heavy machine gun. The best bailout heading is zero nine zero, feet wet; closest emergency field is Hue Phu Bai, due east for about fifteen miles. The run-in is your option of east-west or west-east to parallel the friendly lines and the FEBA [forward edge of the battle area], and you'll need to pull off to the north to avoid the mountain and overflying the friendlies. We'll start with your Mk-82s in pairs, followed by the nape, and we'll clean up anything that's left with the 20 mike-mike. The FAC will hold to the south of the target at approximately thirty-five hundred feet, clear of the hill. Any questions?"

"Negative, Bilk. Looks like the sky is clear enough for us to stay above the clouds and work through the breaks."

"Roger, Gunfighter. Go ahead and set up your wheel. I'm gonna check in with the guys on the ground. Be right back with you."

The wheel was a circular pattern over the target. Fighters came into the area and took up an orbit that allowed the FAC to bring them in from random directions. This was useful if the enemy was pounding away with antiaircraft fire, because it kept him in motion, wondering who was coming from where, and when. Unfortunately, with friendlies on the ground, I had to be more orderly about bringing in the fighters.

"Okay, Delta, I'm about thirty seconds away from rolling in and firing a smoke rocket. You guys need to close ranks and get as low as you can. But keep an eye on my smoke. If it looks good, it'll be followed by 500-pound bombs, some napalm, and maybe some 20-mike-mike cleanup. You got it?"

"Yes. Got it, Bilk. We ready for smoke—smoke and big bombs."

"Gunfighter flight, the FAC's rolling in to mark the target."

I tipped my wing slightly for a final look-see at the terrain, the river, and my intended target. I didn't have to be 100 percent accurate with my smoke rocket; I just had to provide a viable point of reference. Losing altitude, I eyed the ground through my windscreen and gunsight, trying to gauge just the right angle and moment to let loose with a Willie Pete—a white phosphorus rocket. As my altimeter unwound toward 1,000 feet, the ground below me lit up, and both my FM and UHF radios jumped to life. Shouts and gunfire echoed through my headset, and I strained to decipher the words.

Shit, the friendlies have been overrun. No, wait, that's not it. What the hell are they yelling about?

The friendlies weren't in trouble. I was.

"Bilk Two Four. They really coming at you! We see many ground fire—much guns, much guns. You be careful!"

The ARVN commander knew as well as the NVA that if the FAC bought the farm, the whole air strike ended. And he knew that, without me, his unit had a life expectancy of about twenty minutes.

"Hey, FAC, you're taking some *serious* ground fire. Watch it, Bilk, they're all over you like stink on shit," came the unusually colorful report from the fighters.

Getting shot at had become something akin to breathing: It just happened, and I didn't waste much effort or energy thinking about it.

But I could count on both hands the number of times I had been hosed this badly. I was half convinced that the trees themselves had pulled out guns and started firing at me.

My peripheral vision caught a couple of tracers splitting the air on either side of me, but I felt no impact and heard no whiz of bullets. My heart pounded as though it was trying to bash its way out of my chest and head for higher ground; sweat trickled across my forehead and over my eyebrows, threatening the only real defense I had—my own visual acuity. Not that good eyesight meant anything if these guys launched a heat-seeking SA-7 my way. In that event, my ability to see what was coming would only provide an extra second or two of angst before the end. I shook my head sharply, trying to fling away the streams of sweat as well as the unpleasant thoughts. My job was to mark the target and get out of the way, and, by God, that's what I was going to do.

Ignoring the shouts into my headset and the unnerving realization that I could be enjoying the last few seconds of my life, I lost more altitude and refocused my attention on the wall of rocks that trailed away from the north riverbank.

That's it, Scoop. There's your target. Hold her steady and let it go; you don't want to have to do this twice.

I hit the button that sent a Willie Pete screaming from under my wing. I yanked the plane up and to the left, remembering the old fighter maxim "never watch your rocket hit, or your plane will hit right after it."

Come on, baby, where ya gonna hit? Make it good. YES! Who says I'm not great under pressure?

Smoke billowed up from just north of the river, and I twisted the O-2 back toward the south as I pressed the radio button.

"Delta Two Eight, this is Bilk Two Four. Do you have my smoke?"

"Roger, Bilk. The smoke is good!" For the first time today, there was a hint of animation in the weary Vietnamese voice.

"Gunfighter Three Six, do you have the smoke in sight?"

"Affirmative, Bilk."

Behind me the ground continued to glitter, and my throat tightened anew with the knowledge that Charlie was throwing everything he had at me in a last-ditch effort to knock me out of the sky. Heading away from the onslaught was almost worse than flying into it; nothing moved fast enough now. I had to physically restrain myself from jamming my feet against the rudder pedals. I was like a little kid who figures if he leans forward and pushes on the dashboard, the car will move faster. It was tough to keep from surrendering to a total mental and physical meltdown. But I wouldn't do it. I couldn't; too many people were counting on me. I shook off the creeping panic and continued my rapid-fire direction.

"Okay, Gunfighter, turn in from the east and hit my smoke. Be advised, I'm still seeing heavy ground fire north of the river and about fifty meters on either side of the smoke. I'll be holding south of the river." *Like maybe over Borneo.*

The first Phantom peeled out of the wheel and dipped across the sky. I watched his roll-in and dive until I was satisfied that he was lined up on the target. I signaled my approval with "Okay, lead, you're cleared hot." He dumped his Mk-82s slightly north of my smoke. *Close enough, Gunfighter. I'd rather see the first one fall too far afield. Gives me the chance to ease 'em in closer without scaring the shit out of the friendlies, or blowing them to hell and gone.*

The bomb tore into the jungle dirt and sent a spray of debris and white smoke shooting into the air a couple of hundred feet.

"Delta Two Eight, Bilk Two Four. How did that look?"

They were coughing but very much alive, and elated. "Everything fine! You do it again, okay?"

"Roger that, Delta."

I switched back to UHF and turned my attention to the orbiting F-4s.

"Good hit, lead. Gunfighter Two, you see the distance from his hit to the river? Call it forty meters. I need you to put two more high drags about ten meters south and twenty meters west of lead's. Continue."

"Two's in. FAC's in sight!"

It was another good, clean run and I chimed my approval with "Two, you're cleared hot!"

Again the bizarre ballet of destruction unfolded as I rolled my O-2 around in gentle circles. My eyes darted back and forth in 30-degree increments, looking for fleeing hostiles, definable damage, or further attempts to blast my ass to another time zone.

In the brief seconds between clearing Gunfighter 2 and directing lead again, I stifled a nervous laugh as I pondered just how the average guy would react to being told, "I want you to fly an unarmed civilian airplane with no ejection seats and next to no defensive or offensive capability over some of the most well-armed turf in the history of warfare. Oh, yeah, and I want you to fly it really, really low—and really, really slow. As a matter of fact, while you're up there, why don't you just fly in circles over the same spot and see what happens."

Yeah, I can almost hear the laughter. "Sure, buddy, no problem. I'll try it once—just hand me my $10 million up front and I'm good to go." Right, and here I am doing it daily, for powdered eggs and minimum wage.

My perverse humor was interrupted by the FM radio.

"Bilk, we are good. Another good hit. You do it again! We see them running. You do again!" I could hear background noise now—other voices, movement. It was apparent that the immediate threat had been remedied.

"I understand, Delta. I'll bring in lead a little farther north. You guys stay south of the river. *Do not* cross the river!"

"Yes, yes, Bilk. We do that. Thank you, thank you. You number one!"

Don't thank me yet. Until the bad guys are dead or hoofing it back to Hanoi, there's always the potential for disaster.

In fact, it was at this point that I usually felt my chest tighten and my ass clench. If the bomb hits were good and the friendlies were happy, my mind inevitably darted ahead to all the potential flies in the ointment. It wasn't a process I enjoyed, but at least I was mentally prepared in case the bottom dropped out, which inevitably happened just about the time I decided to relax.

"Gunfighter lead, this time you need to move it about twenty meters north of Two's last bomb. Continue."

"Gunfighter lead's in. FAC's in sight."

I watched his path and cleared him hot as I uncapped my water bottle and took a much-needed swig. The water was tepid and tasted slightly off, but almost everything did after festering in the jungle heat. It quenched my thirst and loosened my dry throat; that was good enough. I longed to dump the whole bottle over my head and drench myself with something moist that hadn't seeped from my own pores. But in the throes of a combat situation, water was a precious commodity. If I got shot down and had to escape and evade (E&E), that water would become my lifeline, a source of energy and renewal. I remembered with sudden longing the cool, chlorinated swimming pools of my youth. It was a bittersweet recollection as I realized that childhood would probably never be further from my grasp than it was at this moment.

Memory lane would have to wait. The here and now beckoned urgently.

"Good hit, lead. Two, you need to move yours about twenty meters to the west of lead's."

"Two's in. FAC's in sight."

Whoa, cowboy. At what point did I say, "Waste the good guys?"

Gunfighter 2's trajectory was unsettling at best, downright sloppy at worse. He was barreling in on a southerly heading that was dangerously close to the river and to the good guys he was supposed to be saving.

"Two, discontinue. I repeat, discontinue! We need another pass, and this time let's keep it as far north as lead's and twenty meters to the west."

"Roger, Bilk—discontinue."

His voice sounded terse and annoyed, and it ticked me off.

Okay, pal. We can rush through this and knock off a few of the good guys if it saves your pride. I'm sure they'll understand that you're just too much of a hotshot to acknowledge a bad pass. Geeze, lighten up.

Gunfighter 2 licked his wounded pride and jumped back on the wheel while I sent lead a little farther north to unload his remaining bombs on the fleeing bad guys.

As Gunfighter 2 came back around, I watched and waited, holding my breath until his path collided with my expectations.

"Okay, Two, you're cleared hot."

Easy, easy. I don't want to have to do this again any more than you do. Perfect! Maybe you'll upgrade to lead after all.

The high drags found their mark and ignited a series of secondary blasts, probably a weapons cache. I ordered the fighters to hold their orbit as the various parts and pieces cooked off in an explosive trail southward.

Widening my circles, I lost about 500 feet of altitude to get a better view of the damage. It was a nasty tangle of dirt, debris, and body parts. Once the air strike was over, I'd get to count up the body parts and try to estimate the number of people they once belonged to.

"Okay, Gunfighter lead. You should be Winchester on bombs. Now let's lay some nape on them and see if we can burn out the stragglers."

It was a good run, and I watched mesmerized as the napalm swept over the landscape like liquid fire. There was an odd beauty to the fluid precision of a nape drop, though I knew that anyone still alive on the ground would experience a living hell as the jellied flame attached itself to clothing, skin, and hair, consuming everything in a matter of seconds.

I shook off the brief, unsettling empathy. It was all over by now anyway. Back to work.

"Good hits, lead."

A couple more passes with the remaining ordnance and the 20 millimeter served to wrap up the assault and scare away anyone still hoping to hang tight and reassemble.

The ARVN troops were ecstatic, yelling and whistling into the radio, offering repeated and fervent thank-yous, "number one," and "merci." I grinned, genuinely pleased that I had been able to make a difference. On balance, I found that I routinely saved more lives than I took. Somehow that made the whole mess seem a bit more palatable.

As the Phantoms headed eastward and the ARVN unit spread out to evacuate the wounded and secure their position, I banked my O-2 back to the north for a quick bomb damage assessment (BDA), peering through plumes of smoke and dust at the devastation below me. From my vantage point I could see bomb craters, scorched boxes, weapons, and what appeared to be twisted bicycle wheels perched beside the blackened shells of trees and men, still smoldering on the charred ground. I quickly counted legs, arms, and torsos as best I could, and radioed the BDA results to my fighter cohorts.

"Gunfighter Three Six, Bilk Two Four. Here's the BDA on your mission: twenty-five dead, two automatic rifles, twenty rifles, three secondary explosions, and two sustained fires. Eight minutes time on target, 100 percent of ordnance on target, 100 percent of target covered, no duds."

"Roger that, Bilk. Nice work back there. You slow guys draw a lot of ground fire. The beer's on us when you get back."

Yeah, right. I'll take mine right now, guys.

OTHER VOICES: Colonel Arthur C. Evans, USAF (Ret.)

FACs had different agendas in I Corps. For some, the objective was to survive. Those individuals tended to fly their AO at 5,000 feet, where small arms, Strelas and AA had a much harder time tagging you. One FAC had a reputation of flying his missions out over the South China Sea. There weren't any seagoing Charlies. I must say that NONE of the young BILK FACs with whom I had the privilege of flying at Hue Phu Bai and Da Nang were of this ilk. They were all dedicated, professional and skilled. They knew their AOs like the backs of their hands.

You could always tell which FACs were "pushing it" by looking at the windscreens of their aircraft after they landed. There are no flying bugs at 5,000 feet; therefore, the windshield of a "high flyer" always came back clean. Guys who were down in the weeds had bug juice all over the windscreen. A busy 4.5 hours always resulted in grease pencil hieroglyphs all over the inside of the windscreen and smashed bugs all over the outside—making all returns to home base a partial IFR experience. Mike probably does not recall this and may not even know it, but his crew chief called me out to the flight line one day just after Mike RTB'd [returned to base] and was debriefing intelligence. The chief, grinning, pointed to the left wing strut where a small tree branch, complete with leaves, had been snagged. I think Mike may have been the only FAC who knew the Charlies in his AO by their faces!

When the daily fragmentary order came out declaring large areas of our AO as "no-fly" zones, it also included the daily comment "except FACs." We and our 7th Cav partners (the chopper pilots of the 2/17 and the 3/5) lived where most feared to tread. Call it stubborn. Call it unwise. Call it what you will. Mike did his job with a vengeance. He did it all-out. He held nothing back. He had a powerful sense of duty and burning desire to be the best at what he did. He flew once, twice or even three times a day—every day, and his windscreen was ALWAYS dirty!

My body was drenched with perspiration and my hand shook slightly as I shoved the throttles forward, seeking the comfort of altitude.

This would be a great time to call it a day. I suppressed a yawn as I eyed my fuel gauges. *No such luck, Scoop, you've got at least two and a half hours of fuel left. Gee, I wonder if there's anything going on out over the ocean?* I grinned. *Nah, that's not why they pay you the big bucks, Bilk. Get your ass back to the A Shau Valley and see what Charlie's been doing.*

I shook off the post-adrenaline gut cramps—a chore that grew increasingly difficult with the passage of time—and resumed my low and slow pursuit of the bad guys. My eyes were still alert, nerves still spring-loaded, but my stomach rumbled uneasily and my mouth watered for one of those good old American hamburgers that sizzled and steamed somewhere back in the world.

Damn Communists.

CHAPTER THREE

A COCOON CALLED TIPP

THERE was a time when Vietnam didn't define my life. I think I was probably about three. That may be a slight exaggeration, but not by much. I do remember listening to a Brenda Lee song when I was thirteen years old and being absolutely certain she was singing about Vietnam. I later learned from personal experience that there wasn't much to sing about; years after that, I discovered that Brenda was actually singing the words "being in love" with a southern twang. Go figure. But it proves, at least, that Vietnam was on my radar screen even in my early teens.

Still and all, Vietnam didn't consume my life. Not in the beginning, anyway. That would come later. I spent my childhood safely swaddled in a sturdy cocoon called Tipp City, Ohio. Not that being in a cocoon was a bad thing. In fact it was great—something most kids today don't have, something they need.

I guess it was the kind of life—secure, cozy, and friendly—that survives only in reruns of old TV shows. Equal parts *Leave It to Beaver* and Norman Rockwell. Everyone knew everyone else, and there was comfort and symmetry in that kind of world. I was a fifth-generation Tipp Citian. My grandfather had been the town's first mailman; I had first cousins and second cousins and aunts and uncles and "twice removeds" and "related by marriages" sprinkled throughout the Tipp population. I could claim at least a passing knowledge of almost all occupants or their kin in the old community cemetery on the edge of town. Jacksons had lived in Tipp City practically since the town was founded. Our history was Tipp's history, and knowing that gave me a strong sense of connection and roots.

I suppose there were kids who left towns like mine and grew pretty disillusioned and bitter with the realities of the world. For me it was just the opposite. Tipp City planted something in me that made me feel comfortable and safe, even when I wasn't. Growing up in Tipp gave me an abiding sense that I belonged, even when I didn't.

When you're getting shot at every day, you find yourself returning to childhood memories, to the things that comfort you and give you the incentive to hang on. My buddies and I dreamed of getting out of Vietnam and returning to "the world." For me, the world was everything I'd left behind—my parents, my siblings, my wife, and my friends.

Even in Southeast Asia, planted squarely in the middle of a war zone, I managed to stay afloat in my little Tipp City life raft. The 366 days I spent in-country should have been nothing short of hell on Earth, but they weren't. Don't get me wrong; I didn't want to be there, but I wouldn't have bailed out early if given the chance. And, in fact, such an opportunity presented itself the day I stepped out of my hooch and was thrown twenty-five feet (onto my head, fortunately; it's one of my most thickly reinforced parts) by the force of a rocket explosion that trashed the building next door.

The impact dislocated my jaw, banged up my shoulder, and left me with bone and tissue damage that never fully healed. I knew at the time I was hurt, though I underestimated the extent of the damage. But I could have played the incident for all it was worth. I could have said, "I'm injured. Send me home." Manipulating the system to my advantage was and is one of my favorite parlor games, but not where duty and obligation are concerned. Stepping out of the line of fire so someone else could fill my shoes was, to me, a move that invited—and richly deserved—some measure of divine retribution. So, following a discreet visit to the base dentist, who manhandled my jaw and pronounced me fit, I rested for a day or two, then resumed my FAC duties.

I suppose I knew that doing so might cost me my life; I was certainly aware that death was all around me. In Vietnam, everyone showed up and left at different times, on different airplanes, and with a different group of people. One day a guy would be there; the next day he was gone. You'd figure he just went home—until you saw someone going through his stuff. Then you'd feel a little knot in your gut, and you'd know it was for keeps. But I managed to avoid dwelling on it. Maybe that was how I held on and stayed sane. In my little world, then as now, everything always works out. I guess it's the Tipp City in me.

Back in 1962 my best friend was Joe Catey—lean, quick with a joke, and always in search of fun, mischief, or, if at all possible, both. These days Joe's a little less lean than he once was, but everything else still applies, including the "best pal" status. Back then, we managed to fill our days by cruising the town (going end to end took about three minutes), pondering the mysteries of women (well, girls), and hanging out at the Eickhoff's, our favorite home away from home. Joe and I bent all the rules together in high school. Never really broke any major ones, but pretty much bent the heck out of everything else. It's a habit I've carried with me throughout my life.

OTHER VOICES: Joe Catey

Jackson always had a talent for weaseling. There was never any real malice connected with it, just a certain perverse pleasure he derived from attempting to bend rules and situations to his advantage. Together we managed to charm or blunder our way through high school and a variety of subsequent misadventures. We maintained reasonable grade point averages, made friends with anyone and everyone, and gained just enough teacher trust to be assigned duties that often gave us the run of the school. In fact, we occasionally dodged class and snuck off campus for ice cream sodas and radar range hotdogs, all with the tacit approval of the teaching staff who somehow believed we were tending to school business. Dunno where they got that idea! But, like I say, there was never any intentional meanness about Jackson, just a quirky tendency to defy authority while simultaneously obeying it. In the end, it's probably why he did so well in the Air Force. I like to think I was there at the beginning to help him nurture his God-given talent!

We tried to never weasel into anything that couldn't be weaseled out of with a heartfelt apology or a look of sincere remorse. I simply had no interest in disappointing or defying my parents, despite the fact that such things became fashionable during the 1960s. I don't ever recall having a major blowout with my folks. I'm not sure we ever had a serious conversation, but we got along just fine.

Then again, nasty confrontations with my parents didn't conform to my belief that the world should be as consistent and mess-free as possible. Even as a little kid, I liked order; it's something my mom instilled in me, something that gives me structure and sanity even today. I guess back then I saw the world as a very orderly place, where good is rewarded and bad is punished. That conviction took quite a beating as life unfolded around me, but it's probably one of the reasons I ended up in the Air Force, where there was more than enough order to suit me.

Because of my father's civil service job, I grew up around the military, always aware that Dad had fought in World War II. His military service had left him with a profound antipathy toward flying and toward airplanes of any kind. It wasn't something we ever chatted about; in fact, I don't think I ever connected the two until his civil service job required him to fly to Panama in the late 1950s. Then we heard the whole story for the first time.

Dad left high school in early 1943 and wound up in the Army Air Corps. His first mission was as the left waist gunner in one of the

B-24s that hit the oil refineries in Ploesti, Romania. Talk about a trial by fire; that mission alone would have given him enough war stories for a lifetime. But Ploesti wasn't the half of it. On Dad's eleventh mission, he was wounded and ended up in the hospital. Two missions later, he was treated to an unsettling dose of déjà vu when his airplane took heavy flak damage and was forced to fall back from its formation. The B-24 limped along, taking a relentless pounding from German ME-109s and FU-190s. Twenty-two shards of shrapnel found their way into Dad's right arm and wrist. He was a mess and his airplane was even more so, having lost two of its four engines. B-24s don't fly so well at half power.

Communications had been knocked out between the front and back of the plane. Heavy bombers weren't designed to allow you to march into the cockpit and ask "what's up?" So no one knew what was going on or just how bad the damage was. The bombardier patched up Dad as best he could using a tourniquet and an antibacterial drug called sulfa. The guys in back with him were convinced that everyone else had bailed out, so they asked Dad if he could manage to pull the ripcord on his parachute. Well, what was he going to say? It beat the alternative. So they strapped him into a parachute, slapped the ripcord in his good hand, and threw him out of the plane. As he went out the hatch, he slammed his head against the door—so suddenly he was not only shot up but nursing a head wound to boot. His crewmates held their collective breath, waiting for the chute to pop and hoping that Dad hadn't been knocked out cold. But he was still conscious and managed to yank the ripcord in time to land safely.

The remaining guys in back bailed out too. They were all picked up by the Yugoslav underground, Marshal Tito's guys, who were half convinced they'd rounded up a bunch of spies. Dad and his two crewmates had no idea where the B-24 had gone, and their Yugoslav hosts had some difficulty swallowing the story of an abandoned plane that couldn't be found. For a brief time Dad faced the very real possibility of surviving a bailout over enemy territory, only to meet his fate at the hands of a Yugoslav firing squad.

In reality, the remaining B-24 crew members had never left the aircraft. They figured the crew in back was too seriously injured to bail out, so they crash-landed the plane and were promptly taken prisoner by the Germans. I guess the Yugoslavian partisans finally accepted the truth, because they spent the next thirty days helping Dad and his crewmates evade capture.

It was like something Hollywood might have dreamed up, except that Dad would have gladly surrendered his starring role to any willing matinee idol. Traveling by night and hiding in haystacks during the day, the Yugoslavs and their American charges finally reached a clandestine airstrip. The partisans ignited runway torches and signaled for a C-47 to sneak in under cover of darkness and rescue my father and his crewmates.

The whole experience left Dad pretty shaken up. He was no longer emotionally prepared to climb back into a B-24 and repeat the whole episode. He told his superior officers just that, adding that they could court-martial him or cut to the chase and throw him in front of a firing squad, but Ed Jackson's days as a gunner were over. Period.

I think his superiors must have looked at his record and his injuries and figured that he'd paid his dues. But Dad wasn't so sure. Even after he returned to the States, he was convinced that a court-martial was inevitable. He and Mom were living in a converted chicken coop at a training base in Kansas when Dad's training work required that he make a flight. He couldn't do it. He just froze up, and decided the whole thing was more than he could face. Dad insisted that the pilot land the plane, after which he refused to go up again. A few days later he got word that he should report to the base headquarters building wearing his class A uniform. He told Mom, "I'll see you whenever; they're going to court-martial me and I'll probably end up in jail."

Well, they didn't court-martial him; in fact, when he arrived at headquarters, he was awarded the Distinguished Flying Cross. Mom didn't get to see it because she was at home waiting to hear what jail they'd tossed him in.

Eventually Dad did fly again, but it took a very long time and, to this day, he's not wild about it. When I made up my mind to become a pilot, he didn't try to talk me out of it. I think he probably had his misgivings, but I also know he was proud of my decision.

We were and are a military family. All but one of my brothers served in the Air Force. Duty and honor weren't just words; they really meant something to us. We grew up believing that military service is part of your obligation in exchange for the freedoms we enjoy as Americans. I've never viewed the draft as a bad thing, even when it was tightening its grip on my young tail. In a way it was the great equalizer; almost anyone could end up in the military. The high school kid next door might show up one day wearing a uniform because he'd either been drafted or had enlisted.

I suppose that sounds unthinkable to today's kids, who expect to have their lives mapped out by the time they're high school sophomores, but the draft was a good thing because it pulled from a cross section of society. It's easy to criticize the military when you haven't worn a uniform or known someone who has or does. Once you start to understand the hows and whys of military service, you gain a better appreciation of your rights and responsibilities as an American.

When I was a young kid, military families were everywhere. That's not true today, and it really wasn't true when I joined the Air Force. I was definitely out of step with the times, and maybe I wasn't the brightest guy in the world for joining, because the idea back then (and almost always) was to avoid planting yourself in the line of fire. But I just couldn't think in terms of weaseling out of the service. Naturally, in keeping with my personality, I wasn't above trying to manipulate the system to my advantage. But the fact is, if I'd wanted to stay out of Vietnam, I had plenty of opportunities to do so.

In the beginning, though, I couldn't imagine that we'd still be there by the time it was my turn to go. I mean, wars last—at the most—four years, right?

So when I was in high school I figured, "Hey, it's gotta be over by the time I graduate." *Well, wrong.* But for certain I knew that it would be over before I finished four years at Ohio University. *Well, no, not quite.* So then I joined the Air Force and headed for Officer Training School (OTS), which took three months. *Nope, still not over.* But after a year of pilot training, I figured, "It's definitely gonna be over by then!" *Wasn't over then.* Next I headed for my first assignment with a stateside

FAC squadron, where I thought, naturally (I guess it had gotten to be force of habit by then), "It's gotta be over soon!" *Wrong again.*

Finally, after all that, I was handed a choice to go to Vietnam or take an assignment in Korea. It didn't require a great deal of thought or soul-searching. There was a war going on, and I'd spent the last two years training for it. It seemed silly, if not downright disingenuous, to go any-where other than where I was most needed. So I stepped up to the plate and said, "Send me to Vietnam." And the Air Force eventually complied.

But I *did* have choices and I *could have* chosen differently. Draft deferments forestalled the inevitable, sometimes indefinitely. As a college student, I had been deferred from service for four years. Armed with a teaching certificate, I could have taken another deferment, possibly permanently, or at least until the war was over.

It was 1968, the year of the Tet Offensive, the year America was coming apart at the seams. And there I was, weighing my options—except that I already knew what I wanted. On the surface I had it made; I'd been offered a teaching position in my hometown. I was heading back to the safety and security of Tippecanoe High School. Teaching had become a popular profession during the Vietnam era; so had getting married and having kids, because they each came with a nice, juicy draft deferment attached.

If I'd just kept my mouth shut and taught school, I probably would have been deferred forever. But my restless side reared its ugly head and started asking a lot of questions about where I'd be and *who* I'd be twenty years down the road. Although I loved growing up in Tipp, I couldn't quite face the idea of heading straight back there and waking up several decades later wondering what I'd missed in life, the places I might have seen, the things I might have done. It didn't take a lengthy internal struggle; teaching lost and the Air Force won. But at this point, things started to get complicated. My heart belonged to the Air Force, but I soon found out that the Army wanted the rest of my body.

I could have kept quiet once I turned down the teaching position. Nobody would have been the wiser, and it would have bought me the time I needed to get into the Air Force. But, believing in the rules, I went straight to the draft board the same day I rejected the teaching position—the *same* day, because that's what you're *supposed* to do. I told the draft board officials that I had decided not to teach and that I'd taken the Air Force Officer Qualifying Test.

"I'm going to be an Air Force pilot," I proudly announced, only I wasn't clear yet on where, when, or how.

The guy at the Miami County draft board seemed seriously unimpressed with my declaration.

"Have you been given a date when you go in?"

"No."

"Have you been sworn into the Air Force delayed enlistment program?"

"No."

"Well, guess what, Jackson? Your draft status is now 1-A—top of the heap—and since you've had a four-year deferment for college, you're at the *tiptop* of the pile and you're gonna be drafted just as soon as we can get you lined up."

I was stunned. This was not the accommodating response I'd expected. Convinced that they simply misunderstood the gravity of the situation, I proceeded to explain that, as an Air Force pilot, the military would get me for a minimum of six years, "but if you draft me into the Army, you've got me for only two years."

Apparently, my tenure in uniform was of no consequence to anyone on the draft board. They remained unmoved, so I pulled out my ace in the hole.

"I'm a college graduate," I argued. "Doesn't it make more sense for me to enlist in the Air Force as an officer *(and do great and wonderful officer stuff)* versus tromping through the mud as an Army grunt?" Of course I was painfully aware that someone had to do the tromping, but no one was especially wild about doing it, and if I had four years of education and could do something different, why not let me? It sure made sense to me.

Unfortunately, it made little sense to the draft board.

"Nope. You've been deferred for four years. Unless you are magically accepted into the Air Force and sworn into the delayed enlistment program in a matter of days, you're gonna get drafted and it's gonna be soon."

The gauntlet had been laid down. I had clearly been told "you can't," which initiated a chain of events and a struggle of wills that I did not intend to lose. Thus began the story of how I ended up in the Air Force, or, more accurately, how I *didn't* end up in the Army.

I have a quirk of character that imposes all kinds of rules and restrictions on myself—but resists vigorously if someone else tries to do so. When the draft board official declared, "This is what's going to happen and there's nothing you can do about it," he ignited my competitive spirit, and I was off and running. It was Jackson versus the draft board. I might suffer a bitter defeat, but not before exhausting every possibility.

At this point, I was fed up with waiting for the system to work for me, since it now seemed hell-bent on working against me. Taking matters into my capable, though decidedly naive, hands looked like my only option, although just how I would do this remained a mystery. But even at such a young age, I had already developed a personality trait that would serve me well in life: I simply refused to give up. If I wanted something, I would go under, over, or through any obstacle to get it. I wanted to be in the Air Force. Somehow, some way, I was going to make it happen.

In the meantime, I got the notice to go for my draft physical. It was not a pleasant experience. I had the uneasy feeling that we were being herded through a cattle yard and dressed for slaughter, which, in retrospect, was probably an accurate analogy.

I did manage to pass the physical, which wasn't necessarily a plus, because they informed me that my Army career was looming closer than ever—the next month or so. By now I had started to panic in earnest. I knew I wanted to be a pilot. I suppose I also knew that the body counts in the Army and Marine Corps were pretty high at that time. Admittedly, there was probably some measure of self-preservation at work, but I honestly didn't see it that way. I didn't object to being in harm's way; I just thought I'd be more efficient if I was in harm's way on my own terms—in an airplane.

I built up the courage to find out my status from the draft board. The news wasn't good. They guessed that within the month I'd be singing "You're in the Army Now." I'd already made up my mind that it was a song I didn't intend to learn, but my options were limited.

Deep in the throes of misery and desperation, I became suddenly aware that the secretary at the draft board was my age and quite attractive. It occurred to me that asking her out was a sensible thing to do: If she didn't have any answers to my draft dilemma, at least she'd be pleasant company until my name came up and the world crashed down around my ears. As I walked out of the draft board office and down the steps, a very distinct inner voice said, "Oh, what the heck, what have you got to lose?" I couldn't come up with any argument to the contrary, so I turned around and headed back inside.

She was pretty and attentive and, most important, she was interested. We talked for a while and she agreed to go out with me. We had a good time together, and I knew I wanted to see her again. I should point out that microcomputers hadn't been invented yet; everyone's files were kept in plain old manila folders. I should also point out that I was pretty quick to tell her all about my conflict between the Army and the Air Force. Well, being a patriotic American, she felt compelled to store my draft folder safely at her home. I honestly never asked her to do it, but it sure was comforting to know it was there—and of course it offered plenty of incentive for me to show up for our next date.

I suppose there are people who would tell me I cheated the system. Maybe I'm kidding myself, but I didn't see it that way then, and I still don't. It wasn't as though I was trying to avoid military service, or even combat. I think by this time I figured I'd end up in Vietnam one way or the other. But I *wanted* to be a pilot and I *wanted* to sign up for six years versus two and I *wanted* to be in the Air Force. It just made sense to me. I couldn't imagine why my joining the Air Force versus the Army would have any long-term impact on the course of the war or the future of the military.

By August 1968, Uncle Sam had finally begun to see my logic. I'd met all the qualifications for Air Force undergraduate pilot training (UPT) and was promptly sworn into the delayed enlistment program. At last, I was in the Air Force, and I could stop holding my breath. Shortly thereafter, my draft file mysteriously made its way back to the draft board office in Troy, Ohio. The pretty draft board secretary and I eventually went our separate ways, but I remained forever grateful to her for taking pity on the eager kid from Tipp City who just wanted to fly airplanes. Like most events in my life, I didn't have any grand design in mind—I simply wasn't that devious. I just knew what I wanted and was determined to exhaust all possibilities before giving up.

I never heard much more about the traveling draft file until one day a few months later when I was wandering down the street in town and ran into a friend of my dad's named Hack Yetter, who just happened to sit on the draft board. As we exchanged pleasantries, he cocked his head and eyed me curiously.

"Y'know, it's the strangest thing. We managed to miss you. You were due to be drafted a couple months ago and somehow you got overlooked. I'm not sure how that happened."

I knitted my eyebrows and shrugged. I was never sure whether he knew more than he let on, but I didn't care. I was in the Air Force!

CHAPTER FOUR

AN OFFICER AND A GENTLEMAN?

LEAVING home for Officer Training School (OTS) turned out to be an emotional minefield that I was unprepared to navigate. For four years I'd made the 150-mile jaunt to Ohio University every September—no tears, no fears, no fuss. Although San Antonio was a considerably longer journey, I reasoned that it would be just one more "see ya in a few months."

But as the days slipped away and the hour for my departure grew close, it became apparent that this good-bye would be altogether different from my college farewells. My family grew increasingly quiet and pensive in the week preceding my OTS junket. An awkward uneasiness settled over the house, as though everyone knew that something was being lost and might never be regained. In large measure we were each confronting the specter of Vietnam, combined with the emotional uncoupling that has to occur before a family can send off one of its own to face an uncertain future.

On the evening of November 6, 1968, I called my girlfriend, Karen, at Ohio University to say my first round of good-byes. It wasn't easy, but I was beginning to understand that the greatest challenge wasn't leaving—I'd done that before; the real hurdle was watching the family dynamic shift, knowing that one phase of life was ending and another was beginning.

The morning of November 7 found me awake and packed by 5 AM. Even if I'd had the luxury of a few more hours of sleep, I couldn't have enjoyed them. Instead I paced and I sat and I fiddled with the ties on my travel bag, awkwardly awaiting the moment when Dad would shuttle me to meet my recruiter in the parking lot of the Royal Castle Restaurant, just a few blocks from home. From there, the recruiter would drive me to the Military Entrance Processing Station in Cincinnati, after which I'd board a plane bound for OTS training at Lackland Air Force Base (AFB) in San Antonio, Texas.

In the first light of that chilly November morning, nothing I could imagine about the days ahead was as daunting as saying good-bye to my family. Looking into the eyes of my mother, my sister, and my brothers, I saw the reflection of every fear, hope, and regret that no one knew quite how to express, least of all me. We hugged. We murmured words of support and encouragement. Our voices caught slightly and cracked at the wrong times, but we pretended not to notice.

I headed out into the morning chill, tossed my bag into the backseat, and climbed up front with Dad before stealing a last, lingering gaze at the house. Bad move. I felt an uncomfortable stinging sensation in the corner of my eyes as I stared at the front window, where my mother and sister were holding each other—and crying. I rarely saw my mother cry, and watching her do so now gave me a sense of helplessness and longing that I have never forgotten. A sharp breath caught in my throat, and my heart twisted painfully. Clenching my jaw, I fought to steady my breathing and clear my head. Dad stared straight ahead and drove in silence as we moved slowly down the block. Our house was a tiny oasis of light on a dark, quiet street, and I wondered miserably how it would feel to be in one of those other houses, sleeping comfortably and waiting for a new day to begin that would be identical to the day before and to all those that would follow.

As we waited in the restaurant parking lot, Dad struggled to fill the awkward emptiness by offering advice on how he had survived basic training. I wondered whether he was reliving his own wartime enlistment, some thirty years prior, and thinking about the combat that lay just beyond the training. But we kept the conversation light and clipped, neither of us willing to revisit the emotions that had tackled us back at the house.

When the recruiter showed up, I transferred my bags, then said good-bye to Dad and extended my hand in his direction. He shook it firmly, then wrapped me in an uncharacteristic embrace. "You'll do fine, Mike," he said in a low, gruff voice that barely hid the weight of his emotions. I was suddenly, acutely aware of the degree to which life was changing. I hesitated for a moment, then slowly pulled away from my father and climbed into the recruiter's car, this time knowing better than to look back.

Fortunately, OTS would offer plenty of distractions to pull me from the jaws of creeping homesickness. After arriving at Lackland's Medina Annex, I struggled along with everyone else to fall into some kind of comfortable rhythm. The days were long—and lonely; the nights were short—and lonely. Lackland AFB had been plopped down in the rolling but isolated hills due west of San Antonio. Not that geography was an issue; Lackland could have been nestled neatly in downtown Las Vegas, for all the good it would have done us. As lower-class officer trainees (OTs), we rated somewhere beneath brine shrimp on the food chain. Privileges were something enjoyed by civilians and OTS grads. Those of us who fell into neither category just held on for dear life, hoping for the best and settling for whatever we got that was marginally better than expected.

True to form, I started looking for ways to outsmart the system. I had no desire to completely bypass it, just circumvent the more inconvenient aspects. It occurred to me later in life that learning how to work the system while living within its boundaries was part and parcel of the military education process. The Air Force hierarchy understood that rules and regimentation are critical to a fighting force. They also recognized the value of learning to efficiently manipulate those rules to your advantage and your unit's flexibility.

Ah, I had found a home at last!

For the lowerclassmen, an average day in OTS involved equal portions of study and abuse. Once we graduated to upperclass status, some of the pressure eased, and we were able to split our time between studying and working at job assignments designed to give us a taste of military policies and procedures. And, yes, we still had to carve out time for abuse, but by now we were on the giving end.

Even as a lowerclassman, I kept my eyes and ears open, hoping to identify my ideal upperclass job: something that would give me a measure of freedom without requiring excessive work or interfering too much with my studying, which had suddenly become the focal point of my existence. For the first time in my academic career, I found myself unable to simply coast. I couldn't recall cracking a book in high school. College was much the same, although I could divide higher education into two eras: pre-Karen and post-Karen. Prior to meeting the girl I would eventually marry, I had measured my academic performance against a motley crew of buddies. I'm doing better than any of these guys, I reasoned. I must be doing okay.

It eventually occurred to me that the attrition rate among my role models was pretty high. Maybe I was measuring myself against the wrong people. Karen, on the other hand, actually studied, and had the scholarships and dean's list ranking to prove it.

As with every other endeavor in my life, I had the brains and the ability; I just needed the motivation. A smart, attractive brunette who was two years my junior was more than ample inspiration, and my last two years at Ohio University actually produced some dean's list results. But even in college, I was never challenged beyond my ability to goof off and still get the job done.

Officer Training School was proving to be a little different. I still wasn't worried about failing, but success played a more compelling game of hide-and-seek. I knew without question that I needed to find a job that would insulate me from some of the sillier aspects of officer training.

By the end of my six-week stint as a lowerclassman, I had reached the limit of my tolerance for stupidity. Then again, I had never expected that OTS would be fun; it is essentially basic training for officers, more academic than physical, but with plenty of harassment and discomfort. We were treated to a variety of indignities, the stupidest of which may have been "woolly marches." Typically, these took place in the evenings after the commissioned staff had abandoned the facility to the upperclassmen and headed home for the day.

Woolly marches were great fun, for the guys commanding them. Our "superiors" (superior only by virtue of six weeks' seniority over us) organized us into work details and marched us shoulder to shoulder across the grounds, demanding we pick up anything that wasn't grass or dirt. "Woolies" were the prime objective, tiny lint pieces hiding between blades of grass; they were almost imperceptible to the average human eye—but apparently highly offensive to the discriminating glare of an OTS upperclassman. If our group missed so much as one woolly, we were subject to numerous disciplinary actions and the dreaded demerits. It was, from my seasoned and worldly perspective, the silliest, most pointless exercise anyone had ever asked of me. Ironically, it was also the first step in teaching me detail and discipline. We quickly learned to anticipate. Where will they look now? What have we missed? And every time we thought we'd broken the code on their system, they'd do something unexpected.

Gradually we were being stripped of the remnants of civilian life, learning new ways to behave and respond. It was an unfamiliar social structure and system of rules, where we learned that even the stupidest of orders might have its context and purpose.

The system thrived on obedience and organization—not a bad deal for a Catholic kid who grew up believing that self-discipline is its own reward. My mom's penchant for order and regimen had rubbed off on me, and I had no trouble accepting the spirit of the Air Force commitment to structure. But even I balked at embracing certain elements of the system that seemed hell-bent on setting us up for failure.

Theoretically our days began at 5:30 in the morning, when the Charge of Quarters (CQ) stalked down the corridor bellowing, "The time is 0530! Your overhead lights should be on! Today is the forty-second day of training for the upperclass and the tenth day for the lowerclass! The uniform of the day is 1505s with flight caps." At this point, no matter what, your feet hit the floor. But if you were smart, your day had actually started much earlier. It almost became a game. As the system tightened its grip on us, we desperately tried to conjure ways to wriggle free. Something as simple as making the bed became a challenge to my conviction that rules were designed to be pliable. The secret, I decided, was to make my bed to perfection the night before, then sleep on top of the blankets instead of between them. Come morning, I could hit the ground running, resmooth the covers, and have the perfect Air Force bed.

Clothing posed yet another challenge. For reasons that escape me even today, the Air Force believed there was some merit to owning underwear folded into exact six-inch squares. T-shirts were to be similarly folded, with everything precisely grounded to the four corners of your drawer. Washcloths and towels also received the Air Force treatment. And somehow this level of perfection had to be achieved during the half-hour preceding morning chow.

As with the perfect Air Force bed, I managed to connive a measure of perfection without driving myself completely insane. In short order I had ironed all my earthly belongings into the requisite Air Force squares. Once these had been placed in my dresser in an appropriately aesthetic manner, I began living out of my laundry bag. That, of course, was yet another gross violation of OTS protocol—if they caught me. I relished the challenge of thwarting authority, even as I was learning to acknowledge and respect it.

By 0600 each morning—whether you lived strictly by the rules or skated deftly around them—you were expected to have your housekeeping chores finished and be ready to march with your flight to breakfast. Mealtime offered still another exercise in humility, or humiliation, as lowerclassmen were herded to the chow hall for our ten-minute dining ordeal. In we marched—straight, silent, and appropriately cowed. We marched at attention and shifted to parade rest when standing still.

We didn't speak, didn't smile, didn't look around. We took the food we were given and marched to the nearest table, where we ate in silence, staring only at our plates, then exited the mess hall as quickly as possible. Mealtime in OTS was not an event to be savored.

Once we became upperclassmen, life improved and we earned the luxury of relaxed meals, which permitted some level of walking, talking, and looking around.

But to truly reach coveted upperclass status, we had to make it through the holidays, which wasn't as easy as it sounded. The reigning upperclass graduated on December 20, leaving us with words of encouragement ringing in our ears: "Man, I'd hate to be stuck here at Christmas" and "Tough break. You guys are really gonna be lonely and miserable." Although we immediately became the new upperclass, there would be no restocking of the lower ranks until early January, so we got to do double duty. Twice the work. Half the fun.

We had tried to ignore the reality that we would be held hostage for all of December. Now there was no dismissing the inevitable. And no taunt from the graduating class came close to describing how I actually felt on December 25. It was the emptiest, most isolated Christmas I'd ever spent.

Theoretically I had a few hours of freedom that day, but I didn't have a car and I didn't know anyone, so I wandered the base in silent despair. My mind wandered even further, back to Tipp City, back to the holiday gatherings of yesterday. Christmas within the Jackson-rich Tipp community wasn't simply an event; it was a family free-for-all. We crammed into one another's houses, ate one another's food, and broke one another's toys. And once the family entertainment had been exhausted, I'd head over to Joe's and we'd cruise the town collecting high school friends and whittling away the remaining holiday hours until local stores and restaurants reopened. It was the kind of Christmas you'd see on the cover of *The Saturday Evening Post*: uncomplicated, joyful. I had never fully appreciated its simplicity until this moment. My visit across the years and miles only darkened my mood and I wallowed in misery, wondering whether my life would ever be the same again, whether I would ever completely return to Tipp City.

I would, eventually, but nothing would ever be *exactly* the same again; *I* would never be exactly the same again.

After the holidays, life took on a rosier hue as the new class of OTs came on board and my group officially donned the mystical mantle of upperclassmen. Now more than ever, I was determined to insulate myself against the idiotic and the ill-conceived for the remainder of my OTS tenure.

Somewhere deep inside me, yesterday's earnest altar boy comfortably coexisted with today's puckish opportunist. Both identities were infinitely pleased with my decision to pursue the position of squadron chapel representative. As near as I could tell, the chapel rep didn't answer to anyone except the chaplain, and how bad could the chaplain be? By definition he had to be a pretty decent guy. Besides, chapel reps got their own rooms and walking privileges (which meant they could wander unsupervised around the base), and, best of all, nobody much bothered to inspect them.

Once my objective was clear, I had to carefully plan the attack. This maneuver cried out for artful strategy. Officer Training School was divided into "flights" of sixteen to twenty students. Between four and eight flights were a squadron; four squadrons made a group; and two groups formed the wing. By securing a squadron-level position, I'd be sandwiched comfortably between the underachievers and the wing hierarchy.

Cagey to a fault, I reasoned that if I appeared to set my sights too high, I'd be perceived as aggressive and would be simultaneously rewarded and punished by being granted the position I sought, only on a much smaller scale. But, of course, the joke would be on the OTS hierarchy, who were blithely ignorant of my plot to disappear into the no man's land of middle management.

When the time came to declare a job preference, I marched in like an idiot and announced that I wanted the position of *wing* chapel rep, the top guy on the God Squad, second only to the chaplain himself. What gall. What chutzpah. I could barely contain my glee at this cunning manipulation of the system. The OTS officials, unknowing pawns in my clever shell game, seemed neither enthused nor offended by my declaration. A series of questions followed. "Okay, OT Jackson, wing chapel rep is an essential position, a pivotal link between the chaplain and the OTs. If an OT has a problem, he'll take it to one of your chapel reps, then they'll hand it off to you. You might have to advise someone who thinks he has violated the OTS honor code or someone who doesn't feel he can successfully complete OTS. The issues you might have to address are incredibly diverse. For instance, OT Jackson, how would you respond if an OT confides to you that he is having problems with his marriage?"

I pondered the question thoroughly, turning it over in my mind and applying all my hard-won analytical skills before answering, "I don't know. I'm not married. I guess I'd send him to the chaplain."

Okay, so maybe it wasn't a shining example of my analytical genius. At a minimum, however, it was honest.

I left the interview thinking, geeze, I really fell on my face with that one. But I still clung to the hope that maybe they'd take the plunge and trust me in the lowly squadron chapel rep position. Apparently honesty counted for more than I'd anticipated. Two days later I got the word that I was the new *wing* chapel rep. Although it was a little more responsibility than I wanted, it elevated me to wing staff as an OT major and to a much loftier spot in the strata than I had envisioned or probably deserved.

Despite my ineptitude at outsmarting the system, my new job turned out to be almost exactly what I was looking for—plenty of privileges with minimal responsibilities. Once each week I met with the chaplain, who seemed to expect even less of me than I did. I also spent a couple of hours a week with my eight squadron and two group chapel reps, who displayed skill and dexterity in addressing OT issues before they had a chance to land in my lap. And, as a member of the wing staff, I helped lead the OT corps of cadets. That was about the sum total of my duties—basic, uncomplicated, and sans any hint of mental or emotional challenge. In other words, perfect.

I roomed with the wing athletic officer, Kraig Lofquist, who had been playing football for the Pittsburgh Steelers when he apparently took a few too many blows to the head and decided that being an Air Force fighter pilot was less dangerous and more glamorous. Unlike me,

Kraig didn't simply bend the rules he found inconvenient, he completely ignored them. But he managed to do so with a genuine finesse that made him difficult to dislike. Our two wing staff positions were polar opposites, but we hit it off immediately. Confident, motivated, and a few years older than I was, Kraig was like a worldly big brother who surprised and entertained me with his insights and experiences across the vast landscape of the female gender. Always the altar boy, I made no effort to compete with Kraig's conquests, but I admired his self-confidence and savvy, and I vicariously reveled in his exploits. In fact, we would unintentionally see to it that we ended up in pilot training together, where Kraig would heroically save my bacon when my mouth overloaded my muscle in a little barroom disagreement with a guy twice my size.

Thus endured the Jacksonian habit of stepping into crap and ending up with rose petals. Having secured a decent roommate and an esteemed spot on the wing staff, I began to relax and enjoy the view from the top.

With upperclass status came a certain level of arrogance. We had weathered the storms of servitude and were rapidly proving ourselves as leaders of men. In five short weeks we would be officers and, presumably, gentlemen. At the ripe old age of twenty-two, I would outrank 90 percent of the people in the Air Force. On top of that, many of us were headed to pilot training. If there's anything more overtly cocky than an (almost) brand-new officer, it's an (almost) brand-new officer who fancies himself a fighter pilot.

The spare time we had finally acquired as upperclassmen gave us a chance to ponder the future. Our flights of fancy rarely extended past pilot training, however. No one wanted to peek too far into the shadows for fear they'd find Vietnam staring back at them. It seemed unthinkable; with fifty-three weeks of pilot training ahead, surely the war would be over. Wasn't it time for this thing to end? Hadn't we been playing this game since high school? I still stubbornly maintained my "if you ignore it, it will go away" stance, but my confidence was beginning to waiver. The OTS faculty had the unsettling habit of hammering us with combat or Vietnam scenarios during every classroom session. We got the distinct impression they were trying to tell us something.

Rather than dwell on the unthinkable, we turned our attentions to how and where we would earn our wings. We didn't know exactly what to expect, but we knew we would be entering a strange new world. On the surface, we swaggered and sneered and made light of the process; underneath, we each privately questioned our own ability to make the cut. My personal preference was to avoid the issue altogether. I'd never had a problem envisioning myself as the consummate Air Force officer, but adding wings to that image was a bit more challenging. I knew I could act like a pilot; I just wasn't certain I could fly like one.

But we sucked up our doubts and plotted ways to maximize pilot training. The first order of business was to seize control of our geographic destinies. There were certain desolate, godforsaken places where you didn't want to spend fifty-three weeks of your life. The two that leapt to mind were located in Texas: Laredo Air Force Base, squatting just this side of the Mexican border, and Laughlin Air Force Base, located in Del Rio, also a border town. They were isolated and barren, offering nothing in the way of pleasurable distractions for a high-energy pack of bachelor pilot wannabes.

In my exalted position on the OTS wing staff, I crossed paths with a variety of people, all of whom surpassed me in their understanding and skillful manipulation of Air Force policy and procedure. Many on the wing staff were enlisted men who had gotten their degrees, then applied for OTS. Some of them were master sergeants with years of Air Force service already under their belts. These guys knew the ins and outs, right?

We spent a fair amount of time talking about our options and composing our flight training wish list. Like everyone else, I was hoping to be sent to Williams Air Force Base in Phoenix. It was warm and inviting, a virtual vacation spot. It offered an active nightlife and a certain mystique. A guy could really kick-start his piloting career with panache if he trained at Williams.

I confided my objective to a fellow wing staffer, a guy with more than a couple Air Force years under his belt. He was quick to offer the benefit of his military wisdom, and I was quicker still to latch on to what seemed like another brilliant game of "subvert the system from within."

"You guys need to head over to Randolph Air Force Base and pay a call on the headquarters of the Air Force Military Personnel Center. Just tell the personnel office that you want to go to Williams and they'll take care of it."

Who knew it could be so simple?

Several days later, five of us, including Kraig Lofquist and Bill Orellana, the OT wing materiel officer, put on our crisp little OTS uniforms, piled into a battered '62 Chevy, and headed down the yellow brick road toward the opposite side of San Antonio where, presumably, we would ask the wizard of Randolph to grant our heart's desires. As it turns out, we would have been better off asking for brains.

It just happened to be New Year's Eve—which was the only way we could have carved out the time necessary to make the trek across town and back. In retrospect, we should have waited for a day when people weren't rushing to head home to celebrate (if they hadn't already started), but, no, we showed up at Randolph and rolled into the Military Personnel Center, blissfully ignorant and supremely confident.

With all the authority that our eight weeks of OTS could summon, we announced to a perplexed two-striper that we were there to reserve our slots at Williams Air Force Base. The two-striper dropped his jaw and stared at us as though we were insane, suicidal, and/or speaking in some obscure, dead language.

Then came the explosion. It was subtle at first, the shuffling of papers and the urgent squeak of a chair scooting backward. From the corner of my eye I glimpsed an angry red face attached to a uniformed body. It burst from the corner office and made a beeline for the counter where the five of us stood like confused cattle in a slaughterhouse line.

The voice was deep and clipped and unmistakably hostile. Standing in front of us, sputtering like a bad engine, was a full bird colonel, the highest-ranking officer I'd ever seen. And man, was he pissed.

"You OTs are here to do *what?* Of all the stupid, mindless arrogance! Do you understand what I can do to you? I can call the OTS commandant. I can have you expelled. I can see to it that you never serve as an officer in the Salvation Army let alone the United States Air Force. Where the hell do you get off trying to manipulate the Air

Force assignment system? It is pure as the driven snow! When the time comes, your names will go into the same pool as everyone else and you'll take what you're handed and be damned glad to get it, and that's *if* I don't decide to kick your sorry asses out of the Air Force right here and now!"

The ranting continued, but my mind's ear had snapped shut, along with other parts of my anatomy. I caught a few additional phrases, lightly peppered with four-letter words and that annoying refrain "pure as the driven snow."

Before returning to Lackland with our tails tucked squarely between our legs, we had to surrender our names to the two-striper, who managed to look sympathetic and smug at the same time. The ride back was quiet—and long. Nobody knew what fate, or the raging colonel, had in store for us.

We silently slipped back into the OTS routine and tried not to think about whether one stupid mistake would abruptly end our military careers. None of us thought we'd abused the system; we just thought we'd been lucky enough to stumble across the formula for harnessing its power. I don't think I ever confronted my well-meaning wing staff buddy with the results of our road trip. I probably should have; God knows how many other hapless cadets he sent to Randolph for the "pure as the driven snow" speech.

Days passed. I studied. I worked. I provided spiritual guidance as needed. Fortunately for me, and the lost souls who sought my counsel, the issues laid on my doorstep were never especially weighty or complex. As I counted down the days until OTS would be a happy memory, I paused occasionally to ponder how and when the angry colonel from Randolph might choose to extract his pound of flesh.

I didn't have to wait too long. On the day that base assignments were released, I discovered for myself the "sanctity" of the Air Force system. Although other OTS buddies were scattered to the winds at various bases throughout the country, the five of us who made that fateful road trip to Randolph were—ironically—split between two locations: Laredo and Laughlin.

So much for "pure as the driven snow."

CHAPTER FIVE

THE YEAR OF FIFTY-THREE WEEKS

DESPITE my concerns about measuring up, I graduated in the top 10 percent of my OTS class, earning the status of "Distinguished Graduate" no less. It was, perhaps, the first time I had ever seen a direct correlation between my academic success and pure, unfettered study. My Johnny-come-lately college triumphs had more to do with Karen's influence than my own motivation. This time, however, there was no female presence to either distract or inspire. I had done it by myself.

Graduation day was satisfying but lonely. With three kids still at home, my parents had neither the time nor the money to jet to Texas and watch their eldest earn his second lieutenant bars, and Karen was tied to her college schedule back in Ohio.

As it turns out, I had little time to savor my academic "personal best." Immediately after the graduation ceremony, I was hoofing it toward the cab that would deliver me to the airport for my triumphant return to Tipp City.

It was a homecoming I relished. I didn't expect people to swoon in my arms or throw rose petals across my path, but somehow I expected them to absorb and reflect the tremendous pride and satisfaction I felt as an officer in the United States Air Force. When I put on that uniform, I could almost sense a tangible difference in who I was and how I carried myself. It meant something to me, and it wasn't a "look at me, I'm special" sentiment. I felt a deep and genuine obligation to protect and serve my country. The uniform represented not only everything I believed but everything I wanted to be. For all my smart-ass tendencies, the unspoken obligation of those dress blues was something I took—and continue to take—very seriously.

Unfortunately, my "triumphant" return to my hometown was decidedly more low-key than anticipated. I wore my uniform to church Sunday morning, but ended up disgruntled by what I perceived as a lackluster reception. Everyone offered support and encouragement, but few understood what I had endured or achieved as an officer trainee. For the first time in my life, I felt oddly out of my element among civilians. It was disturbing but empirical evidence that OTS had, indeed, begun to mold an officer out of some fairly unrefined material.

My brief visit home also presented Karen and me with an opportunity to discuss our future. We decided to get married once she graduated from Ohio University. If she attended summer school and carried extra credits each quarter, she could graduate in December, two months before I wrapped up pilot training. We agreed that the wedding would take place sometime toward the end of pilot training, assuming I actually made it through the full fifty-three weeks. I didn't verbalize that particular concern (this sweet, unassuming girl was no doubt dazzled by the prospect of marrying a fighter pilot; why threaten her illusions unnecessarily?), but it continued to weigh heavily in the corner of my mind that hosted secret doubts.

After a little more than a week at home, I packed my bags again and piled into my semi-new 1966 Ford Galaxy 500XL convertible. I was certain that somewhere in the unwritten rules of aviation was a section that dictated "no man shall be taken seriously as a military pilot unless he is driving a snazzy ragtop." Somehow it fit the whole Air Force officer/fighter pilot mystique.

I rolled into Del Rio, Texas, ready to take Laughlin Air Force Base by storm. My limited experience navigating the rural suburbias of the Midwest did nothing to prepare me for life in a sleepy Texas border town. *Sleepy, hell, this place bordered on catatonic.* A patchwork of wood and adobe sprinkled between alternating paved and dirt roads, Del Rio had little to offer in the way of distractions—one theater, next to no shopping, and precious few restaurants. If Colonel "Pure as the Driven Snow" had hoped to extract a lasting pound of flesh, Del Rio was just the place to do it.

I changed into my uniform at a beatup old service station and pulled up to Laughlin's main gate, where I felt my resolve begin to waiver. From my vantage point at the entrance, I watched the T-37s and T-38s roll out under the bright Texas sun. They were sleek and shiny and as close to aviation nirvana as anything I'd ever seen. Where did I get off thinking I had the skill and smarts to fly one of these things? Where did I get off thinking I could fly *anything*? In my whole life I had taken only a few airplane rides and always in the cushioned comfort of a commercial airliner—hardly sufficient preparation for flying Air Force jets at mach one. Every self-doubt I'd ever had swept over me and lodged in my throat like the dust and grime of the highway.

How much hard work have you ever really done, Jackson? You've managed to skate for most of your life; even in OTS you weaseled your way around the majority of the rough spots. This isn't going to be like college or high school or even OTS. If you can't figure out where your potential is, and work past it, you're gonna be out on your ass.

This wasn't the pep talk I needed at the moment, but the voice inside my head knew me better than anyone else. We were both worried.

I'd never been much of a whiz at math and science; how would I fare with the technical challenges of flying? And what if I hated flying? That thought hadn't even occurred to me until now.

Keep it up, idiot, and you're gonna turn this into a self-fulfilling prophecy.

I squared my shoulders and muzzled the fears that were nipping at my heels. I announced to the gate guard that I had arrived for pilot training, and he responded with a wave-through and a smart salute. Tradition dictates that the first guy who salutes a new officer earns a silver dollar for his effort, but I was too flustered by the magnitude of the moment to even remember to fish the coin out of my pocket.

The housing office quickly set me up in what would be my home away from home for, I hoped, the next fifty-three weeks: typical Air Force bachelor officers' quarters (BOQ) accommodations, spartan by anyone's standards. I soon found that I was the proud owner of a bed, a desk, and a battered ranch oak chair that had been crammed into what may have once been a walk-in closet. My quarters opened into a common area, on the other side of which lay a similar closet with similar furnishings and yet another hapless new officer hoping for a shot at his wings. Somehow the process of settling into my own space buoyed my confidence, and I ventured over to the base officers' club. The stroll to the O-club was invigorating. Here I was in my brand-new officer's uniform about to be welcomed into the inner sanctum of "officerness." Heady stuff. Maybe I could fly those planes after all.

From around a corner, another officer headed toward me, closing quickly. *Yikes. Remember the drill, Jackson. Fingers together; hand slides crisply up the silver buttons, snapping smartly to the eye, index finger and middle finger just grazing the outer edge of the eyebrow; then a hasty jerk back into place. Great job, Lieutenant. Perfect salute!*

The other second lieutenant I had just saluted returned my gesture with a look that was equal parts quizzical and suspicious.

Okay, Jackson, you idiot, you just saluted an officer of equal rank. Bad form. Why not wear a sign that reads, "Hi, I'm a freshly minted officer; color me clueless." Just keep walking and pretend you knew what you were doing all along. Joke's on you, buddy; I just wanted to see how you'd react.

I quietly comforted myself with the story of an OTS classmate who, on one of his early uniformed forays off base, was completely rattled by the sight of an approaching officer. He snapped to attention and delivered a salute worthy of Gen. Hap Arnold himself, only to discover that he had just saluted the mailman. The mail carrier grinned playfully and returned the gesture, no doubt shattering the future lieu-tenant's confidence for years to come. At least the guy I'd saluted was a real Air Force officer.

I wasn't about to let one tiny breach of protocol mess with the revival of my ego. College hadn't beaten me; OTS hadn't beaten me. Pilot training wouldn't either. *I'm an Air Force officer, for Pete's sake; I can do this.*

The ensuing days and weeks seemed hell-bent on making me eat my words. If OTS had been intense, pilot training was all-consuming. Every minute of every twelve-hour day was dedicated to one of two things: academics or flight training. And once your twelve-hour shift was over, you kicked into study mode. Aircraft systems, weather, navi-gation, aerodynamics, instrument procedures: somehow I had to stuff it all into my head, and make sure it stayed there.

Okay, Jackson, what's the difference between calibrated air speed, equivalent air speed, indicated air speed, and true air speed? Huh?

The fears I'd flirted with at the base entrance quickly took up residence in my room and dogged me like Edgar Allan Poe's raven. I was less than unprepared, less than uninitiated; I was pathetic, and there were plenty of people eager to remind me of this on a daily, if not hourly, basis.

Pilot training began with an introduction to the T-41, which was nothing more than a military version of a Cessna 172—the plane that practically every civilian pilot in modern history cut his teeth on. At Laughlin, however, this docile little aircraft had earned the sinister nickname "the attrition machine." The Air Force apparently reasoned that if someone was going to wash out as a pilot, he might as well do it in an airplane that was inexpensive to repair and operate.

Military flight training bore little resemblance to the easygoing, work-at-your-own-pace instruction of the civilian sector. The whole idea of each lesson was to give you one more task than you could rea-sonably accomplish, then watch you battle the twin demons of inexperience and panic.

The guys who came into the game with a private pilot's license in hand had a definite leg up on those of us who didn't know an elevator from an aileron. And everybody, it seemed, had the advantage over me. Not only was I unfamiliar with aviation terms and equipment, I had managed to draw the one instructor nobody wanted, the one guy I had been warned about, the guy who made the Marquis de Sade look warm and cuddly.

George was one of those guys you always see in movies about military training—the washed-up, bitter drill sergeant type who takes great pleasure in tormenting his charges. He screams; he belittles; he acts like a giant, flaming asshole. Except in the movies, it turns out that the washed-up, bitter old drill sergeant has a heart of gold, that he's secretly a Medal of Honor winner who lost both kneecaps and a kidney at the Bulge and now dedicates his life to thoroughly preparing his charges for the horrors of war so they never suffer a similar fate. Likewise, as the movie unfolds, we learn that the young officer he most torments actually reminds him of himself as a youth. Following a manly fistfight and a pint of Old Overcoat whiskey, the two adversaries acknowledge a grudging respect for each other and enter a new phase of cooperation and teamwork. The young officer goes on to win his wings, the girl, the war, and a spot on the Republican presidential ticket, and everyone lives happily ever after.

Okay, so the only thing my situation had in common with the movies was that George screamed, belittled, and acted like a giant, flaming asshole. I had even overheard him bragging to his cohorts about the number of students he'd sent packing. It wasn't exactly a confidence builder.

The truth was that none of the T-41 instructors nursed any particular affection for their eager young charges. They were civilian contractors, and most of them seemed to resent training a bunch of overeducated little Air Force pukes. It didn't matter who we were, how we behaved, or whether we performed beyond all expectations; we were Air Force pukes and, as far as our T-41 instructors were concerned, the name of the game was washout.

In my case, performing beyond all expectations was not an issue. I'd resigned myself to the fact that I might really have to struggle to make the grade. I was completely unprepared for the more technical aspects of flying. My first flight was an instructional lesson, and I was expected to treat it as such. The problem was, for me—the kid from

Ohio who had never seen the inside of a Piper Cub let alone a Cessna—it was more like a sightseeing tour. As the dusty roads of Del Rio fell away beneath me, I stared in wonder at the crisscrossing patterns of fields, trees, fence lines, and streets. Everything was different, yet the same. I sat in quiet awe, consumed by the "I can see my house from here" syndrome.

I vaguely heard my instructor barking orders, instructions, and information, but the whole "miracle of flight" thing was too overwhelming. I walked away from my first lesson having absorbed precisely nothing. I was now standing squarely behind the undergraduate pilot training eight ball.

The Marquis de George was less than amused. He seemed to interpret my distraction as a challenge to his teaching skills. The pointer he carried with him got quite a workout as he rapped my knuckles, arms, and head to gain my attention.

Every lesson thereafter had a similar theme: I struggled to focus on the work at hand, still sneaking occasional awestruck gazes out the window, as George voiced his conviction that I had no redeeming value whatsoever.

"Hello? Lieutenant Jackson? Anybody in there?" Rap. "Pay attention, Lieutenant. Your life depends on this—boy are you in trouble!" Rap.

Nothing he said buoyed my sinking spirits. Nothing he did gave me any assurance that I might eventually master this machine. If I was already falling behind by the end of my first flight, by the end of three flights I was arguably more clueless than before. I was thoroughly frustrated by my own inability to comprehend and by my instructor's complete lack of empathy for my confusion.

"I think this guy really enjoys watching me go down the toilet," I told Kraig Lofquist, who had also ended up at Del Rio, courtesy of our little New Year's Eve trek to Randolph. "This jerk really wants me to fail. Nothing I do is right or even close. He ridicules me, he insults me, and, on top of that, he's a lousy instructor. I don't know what the heck to do."

I wasn't expecting answers. And Kraig didn't have any. Everyone was dealing with his own private hell, but the other guys pretty much agreed that I had drawn the shortest straw of all when I got handed George.

As the days dragged on, I applied myself with an intensity that startled even me. I'd never worked so hard yet felt so stupid. Every waking moment, every ounce of energy and brainpower went toward mastering my studies and overcoming the deficiencies that seemed to multiply daily. I couldn't fail at this; I wanted it too much. Surely that counted for something. Surely my hunger and drive would be the grain of sand that tipped the scales in my favor.

But wanting it and understanding it were two vastly different concepts. How did the aircraft attitude control air speed while the throttle controlled altitude? It made no sense. And what the heck was the difference between a traffic pattern stall and a power-on stall? And why in the world were they teaching me how to stall? Wasn't that kind of like a driver's ed teacher showing his students how to crash? None of it made sense. Hell, I couldn't even figure out how to hold the controls when I was taxiing let alone master the complexities of airborne maneuvers.

Every night I'd close my eyes and feel a gnawing, hollow ache in the pit of my stomach. Every night the little voice in my head grew more urgent and shrill. *You can't do this. You've given it your best shot, but you're just not as good as the other guys. Walk away now and hold on to some shred of dignity. You're no pilot, Jackson. It's just not gonna happen.*

It didn't help that I heard much the same thing during the day from my T-41 instructor. It finally began to wear me down. Nagging doubts blossomed into a full-blown mental block, the self-fulfilling prophecy that I'd worried about on my first day in Del Rio. I felt myself slowly giving up. You can survive only so long with no positive reinforcement before you start believing your own worst fears. I'd reached that point. I was swimming in quicksand; the harder I fought and kicked, the deeper I sank. The time had come to listen to that voice in my head.

I knew that one of my options was to file a self-initiated elimination, or SIE, an Air Force way of saying, "I quit before you kick me out." Several guys had already chosen this option, so at least I wouldn't be the first to fail. It was a small comfort, but it was all I had.

As hard as it was to admit to myself that I couldn't make the cut, it would be infinitely harder explaining my incompetence to my mom and dad. No kids ever want their parents to pity them or perceive them as not quite good enough. I had never failed at anything I'd set my mind to, and now I would have to break the bad news to my folks and head home with "failure" emblazoned across my forehead. I could hear the hometown grapevine heating up: "What's up with Jackson? Thought he was gonna be a hotshot fighter pilot, and he can't even figure out how to fly a Cessna." The whole mess made me almost physically ill, but what choice did I have? This was the closest thing to a lost cause I'd ever experienced, and apparently even St. Jude, who supposedly presided over such matters, had deserted me. The time had come to pull the plug and spare myself additional humiliation.

With a lump in my throat and a sense of self-loathing I'd never felt before—or since—I called home and told my mother that I was seriously considering initiating the SIE process. The words and emotions tumbled out as I explained that I had the instructor from hell, that I didn't understand the mechanics of flying, and that I just couldn't keep up, despite devoting every moment to study.

"I'm in over my head here. I'm working harder than I've ever worked in my life, and I'm just not getting it. I just can't seem to understand *anything,* and once I finally do understand something, I find out I've fallen behind in everything else. You know I've never been that great with math and stuff like that. I think this is just one of those things that's probably beyond my abilities."

I paused to take a breath. Mom had been listening quietly as I rationalized my failure. When she finally spoke, her words were slow and thoughtful. I could hear sympathy in her voice, but I also heard resolve.

"Here's what I think. First of all, you're *not* quitting. You've never quit anything in your life, and this is not the time to start."

I shook my head. Had she listened to anything I'd said? Did she understand that I'd given it my best shot? Maybe I had so stunned her with my admission of failure that she simply couldn't accept the reality that her eldest son was a loser.

"It's not your decision to make," she continued. "There are people at Laughlin who are paid to make that decision. They are older and more experienced than you, and it's their job to make the call on whether or not you're good enough. And if you really are as bad as you seem to think, rest assured they'll let you know. In the meantime, all you can do is the best you can do. Michael, you're tired, you're away from home, and you're under a lot of pressure. It's really easy to let all your doubts and fears seem bigger than they are. But you can't let that happen. If your superiors give up on you, that's one thing, but don't ever give up on yourself."

Wow. I was speechless—and oddly relaxed. In a few short sentences, my mother had shattered the anxiety and doubt that had plagued me since I rolled up to the gate. It was one of those distinctive parent-child moments when you sense that you've been handed something that will help redefine who you are and how you function. Mom was offering to pull me out of the quicksand, and she wanted to make damn sure the lesson was permanent. Winnie Jackson wasn't a highly educated woman, but she was as intuitive and street-smart as anyone I've ever known. She understood people; she understood *me*. She knew that quitting was a tough habit to break, that—in the end—victory goes not to the swift but to the stubborn. And she knew better than anyone else that what I lacked in speed and smarts, I more than made up for in stubbornness.

"Okay," I said slowly, still measuring her words against my situation. "I just wanted to let you know what was going on. But maybe you're right. I'll stick with it, and we'll see what happens."

"Whatever happens, you've made the right decision," she said firmly, but I could tell she was smiling.

I have often wondered what she said to my father after she hung up. I never asked, and I suppose it didn't really matter. What she said to *me* had a profound impact on the way I viewed myself and the way I would view success and failure for the rest of my life.

In the days that followed, nothing about my situation changed. George was still an asshole. I still struggled to understand the fine points of flight. Del Rio was still desolate, lonely, and boring. And yet *everything* was different. That horrible decision to give up, to turn and run from my own inadequacies no longer hung over my head. Mom had succeeded in removing the one pressure that I simply couldn't handle, the pressure I was putting on myself. I began to understand that all the external crap was difficult, but it was manageable. In the end, it was my own fear of failure that almost did me in.

Thanks to Mom, I remain to this day the one guy you don't want to get in a fight with. I'm not all that strong or fast, but I just won't quit. You can stop the fight or you can kill me, but don't wait for me to cry uncle. It'll never happen. That's due to Mom's influence, a testament to her quiet strength that wasn't always so quiet, especially if one of her own was threatened or mistreated. She nursed a sense of fair play that sometimes put her at odds with the less balanced factions of the world.

OTHER VOICES: Don Jackson

Shortly after Mike arrived in Vietnam, he shipped me a T-shirt that he'd bought at the Da Nang BX. The shirt boasted a fully loaded F-4 under the modified United Airlines slogan "Fly the Friendly Skies . . . of Vietnam." I proudly wore it to school at the first opportunity and was immediately informed that it violated the school's dress code. I had two choices, remove it or wear it inside out. I refused on both counts and was promptly sent home to change.

Once home, I explained the problem to Mom, who was a force of nature when it came to defending one of her own or confronting an injustice. Without a moment's hesitation, she marched me back to the principal's office for a lesson in freedom of expression. At issue was the school's abundance of students decked out in peace signs, "make love not war" buttons, and "give peace a chance" shirts, which inflamed Mom's sense of balance and equity. I had been singled out based solely on the politics of my T-shirt, she pointed out. She further told the principal that he had a lot of nerve, considering that her eldest son was in Vietnam defending freedom and defending the rights of people to express an opinion or support a cause—whether verbally or via a T-shirt. The principal was forced to acknowledge that a T-shirt featuring an airplane and the name of a foreign country was no more—and probably much less—of a political statement than those actively promoting the agenda of America's liberal antiwar movement. I returned to school wearing my T-shirt, which now meant even more to me.

My mother's common sense was tough to debate. The Tipp principal didn't even try, and Don was free to once again wear the memento of his brother's tour of duty. That was Mom—quietly stubborn, fiercely loyal, and, oh yeah, without question the savior of my piloting career.

What she couldn't salvage was my early fascination with the miracle of flight. My T-41 experience left me somewhat disillusioned by the whole process. I never again viewed flying with the same level of awe and enthusiasm. George had made certain that it was nothing but drudgery. By my tenth training flight, I was prepared for the declaration that I was too stupid to solo and should pack my bags and head back to the black-and-white land of the ground pounders.

The flight began with the Marquis de George running me through my paces and making certain I knew that (a) I was incompetent, (b) I was a lousy pilot, and (c) nothing I did could ever change either condition. We landed the plane, taxied back to the ramp, and sat in silence for a moment. I was miserable and completely lacking in anything that resembled confidence. George looked at me with disgust and said flatly, "I'm getting out. You're going to fly this thing by yourself— and you're going to die." With that, he surrendered the controls, shook my hand, and walked away.

Well, I didn't die. In fact, much to George's chagrin, I even brought the plane back in one piece. I actually did okay, and in the days that followed I did better than okay. I started to gain some ground. The pilot training motto has always been "cooperate and graduate." I applied that lesson with increasing relish, depending more and more on the wisdom and guidance of classmates with prior flight experience. Taking pity on the scrappy little mutt from Ohio, they coached me on flying technique and terminology. I'd walk through my maneuvers using a small model airplane, saying, "Okay, I'm doing a lazy eight and I'm gonna roll the plane to the left and here's where I'll need back pressure. Now I'm going to apply a little right rudder." And they'd correct me and say, "No, no back pressure there—and here's the point where you need the rudder." And day by day, bit by bit, I finally started to get it.

To ensure my success, I began "flying" my missions long before I ever set foot on the flight line. I went to the store and bought a toilet plunger, which I planted firmly on the floor between my knees. Alone in my room, I'd envision myself in the cockpit. Using the plunger as my control stick, I'd walk through every maneuver, practice each motion, until I was certain I had it right.

In the end, Colonel "Pure as the Driven Snow" did me a tremendous favor by shipping me to Del Rio. Never one to ignore a distraction, I was at the mercy of Laughlin's desolate setting. At any other base, I might have been lured away from my studies by nightlife or related indulgences. Not so here. Here my attention deficiency found no fuel. And one day I looked up and noticed that all my effort was beginning to pay off. Attrition had been gnawing its way through our ranks, but I was still standing: still struggling, but still standing, dammit. I hung in—not brilliant, not pathetic—just there, doggedly determined to make it a chore for anyone to bounce me from the program.

Gradually the playing field began to level. The guys who had arrived at Laughlin with a flight training advantage slowed down as the work grew more intense and they came face-to-face with their own unfamiliar territory. The guys like me who had entered at a disadvantage began moving forward by sheer force of will. Somehow we all started to meet in the middle.

After T-41 training, we moved into T-37s and life got even better, although I was still behind the eight ball from a technical standpoint, and my absence of any grasp of physics or mechanics often left me scratching my head while the rest of the class appeared to be nodding in unison.

"Lieutenant Jackson, explain to the class the function of the DC bus, the AC bus, and the central tie bus, respectively."

Sure. No problem.

The only thing I knew for certain about a bus was that twenty cents bought me a ride on the RTA line from downtown Dayton to two miles south of Tipp City. I was pretty sure that wasn't the answer they were looking for.

The good news about moving out of T-41s was that the T-37 instructors were all Air Force pilots. They were in our club and had a vested interest in seeing us succeed. The only way one of these guys would actively try to wash me out was if my performance was so poor that a washout was necessary to save my life. I wasn't out of the woods yet, but neither was I still flailing away in the wilderness.

There was never time to relax, never a point where you could kick back and let down your guard. Flight training stayed intense and precise; classroom time was equally demanding. You were expected to walk into the flight room with all the answers. You started your day with a weather briefing, followed by a standardization briefing, followed immediately by a review of emergency procedures.

At this point, everyone in the room, from the biggest screw-off to the best stick in the house, held his breath and prayed that the instructor would shout out someone else's name. This was the moment of truth, an exercise in pure, rote memorization that separated the men from the boys: if you missed so much as one word of the bold-faced critical action items, you were grounded for the day. If you missed one word too often, you were grounded for good. Inevitably, they zeroed in on the one poor slob who hadn't quite mastered the day's assignment. It was as though the emergency procedures officer had been chosen for his ESP abilities.

"Lieutenant Jackson, you're practicing your acrobatics solo and you inadvertently enter a spin. What should you do?"

Shit.

Jumping to attention, I'd sing out, "Sir! I'd execute the T-37 single spin recovery."

Okay, forty-three words, six steps, every word has to be exactly right. Go!

"Sir! Throttles, idle; rudder and ailerons, neutral; stick, abruptly full aft and hold; rudder, abruptly apply full rudder opposite spin direction, opposite turn needle and hold; stick, abruptly full forward one turn after applying rudder; controls, neutral after spinning stops and recover from dive."

Deep breath. Quick glance to make sure no one is snickering.

Not that there was much room for humor. Whether you were in the classroom or in the cockpit, it was competitive and relentless. And just answering the question with the right number of words in the right places wasn't enough. Then they got picky.

"Okay, Lieutenant Jackson, *why* stick abruptly full aft and hold?"

Crap.

"Because that corrects you from any kind of a spin into an erect upright spin."

"And how far forward must the nose go after you throw the stick abruptly full forward?"

"Near the vertical, sir! Usually at least seventy-three degrees nose low."

"You may sit down, Lieutenant Jackson."

Whew.

They told me that pilot training was a cakewalk compared to combat, but I had my doubts. This was pressure unlike anything I'd ever known. Admittedly, my physical well-being didn't depend on the outcome, but pretty much everything else I'd envisioned for my life hung in the balance each time I answered a question.

Every night, as I drifted gratefully toward unconsciousness, I'd reassure myself that I had just moved one day closer to the end of the year of fifty-three weeks. But next I had to make it through T-38s. T-41s had been hell—a directed, unyielding assault on my confidence. In T-37s, I managed to unravel some of the mysteries, although others remained thoroughly bewildering. But midway through T-37s, I began to occasionally allow myself the luxury of thinking in terms of when rather than if I became a pilot. By the time I climbed into the T-38 cockpit, I had begun to break the code. I was reasonably certain that Air Force wings were in my future, the only variable being the amount of blood, sweat, and tears necessary to win them.

Nothing I had done before and nothing that followed would ever test my resolve and conviction in quite the same way. And although my frantic little dance with the Viet Cong would be one of the highlights of my life, it would never surpass the intensity of going toe-to-toe with my own inner doubts and fears.

Two months before my graduation from pilot training, I made it home long enough to tend to one small detail: my wedding.

Unfortunately, when they say "the needs of the Air Force come first," they mean it. In this case, the Air Force needed Lieutenant Jackson back in class the following Monday, so ours was a ceremony conducted on the fly in every way, shape, and form.

OTHER VOICES: Karen Jackson

I wanted a simple ceremony and reception. Cake and punch at the church would've suited me just fine. My mother had other ideas. Her Eastern European heritage had led her to believe that the only "acceptable" (probably to the relatives, at least) wedding day lasted all day and ended with a rented hall, catered dinner, and lots of alcohol. It was going to be her way or there would be no wedding. What should have been a glorious day for Mike and me was destined to be stressful at best.

Mike's plane arrived around one o'clock on Friday morning. Assorted family and bridal party members arrived in town throughout the day in time for the rehearsal and dinner, followed by a late night of partying with the bridal party at their hotel.

Saturday was a long day. The wedding Mass was at noon, followed by a photography session we thought would never end. Then it was off to the hall, a receiving line, dinner, cake cutting, bouquet and garter throwing—the whole shebang. By the end of the evening, Mike and I were totally exhausted and eager to get away.

After spending Saturday night in a hotel near the airport, we caught a morning flight for San Antonio and then drove the 150 miles to Del Rio. Monday morning Mike was up bright and early and headed back to the flight line for an 0530 briefing.

I didn't enjoy the hectic nuptials any more than Karen did, but it was typical of an Air Force wedding and a fair indicator of the frantic nature of an Air Force marriage. We would both have plenty of adjusting to do.

However, my new status as husband was temporarily overshadowed by my old status as struggling UPT student. The undergraduate pilot training program continued to offer plenty of challenge and intensity, but I had turned a psychological corner and was finally starting to build up a head of steam. In fact, as graduation day approached I found that I had risen into the upper middle portion of the class. I wasn't the "best stick," but I was regaining a certain comfort level. I now believed that I would actually graduate, barring any truly stupid mistakes.

About four weeks before graduation, I got my strongest indicator yet that the Air Force hadn't given up on me either. I found myself front and center with the rest of the guys as both flights of Laughlin's UPT class 70-05 assembled at the academic building to take part in the time-honored aircraft selection process. All airplanes available to our class's "block" were scrawled on a chalkboard at the front of the room. For days we had been wheeling and dealing with one another—"if you take one of the T-37s, I'll take the other"—in the ritual of determining who would end up flying what. Now we sat tensely in the classroom awaiting our opportunity to approach the chalkboard and make a selection. One by one the top students erased their aircraft of choice. In rapid succession one T-38 disappeared, followed by the solitary A-1, followed by a C-141. Two more T-38s left the fold, then the T-37s began to fall. There was a certain fascination in watching who picked which aircraft, as long as you weren't watching your bird disappear off the board under someone else's eraser. Despite my rocky start, I'd managed to get through pilot training without ever flunking a test or a check ride. My perseverance allowed me the luxury of snagging my aircraft of choice, the C-130. I wasn't completely sure why I liked the Hercules, except that it did almost everything from hauling cargo and troops to close air support, search and rescue, reconnaissance, surveillance, and special ops. I was especially intrigued by the idea of tactical airlifts and landing on unimproved fields.

So I was reasonably content. I'd conquered UPT and even managed to lay claim to an airplane I genuinely wanted to fly. Life was good. The way I figured it, my C-130 and I would fly off into the sunset together. That vision lasted for about two weeks, until Pete Dunn, Ted Kolias, and I got a call from our flight training officer (FTO), informing us that our C-130s had turned into O-2As.

"So what's the deal anyway?" Pete Dunn asked as the three of us convened to analyze our new assignment. "What the heck's a stateside O-2? Is it better than a C-130? And for that matter, why us?"

We all shrugged and looked at one another.

"The way I understand it, we're three of twelve UPT grads who got pulled for this program," Ted volunteered. "They're starting two stateside FAC squadrons, one at Shaw and one at Bergstrom. I think if it works the way they hope it will, we'll head over to Vietnam a year or two from now thoroughly proficient in the O-2 and ready for combat."

It wasn't the worst news I'd ever gotten. In fact, it was kind of neat to be chosen for a new program. My love affair with the Hercules had been more of a passing crush, and I was easily swayed by the wink of an O-2, despite having little understanding of what one was.

As always, the needs of the Air Force came first, and I found myself preparing for a new and unexpected role as a forward air controller at Shaw Air Force Base. And so it came to pass that Lieutenant Jackson—awkward, mouthy, impatient little ex-altar boy—somehow managed to scrape by on a wing and a prayer to wear those coveted pilot's wings.

But first I would savor a moment that remains, to this day, the proudest accomplishment of my life: I would graduate from UPT. Despite my own worst fears, despite the Marquis de George, despite the best efforts of Colonel "Pure as the Driven Snow," I had endured, and triumphed. For one of the first and only times in my life, I found myself at a loss for words. That feeling was magnified on February 27, 1970, as my father sat proudly in the audience while Karen and my mother pinned pilot's wings on my chest.

I had never worked so hard for a goal, or fought with such determination to subdue my own inner demons. The significance of the moment resonated in my head. *Mike Jackson. Officer. Graduate. Pilot.*

CHAPTER SIX

I WILL
SURVIVE

HAVING endured the agony and the ecstasy—mostly agony—of pilot training, I braced myself for a brave new world wherein I was an Air Force officer, pilot, and husband. It was damned gratifying, especially because I'd come so close to scurrying home with my tail between my legs and my ego in tatters. I'd fought or finagled my way through most of the tough stuff and could finally concentrate on applying some of the lessons learned over the past eighteen months. With each new assignment, I was beginning to build my military support network, meeting the guys and their wives who would become our friends and would soon join me in the newly formed 704th Tactical Air Support Squadron (TASS) at Shaw Air Force Base, South Carolina.

But before I could fully embrace my new identity as an Air Force pilot, I had to prove my ability to survive under adverse conditions—as if pilot training hadn't provided me enough adversity to last a lifetime.

The Air Force now saw a need to test my mettle under extreme climatic conditions, which *did* make some sense. After all, if I ended up in Southeast Asia, I would need to be physically and mentally prepared to endure extreme heat, exotic insects, humidity, and monsoons. Naturally the military brain trust sent me to Fairchild Air Force Base in Washington State, where I spent sixteen glorious days up to my ass in—snow.

It was Easter 1970 and the fine powder in the mountains near Spokane had been stacking up for months—six feet high in most places, with drifts piled considerably deeper. The whole frigid mess was topped off by a deceptively delicate crust. I tried to reassure myself that escaping and evading in six feet of snow would have certain similarities to escaping and evading in a rain forest cluttered with bamboo spikes and palm fronds, but it was a tough sell. To make matters worse, some survival school weenie had decided that the presence of an icy crust negated the necessity for snowshoes. In fact, the crust was nothing more than—a crust. As we plodded into the wilderness, we spent more time falling through the crust and digging ourselves back out again than we did walking.

Misery consumed me as I slogged face-first into the arctic winds, but I consoled myself that others were considerably more miserable. On day ten, word filtered down that one of the lieutenant colonels had keeled over with a heart attack, courtesy of the relentless physical demands of falling six feet through the snow and scrambling back out again.

We were also treated to the lurid tale of an actual death within our ranks; one of the trainees reportedly defied the cardinal rule of never falling asleep in wet clothes.

True or not, the story motivated me to resist the lure of slipping into my mummy bag wearing anything more substantial than skin. Crawling back out the next day, however, proved to be a bit more daunting. During the night the mummy bag had done its job, wicking moisture away from my tender pink skin and splashing it across the ceiling of my "tent" (a rubber poncho stretched to its limit), where it condensed and froze, along with my breath and any precipitation that might have fallen in the darkness. The result was a cavernous glaze of ice crystals and stalactites that seared my delicate body parts as I struggled into my clothing.

Mealtime proved to be yet another adventure for those of us accustomed to the conveniences of suburbia. My lifeline was a god-awful substance known as pemmican, which had all the appeal of lard-flavored sand. I strongly considered eating bark, and even went so far as to concoct pine needle tea, which tasted every bit as bad as it sounds.

At one point the Air Force supplied us with fresh meat—*really* fresh, as in still alive. We temporarily acquired a traveling companion, a tame young rabbit with fleecy white fur, perky little ears, and bright pink bunny eyes.

As I stood fire watch on Easter eve, wrestling with bouts of boredom punctuated by exhaustion, I committed the unpardonable offense of making friends with my dinner. I scooped up Mr. Whiskers and chatted quietly with him in the darkness, sharing whispered observations about the weather, the campsite, and my snoring companions. Mr. Whiskers tilted his head and blinked his eager bunny eyes at me, telegraphing something I uneasily interpreted as trust.

My awkward alliance with the main course would come back to haunt me the next day as we made preparations for our Easter "feast." The irony of devouring a perky little bunny for Easter was not lost on me, and, despite my creeping hunger, I grew increasingly discontent with the whole process. Hesitance blossomed into full-fledged disgust as we reconvened for dinner.

Our instructor telegraphed his inexperience, or maybe just good old-fashioned stupidity, as he swaggered to the front of our group and announced, "I will now demonstrate how to kill the rabbit." We all cringed inside. *Not Mr. Whiskers! Not the Easter Bunny. Not on Easter!* Naturally no one was willing to endure the ridicule that would accompany such an unmanly admission, but it was clearly scrawled across each and every one of our faces.

Meanwhile, "Sergeant Survival" scooped up Mr. Whiskers as we stood rigid and attentive, like good little soldiers. "You want to get the rabbit relaxed," the instructor explained in his best soothing voice, taking hold of Mr. Whiskers' back legs and stroking him gently. "The objective is to calm him so that you prevent an adrenaline rush that'll impact the quality and flavor of the meat."

"That's a bunny . . . there, there little fellow," he crooned in an obnoxious, singsongy voice. "Just relax . . . that's right."

"Then," he continued his instructions, "when you can feel that his muscles are loose and at ease, you simply. . . ."

Whack!

We all flinched as Sergeant Survival sliced his hand sharply downward in what was supposed to be a killing karate chop. But with ineptitude born of incompetence, he managed to do nothing more than terrify the rabbit, which proceeded to violently twist and writhe in an effort to escape this lunatic, who was now whacking away at him like some crazed jujitsu master.

In the end, man triumphed over beast, but it wasn't pretty, and nobody's appetite was whetted by the whole episode. In typical macho form, Sergeant Survival made certain we knew that all parts of the rabbit were edible. "Okay, guys, who wants dibs on the eyeballs? How about a spoonful of brains? Ummmm, I've got a yummy plate of rabbit balls here."

I was disgusted. This was my buddy they were piecing out and frying up. I stood there, teetering on the brink of starvation, unable to stomach another bite of pemmican—desperate for a heaping plate of beef or pork—*anything* but Mr. Whiskers. Someone shoved a plate of rabbit crispies into my hand, and I stared at it blankly before shaking my head and stalking away.

As we entered the final phase of our training, I didn't have much time to dwell on the indignities suffered by Mr. Whiskers or on my own hunger pangs, which were gradually being replaced by a dull gnawing.

On day thirteen, our daily map-reading task carried a hidden twist. This time, by design, our directions led us straight into a trap. We were captured and placed in a mock prisoner of war (POW) camp. There was no way to avoid it; part of the purpose of the whole exercise was to acquaint us with the rigors of being taken prisoner.

By 1970, we were acutely aware that Americans were being held prisoner in North Vietnam. Some of these brave men had been there for more than four years. All of them, as we suspected and would eventually confirm, were being viciously tortured and mistreated by their captors, who cared little about the civilities of the Geneva Convention. Each of us understood that today's pretend capture could become tomorrow's real-life extended visit with the enemy.

Our POW exercise went to great lengths to expose us to the indignities of being captured by an opposing military force. We were blindfolded and tethered like market hogs. Our captors carried weapons (unloaded, or so we hoped) and addressed us as "pigs." We were methodically stripped of our humanity and individuality. Although we were never actually tortured, we were subjected to "stress maneuvers"—uncomfortable positions designed to simulate the physical impact of torture. We knew that these guys weren't enemy soldiers. In fact, rumor had it that our "captors" were CIA agents learning the ropes of interrogation. But despite knowing full well that we could not actually be killed, our minds slipped swiftly into the submissive prisoner mentality. We *were* less than human; we *were* pigs. We struggled to maintain our mental clarity and our tenuous grasp on reality.

We quickly learned that even mock POW status carried its own set of physical hazards. One of our routine punishments involved being folded into a narrow plywood box as a means of gaining our cooperation or compliance. I weathered the box discipline reasonably well, courtesy of an already skinny frame, made skinnier by two weeks of exercise and precious little food. Not everyone was as fortunate. One day we heard the screams of one of our fellow "prisoners," a guy I knew from pilot training, being dragged toward the boxes for some real or imagined infraction of the POW rules. He was bellowing at the top of his lungs—not exactly remarkable, because we'd been told we were supposed to resist and put up a fight. But this guy was pouring it on for all he was worth. The guards crammed him into the box and demanded silence, but the screams only intensified: "It hurts! Dammit, help me! It hurts!" Guided by the rules of the exercise, our captors simply screamed back at him.

"Shut up, you dirty pig, and stay in the box until you learn a little bit of respect."

"No, it hurts! I can't!"

One of the built-in, fail-safe measures of the POW exercise was that, at any time, you had the option of calling an "academic situation," which meant that the whole prisoner scenario was suspended and everything stopped.

Why this guy didn't think to call an academic situation is beyond me. It probably illustrates just how rattled, disoriented, and demoralized we all were. It turned out that he wasn't just role-playing the POW theme; he was deadly serious, and in terrible pain. The process of being folded into the cramped box had blown out one of his knees, bigtime. Here was a guy just like me; he'd struggled through OTS, struggled through pilot training, earned his wings, and was on his way to being an Air Force pilot and suddenly, wham! it was over. We heard later that the knee injury got him permanently grounded.

Gradually we each suffered our own mental or physical deterioration, and our captors did their best to capitalize on every weakness. They urged us to read war crime confessions and tempted us with food or blankets—anything that evoked a dim recollection of the comforts of the real world.

If that failed, they took a different approach. At one point I was isolated from my group and led into a small room, where my captors handed me a book of poetry and instructed me to read it aloud. I was puzzled but grudgingly complied, unable to fathom how such a silly exercise could compromise national security. With a distinct lack of enthusiasm, I mouthed a few pages.

Okay, guys, whatever the hell you say. If the fate of the free world hinges on how well I read Walt Whitman, we're all in trouble.

After I finished my recital, I was returned to the POW compound. That night they herded us into a room and played a curious film featuring a stern voice-over that intoned, "Some of your pig compatriots have, in fact, admitted their brutal atrocities, and here is one of your capitalist air pirates reading his confession."

Oops.

There I was up there on the screen, big as life—like a Technicolor Benedict Arnold—my lips moving, my face intent on the words in front of me. No matter that no one actually *heard* my voice, because *Leaves of Grass* just wouldn't have had the ring of a war crimes confession. But the seeds of doubt were effectively planted, and I became immediately suspect within the prisoner ranks. Once again, the line between fantasy and reality was uncomfortably blurred.

We were all on the same side—everyone in camp had pledged allegiance to the same government—yet I was suddenly a traitor, a conspirator, a piece of vermin who had betrayed his country and his fellow soldiers. In fact, a day later my status as a snitch became official when I was pulled away from my group and led into a dingy office at the far edge of the compound. This time the guard sat on the edge of the desk and eyed me for a second before mouthing the words "academic situation." Now a fellow patriot instead of a tormentor, he explained that they wanted me to become a spy.

"In a real POW situation, there will be men among you who cannot be trusted, whose ticket to comfort and nourishment will be purchased at the expense of their fellow prisoners. They are the most insidious danger of all, because they appear to be just like you." He leveled a hard stare at me and continued talking. "Their reports to the enemy of conversations, infractions, or escape plans can endanger those of you struggling to maintain your honor and loyalty. From here on out, I want you to move among your fellow prisoners as a spy, gathering information and observations and bringing them to me. It's not a pleasant assignment, but it could mean the difference between life and death for one of these guys down the road."

So I became Scoop the Snitch, a role that, even as make-believe, I found unsettling and distasteful. On the plus side, there was little for me to spy on, because no one could have escaped to much of anywhere. Anyway, my fellow prisoners were decidedly guarded around me, thanks to my little taped "confession." But I guess I did okay as a spy, because I was asked to stay several extra days for additional training, which, to this day, I can't talk about. Suffice it to say, I'm just glad I never had to apply any of it.

The entire survival training process, especially the POW exercise, was designed to teach us one critical reality: anyone can be broken. It was an important lesson for those of us headed to Southeast Asia. We needed to learn that not only could we be broken, it could be done swiftly and even at the hands of those we knew couldn't really harm us.

The whole POW exercise reinforced what each of us had secretly believed all along: You save one bullet, and you use it on yourself if all hope is lost. We had a new understanding and appreciation of what we would all carry into combat, and beyond: Some things are worse than death.

When at last they dragged our sorry asses back to Fairchild Air Force Base, I made a beeline for the dining hall and loaded my plate as high as I could get it. Then I sat down to gorge—and was overcome by a sharp wave of nausea. All I had been able to think about for days was what I'd eat, and when, and how much. But physical and mental stress had taken such a toll on my body that it now vehemently rejected the introduction of anything as exotic as real food. It was days before my strength and my appetite regained their typical potency.

Once I'd recovered from the rigors of survival school, it was off to Shaw Air Force Base, where one of two new stateside FAC squadrons would be based. With a few weeks to kill before heading to Hurlburt Field's O-2 school, waggishly referred to as FAC University or FAC U, Tom O'Neill, another new second lieutenant, and I got a month-long impromptu introductory course on the care and feeding of the O-2. Tom was my alter ego and favorite drinking buddy; we were both eager to "test our wings," both figuratively and literally.

As the first future FACs to arrive at Shaw, we were greeted by the squadron commander, the ops officer, and an impressive array of shiny new O-2s, poised on the flight line awaiting the eager touch of a brand-new Air Force pilot. Although Tom and I were not yet qualified to fly the birds, each time the commander or the ops officer took one up, we'd get an invitation to ride along. It was an ideal, no-pressure way to familiarize ourselves with the aircraft. And it was an easy aircraft to get to know. After our UPT progression from the T-41 to the T-37 to the complex supersonic T-38, it felt strange to graduate into a simple little machine with nothing more demanding than two seats, two wings, and two props. During my month at Shaw, I pored over the Dash-1—the Air Force equivalent of an aircraft owner's manual. The crew chiefs showed us around, offering us their insights into the O-2's quirks and qualities; and I even carved out some time to just sit in the cockpit and memorize the layout of the instrument panel.

By the time we packed our bags and headed for Hurlburt Field in Fort Walton Beach, Florida, we were reasonably comfortable with the form and function of our new airplane.

After my angst-ridden fifty-three weeks of pilot training, I was almost giddy at the idea of heading into a new round of training with a slight advantage over the other students. In fact, as we began flying the O-2s on a regular basis, I enjoyed a confidence and comfort level that I never thought possible during those tense early days with the Marquis de George. Undergraduate pilot training had already taught us the mechanics of flight, the hows, whys, whens, and wheres. O-2 school simply added a new aircraft to our repertoire, an odd-looking, sluggish little machine that seemed singularly ill-equipped for combat. That the O-2 was not exactly a fire-eating war machine was lost on no one.

"So how do you think this thing will perform in combat?" Tom asked uneasily as we walked from the flight line one balmy afternoon.

I shrugged and glanced back at the row of sturdy little push-me, pull-you airplanes.

"I dunno. I really like the fact that it's an easy airplane to fly. You hardly have to think about what you're doing. It just does its thing and takes you along for the ride. That's gonna mean a lot if we're studying maps, dodging ground fire, and trying to direct an air strike, doncha think?"

Tom nodded but retained a certain keen skepticism.

"Yeah, I suppose, but the damn thing doesn't have an ejection seat or armor or anything remotely approaching speed, and you can barely see out the right window," he argued.

I couldn't debate his logic; I just hoped that the O-2 would prove itself up to the challenges of FACing. And even if it didn't—especially if it didn't—I wanted to be sure I knew everything there was to know about pushing it to the limits of its design.

"Yeah, you've got a point," I conceded, "but I guess we're stuck with it. It wasn't my first choice either, but we could have ended up in something worse."

We began our Hurlburt training in Air Ground Operations School (AGOS). Because we would be working closely with the Army (they were the guys on the ground with whom we'd have to coordinate), we studied the Army's organizational set-up, its terminology and structure. We learned how we would interact through our air liaison officer (ALO), the Air Force officer who served as a link between the FACs and the Army. The ALO attended Army staff and intelligence meetings and coordinated communications and organization between the two military units.

We also got a lesson in how the tactical air control system worked, as well as an introduction to the formal mechanics of being a FAC. After that, we got checked out on M-16s, then headed over to nearby Holly Field, where we climbed into our O-2s and it was "up in the air, junior birdmen!"

The academic aspects of FAC U weren't especially challenging, and I had to chuckle as I listened to some of the guys complain about the frantic, ping-pong attention shifts that were standard operating procedure on any FAC mission. If ever there was a job custom-tailored to my rapid-fire mental gyrations, this was it. I never had the opportunity to get bored, never lost my focus, never needed to shake the cobwebs from my mind. I had been handed the perfect assignment—constant challenge and stimulation. Much to my delight, for the first time in my career as a pilot, I was actually thriving.

Except for the twelve of us bound for Bergstrom and Shaw, everyone else in O-2 school had an immediate ticket to Southeast Asia or Korea as soon as training ended. As I had been doing for what seemed like most of my life, I weighed the possibility that I might actually see combat. If I spent a couple of years stateside, surely the war would be over by then—wouldn't it?

Okay, let's get real, Scoop. You've been playing this game for, how long, five years? Eight? Might as well stop second-guessing fate. Somehow, some way, you're headed to Vietnam. No one seems especially concerned about ending this thing before you get there.

It wasn't as if I could have ignored the prospect of combat. Every classroom endeavor, every moment of flight training emphasized one key element: the unpredictable variables of combat. Most of our instructors were fresh from Southeast Asia, and they made a point of drawing distinctions between how we functioned in the classroom and how different our lives would be under fire.

Once we got the hang of flying our O-2s, we worked with the A-1s and F-4s from nearby Eglin Air Force Base to hone our proficiency at directing air strikes.

Despite the ever-present shadow of war, life at FAC U moved along at a casual and entertaining pace. I was beginning to see the unique "club membership" aspect of the Air Force as I crossed paths with previous acquaintances from OTS and UPT and began building the network that would follow me to Vietnam and through twenty-three years of active service. We were coalescing as a group, forging ties that would endure across many years and miles.

Contrary to the urgent pace of UPT, leisure time suddenly became more abundant. We were determined to make the most of it, savoring afternoons and weekends at the beach or on the water. We discovered the culinary joys of a concoction known as the What-A-Burger; I managed to wear a path between our apartment complex pool and the hamburger stand on the corner. We also became regulars at Earthquake O'Runyan's, where we refined our skill in the art of foosball.

To fully embrace the pleasures of living near the Gulf of Mexico, Tom O'Neill and I took a few extra hours of classroom time to get certified to drive a boat. The Air Force morale, welfare, and recreation program provided a private fleet of rental boats at the Hurlburt Field marina, and we eagerly dipped our toes into the brave new world of water-skiing.

I had never water-skied in my life, but it was great fun to gather the wives and go tooling around the bay in a speedy little motorboat. It was even more fun to challenge my dexterity and muscle tone on the skis. On one of our first boat trips, Tom took the wheel and pulled me through the surf as I reveled in the sun and water. When it came time for Tom's turn on the skis, I carefully backed up the boat—did I mention that I'd never in my life driven a boat?—and gave him plenty of slack rope with which to get situated and poised for his spin in the spray. When he gave me the thumbs-up, I hit the gas and took off at top speed, skimming happily across the waves, pausing only to shout above the din of the engine, "How's he doing?" Both wives answered in unison, "He's not! He hasn't moved yet." *Huh?* I craned my head around and noticed that Tom had all but disappeared between the swells. *Man, either that's the world's longest tow rope or. . . .*

I grinned sheepishly as I brought the boat around and headed back to my bobbing buddy. In all my careful maneuvering and backing of the boat, I had managed to slice up the tow rope with the prop. Well, so much for sun and fun. Without a spare tow rope, we were forced to abandon our outing. Tom never did get his moment on the skis, at least not that day. But such was the relaxed silliness that filled our days at Hurlburt.

All in all, it was a challenging but immensely satisfying existence. The recent past of T-41s and the Marquis de George seemed like a fading nightmare. The nebulous future—one that would surely include combat—was too undefined and, perhaps, too unthinkable to intrude on the comfortable charm of the moment.

But suddenly the moment was gone, and I was cutting my teeth on a new aircraft in a new locale—the AT-33 at Cannon Air Force Base in New Mexico.

CHAPTER SEVEN

FLYING BLIND

IT SEEMED to me that the Air Force had gotten things backward. Here I was, freshly trained on the complexities of FACing and O-2s. But instead of settling in at Shaw with my stateside FAC unit, July 1970 found me heading to Cannon Air Force Base in Clovis, New Mexico. There, presumably, I'd master the AT-33, by which time I would probably forget everything I'd learned about the O-2. Oh well, the Air Force knew best. Even if they didn't, they were the ones calling the shots.

AT-33s were the next step in my evolution as a fighter pilot, and I relished the opportunity to expand my growing aviation competency. My new airplane was an offshoot of Lockheed's highly successful P-80 Shooting Star, a mainstay during the Korean conflict. Despite having been designed by Kelly Johnson's fabled Skunkworks crew, the AT-33 featured some engineering quirks that frequently left me scratching my head and wondering whether Johnson's team secretly hated pilots.

The whole machine reeked of 1940s and 1950s technology, and I soon found myself struggling with boost pumps, instruments, and electronics that were primitive, at best. The cockpit switches were apparently laid out by someone fond of scavenger hunts, making my crosscheck procedures almost impossible. And the intervalometer, which allowed the pilot to alternate between ordnance, had been positioned so that only a contortionist could effectively use it! Once airborne, I struggled to maintain formation while blindly groping behind the seat, hoping to somehow hit the right switch.

But despite its structural idiosyncrasies, the AT-33 was a real confidence builder when weighed against my benchmark disaster in T-41s. Every once in a while, however, the airplane got the last laugh. The snickering started with my first flight as I, the earnest young Lieutenant Jackson, climbed into the cockpit wearing my G-suit and feeling every bit the professional fighter pilot. I settled in quickly, touching the instruments to familiarize myself with location and purpose, and nudging my fanny into a snug though lumpy spot against the seat-packed parachute. But my comfort level began to ebb as I struggled to plug myself into what I thought was the G-suit hose. Annoyed and ever-impatient, I was vigorously cursing the entire staff of Lockheed, their children and grandchildren, when my instructor leaned over the canopy rail and informed me—with poorly concealed amusement—that I was trying to plug into the relief tube. Talk about a humbling experience.

Ah, Jackson, this is a seminal moment in your evolution as a fighter pilot. You are proud, you are calm, you are cocky—and you just plugged your G-suit into the pee tube. Nice going, Ace.

Aside from mild embarrassment, my main reaction was an overwhelming desire to slink off into a corner and sanitize my hands.

But if this new aircraft occasionally got the better of me, I was far from alone—and more fortunate than some. For my buddy Tom McGrath, the AT-33 was a harsh mistress with a puckish sense of humor that left everyone in stitches except Tom. On one of our first solo flights, we discovered that the absence of nose wheel steering could be a source of great amusement to those *not* sitting in Tom's cockpit.

As we headed for the practice range in our standard flight of four, McGrath was the last guy out of the chocks. He completed his final check and started to pull away, whereupon he inadvertently cocked his nose gear to the left. The only solution for cocked nose gear was to run up the throttle and start kicking the brake pedals in an effort to jar the nose wheel loose. Tom rocked the aircraft back and forth with great impatience and frustration, but the gear remained off kilter, until the crew chief came over and pulled it back into alignment.

Freed from his predicament, Tom taxied out to the arming area, where he gently guided the airplane toward the runway, and cocked the nose gear again! So there he sat, spinning the AT-33 around and around in circles, praying that the gear would magically dislodge itself and that no one would notice the befuddled second lieutenant chasing his tail all over the tarmac. No such luck. The guys in the arming area converged on the airplane and pushed its wayward nose gear back into alignment.

It was embarrassing enough to require assistance once; twice was downright humiliating. But Tom managed to shake it off and point his airplane out of the arming area—only to cock the nose gear a third time. By now the poor guy's only hope for deliverance was that the earth would open up and swallow him whole, AT-33 and all. But matters continued to deteriorate as the crew chief gave him the "canopy up" signal and climbed into the instructor's rear seat. An uneasy silence filled the cockpit as the ground pounder willfully seized control, taxied a mortified McGrath out of the arming area, and carefully lined him up on the runway before breaking the silence. "Okay, Lieutenant, can you manage from here?"

Tom nodded, thoroughly disgusted with himself, his aircraft, the crew chief, and the entire military-industrial complex. Those of us who lived, worked, and studied alongside him were the first to express our sensitivity to his distress. In a show of solidarity, we fashioned a special pick-me-up designed to commemorate his blunder—the golden cocked nose gear award.

One thing about Tom, though: he stubbornly charted his own course, even when it meant taking the road less traveled and dragging me along with him. After exiting the practice range one morning, having completed a series of reasonably efficient rocket, bombing, and strafing maneuvers, we headed back to Cannon in "elements"—two two-aircraft formations. Coming off the range, we were to execute a maneuver known as a turning rejoin, wherein the second of two elements swings around and joins on the first two aircraft, allowing a return to base in a four-ship formation.

Naturally the whole rationale for heading back to base was, "I've wrung out the aircraft, I've pressed the limits of my own endurance, and I've pretty much drained the old fuel tank. Time to call it a day."

McGrath and I were in the second element; Pete Dunn and our instructor pilot headed off the range just ahead of us. Still somewhat tentative about making command decisions where airplanes were concerned, I trusted McGrath's navigational skills as I turned my attention toward flying the airplane and maintaining formation. The radio crackled to life as lead inquired about our location. "Do you have us in sight?" the instructor asked.

"Roger," Tom said confidently. "I've got you directly ahead of me. We're executing the turning rejoin."

Well, heck, he sounded darned sure, and who was I to argue? I stuck close and focused on maintaining assured clear distance between him and me.

After a few minutes of silence, lead piped up suddenly. "Three, are you sure you've got me in sight?" he asked, his controlled "instructor voice" fluttering momentarily between curiosity and concern.

Once again Tom responded with cool-as-a-cucumber assurance. "Yessir. I've got you at twelve o'clock, and we should start to close on you any second now."

"Uh, exactly what is your air speed?" came the puzzled reply.

"Three is passing two seven five knots."

Our instructor's voice grew suddenly animated as he evidently realized with dreadful certainty that his young charges couldn't possibly be anywhere near Cannon Air Force Base. "Three, what is your heading?"

"We're at two seven zero degrees, sir, and I can still see you out front," Tom said, his voice continuing to resonate total mastery of the aircraft.

I, on the other hand, was beginning to feel a strange, clawing sensation somewhere deep in my gut. Was there some kind of Bermuda Triangle lurking over New Mexico that McGrath and I had unwittingly stumbled into? And what was he following that gave him so much confidence, and so little fuel? My muscles grew rigid as I watched my fuel gauge tumble toward minimum fuel. To make matters worse, I was suddenly acutely aware of every aviation horror story I'd ever read that ended with "and they were never heard from again."

An endless litany of famous last words ricocheted around my head: "Right on course. Should make landfall soon." "Low on fuel—can't see the island, will circle around and come back for another try." "Can't see the ocean—can't see anything. Where the hell are we?"

Yikes. It all sounded suddenly and alarmingly familiar.

"You're what? Two seven zero?" The instructor's voice was terse and tight. "Well, that would be your first problem, Lieutenant, because *we* are heading zero nine zero degrees, approaching the entry point to Cannon Air Force Base. And we have *you* nowhere in sight."

There was a moment of silence as I held my breath, waiting to hear Tom announce with pluck and vigor that he had everything under control, that he could see Cannon Air Force Base sprawling just this side of the horizon. But Tom's voice was a long time in coming, and when at last it did come, it sounded as though it belonged to someone else—someone awkward and scared, someone embarrassed, someone who had once earned the cocked nose gear award.

"Uh, lead, this is Three. We will be correcting to zero nine zero. There was a . . . uh . . . some kind of bug spot on my windscreen that I mistook for your element. Uh, sorry."

The chatter died. I would have felt tremendous sympathy for Tom (no doubt well concealed beneath a generous portion of razzing) if I hadn't been so terrified that the last drop of fuel was being sucked from my tanks. I braced myself for the engine flameout that would precede an eerie silence, and my own realization that fighter jets make lousy gliders.

Face it, Jackson, the next sound you hear will be the blast of your ejection seat as it exits the airplane. Cripes. When did I become the kind of pilot who walks home from a flight? *Hmmm, well, for starters, when you put your fate in the hands of a guy who can't tell a fighter jet formation from a flyspeck.*

Amid much praying and sweating, we did eventually make it back to Cannon. In the end, the whole ordeal was probably a good thing, because I began to understand that my success in the military, as in life, would hinge on taking matters into my own hands and depending far less on the wisdom of others, especially others no better informed than I. The fly speck epiphany would require additional bolstering in the coming years (and it would get plenty), but I was beginning to see a disturbing trend in my life. I had always believed that things would work out to my advantage in any given situation—and by and large they did. But my military education was teaching me that optimism and trust, although powerful tools, could always benefit from a healthy dose of hands-on manipulation. This realization crystallized the ingredients that would eventually define my career, not to mention my life.

McGrath and I endured significant abuse, thanks to our unorthodox turning rejoin. Not that I cared. I was alive to hear the laughter; everything else was academic. And somehow, over the short but eventful twelve-week curriculum, we all managed to muddle our way through AT-33s without killing ourselves or anyone else. Slowly and often painfully, we were maturing and evolving, gaining confidence and experience, and doing more than our share of "living through" along the way.

Thus it was a more seasoned, self-confident herd of first lieutenants who reconvened at Shaw Air Force Base in September 1970 as members of the 704th Tactical Air Support Squadron. We were not yet tempered by battle but considerably more worldly than the awkward, inexperienced kids who had stumbled through OTS woolly marches with a mixture of awe and confusion. The 704th was a brand-new squadron, made up of a blend of Vietnam returnees and newly minted FACs, who would probably end up in Southeast Asia sooner rather than later. A similar mixed squadron was also initiated at Bergstrom Air Force Base in Texas.

Six of us—Lyndle Price, Tom O'Neill, Tom McGrath, Pete Dunn, Ted Kolias, and I—made up the contingent of the 704th known as "the green beans." This uncomplimentary title sprung from our commanding officer's contention that, as novice pilots, we were somewhere south of amoebas as a life form. It was a nickname offered with contempt but ultimately worn by each of us as a badge of honor.

The green bean designation wasn't common knowledge, at least not until I stumbled across it by accident. I'd gone to look at the scheduling board by the squadron ops counter and discovered that I had been assigned to fly Col. Cy Strain, commander of the 68th Tac Air Support Group, to an upcoming event. As a lowly lieutenant, I would have been intimidated by the idea of flying *any* colonel anywhere, but Cy Strain wasn't just any colonel. He was an unapologetic hard-ass, an iron-fisted officer who ran five miles each day, jumped out of helicopters for fun, and probably devoured eager young lieutenants for breakfast. I wasn't worried about him critiquing my flying, but I was pretty uneasy about my ability to carry on any kind of intelligent conversation with him.

It turned out I wasn't the only one who was concerned. Rounding the corner into the ops office, I overheard our squadron commander, Lt. Col. O. P. Fisher, ranting to the operations officer, Major Field, about whose cockeyed idea it was to assign me to fly Colonel Strain.

"What the hell are you doing assigning one of those green beans to fly Colonel Strain? He's a colonel; he doesn't want to fly around with a damned green bean," Fisher railed, turning just in time to see me cross the threshold of the office. We both stopped short—he in mid-sentence, I in mid-stride. It was too late. I was already committed, so I marched in as though I owned the place and grinned awkwardly at the blustering colonel.

"Green bean? What's a green bean?" I asked, already sure it wasn't a term of endearment.

Fisher stumbled over his words and muttered a few clumsy sentences about how green bean was just another term for new guy.

Yeah, right.

I shrugged and nodded. There wasn't much else I could do. Naturally I made a hasty exit and shared this valuable intelligence with my fellow "beans."

Rather than being angered by our green bean status, we opted to embrace it and make it our own. There were seven of us: six lieutenants and a captain, Stan Buszak, who had served as a navigator before going through pilot training. Although Stan theoretically had more military experience than the other green beans, he was no more or less a pilot than we were. We did, however, waggishly acknowledge his superior rank by designating him the "seasoned bean." Our decision to gracefully accept Colonel Fisher's derogatory nickname reflected a certain level of maturity, which began to gel as we expanded our life experiences and grew more conscious of the rapid approach of combat.

Our recent promotion to first lieutenant had carried with it a heightened sense of confidence and situational savvy, which may have been there all along. But, like the Scarecrow and his diploma, or the Tin Man and his heart-watch, we now had tangible evidence of a certain level of superiority. We gratefully accepted our new position on the Air Force totem pole and breathed a collective sigh of relief that we were no longer the guys squatting at the very bottom.

But it was while Tom O'Neill and I were attending counterinsurgency training at Hurlburt that we were "educated" about the necessity of staging a promotion party. Nobody had told us that we were expected to usher in the promotion process with a night of total debauchery. Never having been promoted before, we were blissfully ignorant until several worldly-wise captains caught wind of the oversight and reprimanded us for our breach of military protocol. And who were we to argue with the idea of partying until dawn and behaving in a manner both raucous and rude?

Returning to Shaw, Tom and I and the other newly promoted green beans took it upon ourselves to right this grievous wrong. We selected a hippie theme for the festivities, probably the closest any of us would ever get to joining the counterculture. The party would also do double duty as a bachelor soiree for Pete Dunn, whose days as a single guy were winding down rapidly.

As the guest of honor, Pete was expected to live up to his status as freshly christened fighter pilot by drinking himself into that narrow state of being somewhere between unconsciousness and alcohol poisoning.

He made it there with surprising speed, and we all followed energetically. The drink of choice that night was, appropriately, a fiery concoction known as an afterburner—tequila in a shot glass, topped off with a lighted match.

The objective was to yell "afterburner" and pound the drink down as quickly as possible, finishing it completely without extinguishing the flames in the process. Squelching the fire meant an automatic "do over," which, if improperly executed, was rewarded with, well, yet another drink. As the evening wore on, the mechanics of drinking became more of a challenge, and we found ourselves slopping our shot glasses all over the bar, which was nothing more than a card table draped in oilcloth. Somewhere between the sixth and the tenth round, it all dissolved into a hazy blur of shouts, slurps, and energetic applause—until Pete hoisted his glass unsteadily, bellowed "afterburner," and managed to completely miss his mouth, tossing the entire concoction onto his face, fire and all.

The room went strangely silent as we all gazed stupidly at Pete, who was now sporting the kind of goofy, half-puzzled expression you'd expect from someone whose face had spontaneously combusted. We stood there for a moment, awestruck not by the presence of our very own human torch but by the lava-like way the blazing alcohol oozed down Pete's cheek and fell toward the floor in flaming clumps, igniting the tablecloth and everything else in its path. Springing to Pete's rescue, we tossed the contents of our glasses toward Pete's face, the table, the floor, and even one another, apparently embracing wholeheartedly the old adage "fight fire with fire." Naturally our actions did not have the desired effect; the flames continued to spread, and we stumbled blindly around flailing our arms, napkins, and jackets in a clumsy effort to extinguish the blaze.

Eventually we succeeded, and Lyndle Price promptly hustled Pete off to the emergency room, where the groom-to-be acquired a lot of curious stares and a huge gauze bandage across his cheek. Pete accepted his injury with typical good humor. His new bride, however, was slightly less forgiving; she anxiously feared that Pete's gauze-draped "battle scar" would shine like a beacon in each and every photo of the upcoming nuptials. Fortunately for the newlyweds—and their future wedded bliss—Pete proved to be a fast healer.

Days passed, and our time as greenhorns—and as green beans—began to dwindle. The parties, cookouts, and mischief continued, but we all had the uneasy sense of living in the shadow of a relentless clock. No matter how urgent our efforts to stay the sweep of those hands, the minutes and seconds kept rolling over into hours and days, each one placing us a little closer to a very uncertain future.

Back at Shaw, we split our time between flying and fun, often combining the two to the best of our ability. Frequently we'd fly over to the Poinsett range to shoot rockets for score, then head out on our own to practice our VR, which stood for visual reconnaissance but actually meant screwing off. For my part, VR involved flying over to Karen's school at the end of the day and following her home. I'd log the flying time as "convoy cover training." Sometimes I'd head out to Fort Sumter and fly over the ocean and scope out the sunbathers. I had the world's greatest job, and I never failed to wring every ounce of fun from it.

When one of my friends from Tipp City and Ohio University, Bob Hinton, joined the Army and swung through Shaw on his way to Fort Rucker and helicopter training, I said, "Hey, let's fly over to the range and shoot some rockets." Because we were a new squadron, populated with brand-new officers, there was a certain relaxed demeanor to our form and function. As a charter member of the squadron, I felt a special ownership and confidence in making executive decisions regarding the use of my plane. It never occurred to me that I should get anyone's permission.

I dragged Bob over to the parachute room, and he strapped on a chute and we headed off into the wild blue yonder. When we were airborne, I pointed to the exterior of the aircraft. "You can have that pod of rockets; I'll take this one." We proceeded to shoot rockets and generally have a good time. Then we decided to check out Fort Benning for lunch. Bob would eventually be stationed there, and I was pleased to be able to give him his first official airborne peek at the Army post. After a satisfying lunch, we headed back via the scenic route, tracing meandering rivers and weaving through rolling hills. It was great fun. I later treated my next-door neighbor, another Air Force lieutenant, to a similar junket. It never occurred to me that the Air Force might not be crazy about Mike's airborne taxi service. In retrospect, I guess we did some pretty stupid things, but I also suspect that they were no more or less stupid than the actions of those who preceded or followed us.

By now the green beans had become a force to be reckoned with. We were secure in our flying skills, giddy with our status as Air Force officers, and completely at ease with one another. Our wives were friends, and our lives revolved around the same places, events, and hardware. Work and leisure blended seamlessly, creating endless activities and spontaneous entertainment.

One spring evening, we beans and our wives retreated to Tom McGrath's house for our semi-regular Saturday party. As often happened, the conversation and the alcohol began to flow liberally, and we were pretty much in our cups when the weather outside began to deteriorate.

"Man, that's some nasty stuff building out there," Ted Kolias said before taking a swig from his beer and pacing back and forth in front of McGrath's front window. The sky had gone from blue to gray to black, and the wind had died down into an eerie stillness.

Not that we cared.

"C'mon, Ted, get with the program," I shouted. "Who cares about a little bit of weather? It's not like we're flying into it—bring it on! But I sure could use another drink."

Ted shrugged and gave the window a last furtive look before heading out to the kitchen to complete his assigned mission.

Lost in conversation and camaraderie, we barely noticed when McGrath scrambled to answer his phone. But we all noticed as he stood wobbling before us, forcing a serious expression to his face.

"That, guys, was our beloved commander, who's been trying to track us down for thirty minutes. He wanted to let us know that the area is under a tornado warning, and we'd better get our asses over to the ramp and hangar the airplanes," McGrath announced with exaggerated eloquence.

We all agreed that the combination of tornadoes, booze, airplanes, and fighter pilots gave the day a certain luster of potential. We decided to further up the ante by dragging our wives along.

Once at the airfield, we handed flight helmets to the women, loaded them into the airplanes, and began taxiing all over the ramp like a squadron of frenzied kiddy cars.

After we tired of taxiing, we started racing the O-2s down the runway, getting up enough speed to briefly leave the ground in order to share the thrill of flight with our better halves. We got permission from the control tower to be on the runway, of course, but they had no idea we were stinking drunk and our wives were flying right seat.

Savoring the humor of the moment, we gleefully raced the airplanes back and forth, oblivious to the towering thunderclouds spilling across the horizon. After a while our wives got into the act and began radioing back and forth, leaving the tower thoroughly confused. Eventually daylight began to fade and we lost interest in the earthbound antics, so we retired our aircraft to their hangars and headed back to McGrath's house to finish the cookout. Surprisingly we never heard a word from the Air Force brass about our runway romp, not even so much as a "what the hell were you guys doing?" There was a war going on; maybe they figured they'd let us have our fun while we could. More likely, however, they never heard from our friends in the tower just how much fun we were having.

We returned to McGrath's, only to discover that our perfectly grilled steaks had grown cold during the airfield maneuvers, so Tom retrieved the steaks from our plates and headed back out to the grill. He came back minutes later with a plate of beautifully charred meat. During his absence we had tossed back a few more drinks and were now in serious need of something to sop them up. The steaks were an ideal sponge, and I tore into mine before anyone else had a chance. But I stopped in mid-chew and caught myself ready to gag. I'd never tasted anything so horrible; in fact, I continued chewing only because I couldn't believe that my taste buds were functioning properly. Nothing could be that bad. As I sat there trying to decide whether to spit the meat across the room or keep chewing and hope it improved, I glanced around the table and noticed twelve equally pained faces in various stages of "prepuke." Thus satisfied that it wasn't a case of Jackson's defective taste buds, I spit the wad of meat into my hand and tried to claw the residue off my tongue as I howled, "This stuff tastes like crap!" My declaration opened the floodgates as everyone else began spitting steak onto their plates, into their hands, and across the table, desperate to rid their mouths of the terrible taste and smell. Having regained our composure, we all stared at Tom indignantly, demanding to know what he had done to our steaks. A seriously inebriated McGrath shrugged and looked at us as though we were a pack of weaselly little ingrates. "Well, I knew we were in a hurry to eat, and the coals had died down, so I squirted lighter fluid right on the steaks and set them on fire!"

Fortunately, the alcohol had dulled our retaliatory instincts. After deciding that Tom probably hadn't intentionally tried to poison us, we pitched the steaks, devoured the potatoes, consumed a few more drinks, and agreed that, henceforth, Tom would toss the salad.

Some of our education at Shaw was unplanned. One night at the O-club, we had all bellied up to the bar and were telling tales of aerial daring and mischief, tales that inevitably grew more exciting and dramatic as the evening—and the alcohol supply—dwindled. Chatting happily with our little group was a captain named Lyn Luebke, one of the guys in our squadron who had done his time in Vietnam and lived to tell the tale. If anyone in our group that night had a right to be telling war stories, it was Lyn. We listened to his tales of "the 'Nam" and lapped up the energy and adrenaline as he recounted firefights and arc light missions and air strikes under the worst weather conditions imaginable. Here was a man who had looked death squarely in the face and emerged unscathed. We were in awe of his bravery and eager to gain the benefit of his experiences.

After a few drinks and more than a few harrowing stories, Lyn excused himself to find the men's room. The rest of us moved on to other topics, analyzing and digesting a number of weighty issues before it occurred to us that Lyn had been gone for quite some time. We dispatched a scout to check out the men's room for disabled captains; he returned to our table shaking his head. No Lyn. We looked at one another and shrugged. Maybe he'd decided to call it a night. Or maybe he'd just wandered away for a bit. If so, we figured he'd eventually wander back.

Sure enough: after about an hour, Lyn returned, looking far more like a chastened little boy than a swaggering fighter pilot. Sliding silently back up to the table, he locked his hands around a cold glass of beer and regaled us with the most harrowing war story yet.

As Captain Luebke had made his way from the bar to the men's room, he had become disoriented by recent O-club renovations that had uprooted and rearranged the bathroom facilities. After getting back his bearings, he found the toilet and settled into one of the stalls for a moment of relaxation and reflection. And there he sat, flight suit swaddled around his ankles, when the bathroom door swung open and a herd of high-pitched, high-heeled individuals clattered in.

Realizing that he had somehow managed to settle into the wrong restroom, Lyn wrapped his flight suit around his calves and braced his legs against the stall door, waiting for the restroom to empty out so he could make a hasty and covert exit.

"But they never seemed to leave, and if they did leave, more took their place," he wailed, sounding like a shell-shocked ground pounder just in from the front lines. "I didn't know what to do. Someone would push on the door and say, 'Oh, excuse me,' and I'd make some strange, shrill 'woman noise' in response. I was sure they'd find me. It got to the point where I couldn't come out, because I'd been in there so long, and I had no idea how to explain why I stayed, without sounding like a pervert!"

Lyn took a long swig from the glass he'd been clutching, and rubbed his hands briskly across his face before uttering what would be his concluding statement on the whole sordid affair: "You guys just would *not* believe the things I heard in there."

Whereas we had earlier quizzed him relentlessly about the savagery of battle, we now fell silent and gazed uneasily at one another. There were some things that man was simply not meant to be privy to, literally.

Suddenly, the clock wound down. It was all over—the learning, the practice FACing, the camaraderie, the parties. We were saying good-bye again, only this time the destination wasn't a classroom, at least not like any classroom I'd ever seen. But I was ready to go. In fact, I had volunteered to go.

Several months prior, we had been given the option of serving in Korea or Vietnam. It wasn't exactly a surprise; we had known all along that we would eventually be "made available for Southeast Asia remote." We understood that we weren't going to be in a stateside FAC squadron forever; in fact, part of the function of the squadron was to create a combat-ready supply of FACs who could be deployed to Vietnam and, once there, could be counted on to hit the ground running.

For me, there was really no choice to be made. I knew where I was going, and I knew why. I was an Air Force officer, trained for combat, trained to defend the principles and values of my country. Why be in the military during wartime and not go to war? It just made no sense to me. There was a strong element of duty and honor wrapped up in my decision, but also an understanding that Vietnam had been stalking me for ten years: the time had come to turn and face the beast squarely. Let the games begin.

CHAPTER EIGHT

BAMBOOZLED

OTHER VOICES: Debbie Jackson Becher

WHEN Mike left for Vietnam I was entering the eighth grade. I had gotten used to my big brother not being around much. I was very young when he left for college; and although he would come home during the summers, he worked full-time and was always on the go. After college, he went into the Air Force. My family understood what was in store for him—Vietnam—but we never talked about it much. When Mike left for Southeast Asia, both Mom and Dad cried, and so did I. I was so scared for him; I prayed every day for his safe return. Mom and Dad never missed the evening news. They had a map of Vietnam on the wall in the laundry area of our basement. Dad liked to keep track of where Mike was, and what was going on around him. It seemed to reassure him. Not me. I hated that map. It was a reminder of all my worst fears. It was just too much reality for my young mind.

My wait at the airport was excruciatingly long—or painfully short; I couldn't quite decide which. For the moment, time lacked any real definition. Whether I sat in the terminal for twenty minutes or twenty hours, my destination wasn't going to change. In a matter of days I'd be flying low, slow missions over a strange country and a whole bunch of angry people with guns, big guns. But that was what I'd signed up to do. I wasn't eager to get shot at, but I *was* anxious to turn the page and see what happened next.

I'd managed to keep my emotions in check during the family farewell. I was more conscious of their pain and anxiety than my own, sensing that any crack in my composure would only intensify their feelings of helplessness and apprehension. It was important to me to minimize their fears. At least I had the luxury of being the guy who was headed into the great unknown. I might not have much fun out there, but at any given time I'd know where I was and what I was doing, and that I was alive. It bothered me to think that there might be stretches of time in the days ahead when my family wouldn't have the comfort of such knowledge. To me, the weight of that uncertainty seemed infinitely more unbearable than the pressures of combat. The greatest gift I could give them right now was my strength, but giving it wasn't easy. I summarily vetoed the idea of a tearful farewell at the airport. Our good-byes were said amid the familiar trappings of home, after which one of my brothers shuttled me to the airport terminal.

Once I'd cleared the airport doors and was on my own again, I made a beeline for the men's room and settled into a stall, where I briefly gave in to my emotions. I've spent most of my life constructing a well-rehearsed, glib exterior. It's not exactly a facade, but neither does it accurately convey the depth of my emotions. My penchant for order and structure forces me to channel my emotions into some kind of streamlined efficiency—most of the time. This time, however, there was no channeling to be done. I needed to let loose and come down from the intensity of the last few hours. By the time I boarded the plane at 1:45 A.M., I had successfully confronted my despair and, for the time being at least, banished my fears to some distant corner of my mind where they could languish until I dragged them back out again in some moment of weakness.

I left Dayton on June 24, 1971, and headed for Travis Air Force Base, near San Francisco. After an overnight stay, I boarded my charter flight for the Philippines. No military aircraft, just a typical 707 with three-across seats and an aisle down the middle. The amenities were sparser than on a standard commercial flight, but it was part of my gradual immersion into austerity. My greatest challenge at the moment was overcoming the daunting prospect of a twenty-eight-hour flight. Any destination, even Vietnam, sounded preferable to the relentless boredom that stretched out ahead of me.

As the hours stacked up, I had plenty of time to ponder the coming months. Maybe I should have been scared, but I was more impatient than anything else. Even by the tender age of twenty-four, I had come to realize that 90 percent of the things I worried about never came to pass; so why waste my mental and physical reserves? I might as well walk out and greet the future with open arms. It's not as though I could stop it from coming. I looked at the whole experience as an adventure.

I didn't dwell on the idea that I might not return from Vietnam, or that my next contact with American soil might come from being lowered into it. I was more curious than scared, more anxious than apprehensive.

By the time our group landed in the Philippines—where we would experience almost two weeks of "snake school" before Vietnam—I'd had it with air travel. Not since T-41s and the Marquis de George had I felt so much antipathy toward a set of wings. I soothed my jangled nerves with the knowledge that the next time I was airborne for that long, I'd be heading back to Tipp City.

The accommodations at Clark Air Base were, at first glance, depressingly primitive. For a wet-behind-the-ears lieutenant from small-town USA, this culture was a stark contrast to anything I'd seen in my native land. Even the hot, grimy border towns of south Texas had a certain provincial charm compared to this place. I would eventually discover that the Philippines had some clear advantages, especially when weighed against my final destination. Over the next year, I would have plenty of opportunity to long for the surroundings I now eyed with contempt. But Clark Air Base in June was nothing short of a sauna: muggy and close, with the kind of heavy air that nearly suffocates you with each breath. It was like sticking your head in a clothes dryer and inhaling soggy socks. Although it didn't occur to me at the time, Clark did have one distinct advantage over my next stop: No one here was trying to kill me.

After a few hours of acclimating and exploring, we regrouped for our first exposure to jungle survival. The biggest single lesson I managed to glean from our early classroom sessions was we were in a world of hurt if we got shot down over the jungle. Just as we'd done in the wilds of Washington State, we listened patiently to a series of detailed explanations about surviving in a hostile environment. Except that this session would have practical applications in just a few days.

"Surviving in a tropical forest is dicey even without a bunch of angry little guys in black pajamas running you like a rabbit," said the staff sergeant who stood before us. "If you get knocked out of the sky over Vietnam, you'd better be damned sure you're as jungle-savvy as the Viet Cong or the NVA regulars, because they'll be on your ass about ten seconds after your feet hit the ground. Your only defense may be your ability to move silently, conceal your trail, and camouflage yourself." The staff sergeant was direct and intense.

The generic gave way to the specific as our instructor launched into a detailed analysis of edible plants and animals. He explained how to taste-test unknown berries, nibble by nibble, to determine their toxicity. Unlike winter survival school—where nothing was edible except rabbit pellets and pine needles—the jungle offered a virtual smorgasbord of tropical delicacies. We learned that we could feast on berries, bananas, bugs, birds, lizards, and various other things that slithered and scuttled past our feet in the undergrowth. We were schooled in the mechanics of skinning, cooking, and devouring a snake.

I deferred from eating our snake companion, as I had with Mr. Whiskers, but not because I'd stayed up all night petting him. More the opposite actually: I'm not overly fond of snakes under any circumstances, and having one placed in front of me on a platter didn't alter my opinion. Fortunately, in this setting I could afford to be a picky eater. There was always something else available.

After the classroom foundation was laid, we packed our bags for a taste of the real thing. Being trucked through the Filipino rain forest had a certain surreal quality to it, as though we'd been dropped into the middle of a *National Geographic* documentary. We rolled past primitive villages and indigenous peoples whose way of life remained unchanged from that of their ancestors 300 years ago. I wondered whether they had any knowledge of who we were and why we were here. Had they ever heard of Vietnam? Did they know about Strela missiles and Ho Chi Minh and F-4s and napalm? Or were their lives so basic and elemental that they couldn't afford to waste precious life energy worrying about the geopolitical struggles between Communists and capitalists. It was an interesting question, and I briefly wondered which of us was better off.

During our first two hours in the jungle, additional snake school teachers took center stage, giving us the skinny on setting up camp in an environment riddled with hungry, dangerous, or deadly flora and fauna. We learned to string our hammock so that nothing could climb into it in the middle of the night. We learned that even the process of eating had to change in this hostile new environment.

"You can't just pop a peanut butter sandwich in your mouth and wipe your face on your sleeve," our jungle guide lectured. "Every rat within fifty miles will smell the residue and figure that you're just one big walking glob of peanut butter. So you'd better be prepared to handle food differently unless you want to storm through the jungle looking like the Pied Piper with about a thousand rodents hot on your ass. Yeah, the Viet Cong won't notice that!"

Our next snake school exercise introduced us to a group of Negritoes, whose job was to track us through the jungle in an escape and evasion drill.

"Each of you will be given a poker chip," said the instructor. "You need to hold on to it and hand it over to the Negrito when— excuse me, *if*—he finds you." Our instructor tossed us each a chip, which we pocketed as he continued his explanation. "The Negritoes provide a tremendous service to us by showing you guys just how tough it is to disappear into the jungle. Every poker chip they bring back can be exchanged for food from the Air Force. It's a good system—keeps the Negritoes well-fed, and keeps you guys on your toes."

We were separated into groups of fifteen and dumped near a patch of dense rain forest, with the simple instructions "go hide."

Okay. How tough can this be? We've got an hour to get lost in a tangled web of vines and leaves. These guys don't realize that Scoop is a master of the calculated disappearing act. If I decide I don't want to be found, that's it, I'm gone.

I lumbered through the dense brush and the endless shoots of bamboo that pierced the tangled treetops until I found a suitably brushy area whose long shadows would certainly make me invisible to the human eye, even the jungle-savvy eyes of my Negrito pursuer. I struggled to recall the "hiding in jungle" tips that our staff sergeant instructor had crammed into our introductory session. Grabbing a broken tree branch, I brushed away all evidence of my tracks; at least it looked that way to me. Then I lay down on my belly and shimmied backward beneath the branches and leaves, pausing to spread loose dirt and grass across my body for additional camouflage.

I protectively raised my olive drab collar around my neck and ducked my chin down to my chest in an effort to prevent any shafts of sunlight from striking my pasty white face. Then I waited, wondering just how long I would have to stay in this cramped and sweltering grotto, and whether someone would let me know when the exercise was over and it was time to come in.

Hmmm, not like the kid games you used to play back in Tipp City, Jackson. I don't guess anyone's going to come tromping through the jungle shouting, "Ollie, Ollie, Oxen Free-o!" Then again, if you do this right, it could save your life down the road. You're better off to play like it's for keeps. In a few days, it could be.

The thought had no sooner formed in my head when I heard the snap of a twig and the faint sound of bare feet skimming rapidly over tangled brush. The branches above me snapped and twisted as they were forcefully yanked aside. I untucked my head in time to see a grinning brown face pierce the foliage, followed by an impatiently outstretched hand. I thought at first he was offering to help me from my hiding spot. Then I realized he was prompting me for my poker chip. I sighed and surrendered it, and he was off again, already hot on the trail of his next hapless victim, leaving me to stumble back to camp dirty, dejected, and less than inspired about my odds of making it out of any jungle alive.

In what seemed like a matter of minutes, all fifteen of us had been rounded up, and our Negrito tracker was happily heading off to exchange his chips for a tropical feast, courtesy of the United States Air Force and our own ineptitude. It was a sobering lesson for all of us.

Okay, Jackson, so maybe the North Vietnamese won't be as cruel as everyone says. Yeah, right. There's your first jungle survival lesson, Scoop: Stay out of the jungle and maybe you'll survive.

The Filipino rain forests were an oppressive fusion of tropical fronds and bushes, punctuated at every turn by tall, dense bamboo forests. They offered a reasonable facsimile of the conditions we would experience in Southeast Asia. Our little escape and evasion exercise proved that surviving in the jungle was nearly impossible if we couldn't even manage to navigate through it.

Tramping through the jungle wasn't the worst thing I'd ever done, though. It beat the heck out of falling through six feet of snow and scrambling back out again. The whole snake school experience had a certain exotic aura of adventure and camaraderie that made me feel as though I was in the middle of a movie. I understood that we were only "play surviving." It was an exercise, a drill, and there was little chance that someone was going to get hurt—well, not badly anyway.

We each carried a large machete and took turns clearing the trail ahead so the rest of our group could pass through. It was hot, tiring work, and the turnover for designated trailblazers was fairly constant. In short order, I found myself second in line, following a guy who was having way too much fun waving that huge blade around, so I made a calculated decision to hang back a few feet and avoid a ceremonial slashing of the Scoop.

We were wearing light fatigues and combat boots as we hacked our way through the bamboo forest. I could feel tiny streams of sweat begin to tickle from my hairline down my neck and back. At least I thought it was sweat, until my imagination began to run wild. *Okay, Jackson, how many different kinds of exotic mites and bugs are trying to burrow into your skin right now?* My back itched and my muscles began to jump and twitch as I mentally fought off hoards of stinging, buzzing, and biting intruders.

Ahead of me, miles and miles of waving bamboo shoots pressed in from all sides, chinkling a strange, hollow tune that sounded as though we were walking through a wind chime. As I stepped into a clearing that our leader had sliced and diced, I felt a slight tingle on my right hand.

"Stupid bugs!" I shook my arm violently, slapping my hands together, only to discover that I was covered with blood—mine! It was everywhere, thick, warm, and moist, pouring from the knuckle of my little finger. There, at my feet, lay a razor-sharp bamboo stake that had apparently gotten tangled in the brush above me and had worked itself loose just in time to pierce my hand with amazing precision. I stared at it for a minute, shuddering as I considered the damage it could have done if it had sliced through my head or shoulder. Taking a few more steps forward, I brought my hands up to my face to try to assess the damage, and discovered that I was now playing host to dozens of nasty little leeches. I don't know where they came from or how they got there so quickly, but they were all over me.

I stood there, fighting the lump in my gut that was rising toward my throat, blindly tugging at the leeches, watching them stretch out and snap back like gooey rubber bands. Occasionally I'd manage to pry one off, only to have it reattach itself to my other hand.

Okay, Scoop, great impression of Humphrey Bogart in The African Queen, *but enough is enough. Get these slimy little suckers off me!*

I decided it was time to call in the reserves.

"Uh, guys, I've got a little problem here."

My companions caught up to me and began ripping off the leeches and flinging them into the brush. We sopped up the blood with rags and towels until the injury became more visible. Examining my hand, I could see a nice chunk of bone peeking through the mangled skin. Everyone agreed that it was a truly impressive wound, worthy of an air evac back to Clark. At first that sounded like a welcome respite, but I was none too thrilled that I might have to repeat the whole exercise once my wounds healed. Still, there was no arguing that the copious amount of blood oozing from my hand was not only unpleasant for me, it had the potential to attract a wide variety of uninvited dinner guests, and infection.

So after only a few hours of actual jungle surviving, I found myself waiting on a mountaintop for a helicopter to whisk me back to civilization, or the closest thing the Philippines had to offer. At Clark Air Base hospital they stitched me up, splinted my hand, and gave me strict instructions not to use it or get it wet. Although I am left-handed, I quickly discovered how tough it is to function sans my right hand. Showering became an exercise in contortionism as I tried to clean all body parts north and south without aggravating my injury.

On the bright side, the Air Force moved me from the stifling hot BOQ into an air-conditioned trailer, a definite improvement in lodgings. I also acquired my very own Filipino houseboy, who showed up each morning to wash my clothes in a garbage can lid for ten cents. In fact, my filthy, battered combat boots, which I had flung across the compound after my abbreviated survival training, reappeared by my door looking as though elves had spent the entire night spit-shining them. They were better than new. I could get used to that kind of service.

My buddies back in the jungle made it through the remainder of survival school without me, despite the fact that I'd been the guy entrusted to carry the food and had carried it in my knapsack straight back to Clark. I pulled the five-pound bag of rice out of my bag and tossed it onto my cot with a chuckle. I was pretty certain the guys would take my name in vain come dinnertime, but at least they had plenty of juicy snakes and bugs to eat. My houseboy, on the other hand, ate well that night; not overly fond of rice, I left the whole bag on my porch along with the day's laundry.

I returned to the flight surgeon a day later and explained that I was having trouble doing even menial tasks because of my injured hand, and was not at all certain I could even carry my bags to the airport. The surgeon took a second look at my wound and granted me an extra couple of days until the stitches could be safely removed. So I got to enjoy Filipino hospitality a little bit longer. What I didn't know at the time was that I would pay dearly for my two days of rest and comfort; it turned out that the guys who left for Vietnam before me ended up being stationed at IV Corps in Vietnam, one of the southernmost locations in the region and definitely the place to be. In fact, the farther south you got from the demilitarized zone (DMZ), the happier—and potentially longer—your life promised to be.

To fully appreciate the irony of where I finally ended up, you have to understand that my life is a constant process of being warned against something and winding up with it anyhow. The one Air Force base I'd been cautioned against was Laughlin, and where did I end up? The one instructor I was told to avoid was George, and who did I get? And, of course, anyone and everyone said, "Stay the hell out of Vietnam," so naturally I volunteered for that assignment. Throughout my tenure at Shaw, the guys returning from Southeast Asia sang one refrain over and over: "Stay away from I Corps. If you end up there, the one place you *must* avoid is Camp Eagle."

Camp Eagle was an Army camp and the headquarters of the legendary 101st Airborne Division. Based on advance intelligence, it was pure primitive, lacking almost everything I had come to regard as a creature comfort. In fact, many of the buildings at Camp Eagle didn't even have electricity. It was dusty, dirty, and oppressively hot, and it made the BOQ at Clark Air Base look like a tropical paradise.

So, of course, I was bracing myself for "Hi-ya, Scoop, welcome to Camp Eagle, where you and four buddies will spend 366 fun-filled days and nights (just my luck—it was a leap year) in the luxurious fourth hooch on the left overlooking the well-appointed officers' latrine. While there, you'll enjoy a daily smorgasbord of olive drab mystery meat, followed by a spirited game of who's going to try to kill me today? Your accommodations will include a rusty metal bed, a moldy gym locker, complimentary mosquito netting, and a variety of scuttling vermin. Welcome to I Corps, Lieutenant Jackson, and thank-you for playing You Bet Your Life.

I may not have been lucky, but at least I was consistent.

CHAPTER NINE

LIFE WITH CHARLIE

I LEFT Clark Air Base on July 8, 1971, and two hours later was treated to my first aerial view of Cam Ranh Bay in the Republic of Vietnam. The air base sprawled across a flat, sandy savannah that had been cleared of its jungle attire by the Army Corps of Engineers back in 1965. Since then, rows of single-story, tin-topped buildings had sprung up across the barren plain, providing a bleak contrast to the clean white beaches and blue-green water that lay just to the east. As air bases in Vietnam went, this one ranked high on everyone's best-case scenario. In fact, the base was considered so secure that President Lyndon Johnson had visited it twice.

As our plane began its arrival descent, my traveling companions piled out of their seats and jockeyed for a view of the sprawling land-mass spilling over the horizon. For ten years Vietnam had flickered across our TV screens every night; suddenly, here we were.

I think I'll keep my seat for now, guys. We're gonna get a real close-up look at this place soon enough. I'm not in any mood to rush things.

In fact, as the plane dipped low over the South China Sea, my main concern centered on the potential that we might be shot down before I even officially made it in-country.

Despite its reputation for safety, Cam Ranh Bay had been breached by the enemy in the past, and would be again—soon. Within weeks of my arrival in-country, Communist forces would successfully blow up the ammunition storage area at the base, trashing more than 6,000 tons of munitions, worth roughly $10 million. But as we glided across the bay on our final approach to Vietnam, my concerns were somewhat less far-reaching. I was considerably more worried that Communist forces might blow up 160 pounds of Mike Jackson, worth roughly $1.25 but highly valued by yours truly.

The plane landed uneventfully, and we crowded onto the tarmac with a visible mixture of hesitation and anticipation. From somewhere beyond the annex of buildings lining the runway, a siren began to shriek and we stared at each other stupidly. *What the hell does that mean? What do we do now?* Someone shouted, "Rocket attack! Hit the deck!" and the next thing I knew I was facedown on the concrete, bracing for my first taste of combat—from the wrong side of the rocket.

Cripes. This is just about as bad as being blown out of the sky on my way to Vietnam. "Dear Mrs. Jackson, after only ten minutes in-country, your husband is now permanently embedded in the runway at Cam Ranh Bay. On the upside, he makes a damn fine speed bump."

I'd been in-country for all of three minutes and, so far, I was not having fun. This didn't bode well for the next 365 days, assuming I made it through the next ten minutes. The sirens continued to wail, but we never saw or heard any rockets. *Was it a false alarm? A drill? A "welcome to the war" opening salvo?* Feeling both foolish and wary, we slowly climbed back to our feet and dusted ourselves off, then headed into the terminal. It was one helluva hello.

During our stay at Cam Ranh Bay, the Air Force provided us a two-day "theater indoctrination school." *Welcome to Vietnam. Here's what you need to know about the people, the customs, and getting back out alive a year from now.* We got a crash course on the care and feeding of guerrilla warriors; we learned that buses decked out in chicken wire and grating were so adorned to thwart someone heaving a hand grenade or satchel charge through the window. We were further cautioned to be careful riding in jeeps, not only because of the potential for grenades and small weapons fire but because some of the Vietnamese would race past you on motor scooters and snatch the watch off your wrist. *So these are the guys we're here to protect? Go figure.*

None of this really surprised me. I'd heard it from the Southeast Asia (SEA) returnees at Shaw, although back then I'd hoped they were exaggerating in order to scare the crap out of the new guy. No such luck. *Welcome to 'Nam, Scoop. Check your naiveté at the door.* We also learned how military personnel should properly utilize the money system. If you wanted to watch someone turn from olive drab to crimson, just hand them an American greenback as payment. It was a sure-fire way to telegraph your status as the latest in a never-ending procession of FNGs, or f—-ing new guys. I was acutely aware of my status as an FNG and had no interest in further drawing attention to myself, so I abandoned my good old U.S. currency in favor of military payment certificates (MPCs), and blended happily into the scenery.

Up to this point, our Southeast Asia indoctrination had told us everything we needed to know, except where we would end up. We knew we were assigned to the 504th Tactical Air Support Group (TASG), which included all the FACs in all five tactical air support squadrons (TASSs), the 19th through the 23rd, but we had not yet been assigned a specific TASS. We did, however, receive our new in-country wardrobe, everything a lovely shade of olive drab. Olive drab T-shirts, olive drab underwear, olive drab handkerchiefs, olive drab slippers, and, of course, olive drab fatigues and jungle boots.

Once we were suitably attired for our new life, we finally got the word on where that life would be lived. I had drawn the 20th TASS, which put me in I Corps, the northernmost military region in South Vietnam and, of course, the region I'd been warned against. If my streak held, I would soon find myself holed up at Camp Eagle, alias "hell on Earth."

I was able to bypass some of the standard flight checkout training due to my combat-ready status, courtesy of my tour with the stateside

FAC unit. Having completed my in-country in-processing at Cam Ranh Bay, I was shipped to Da Nang for I Corps in-processing. At Da Nang, the "ins" continued to pile up as I got my in-theater combat check, which determined my ability to fly an airplane under hostile conditions. I figured that surviving pilot training and the Marquis de George was about as hostile as anything the North Vietnamese could throw at me. That was probably an exaggeration, but not by much.

I marked my time and maintained some faint hope that I might end up staying at Da Nang, which at least offered the security and comfort of cement buildings, electricity, running water, and air conditioning. In my heart, however, I knew my destination. It was inevitable. I was meant for Camp Eagle just as I was meant for Laughlin and George and I Corps. And I was beginning to understand that no matter how bad things looked from my perspective, there was some larger plan at work that followed a logic I was not privy to. What choice did I have anyway? I couldn't talk my way out of this one. And there weren't any pretty draft board secretaries eager to provide assistance and shelter until better accommodations could be found.

In due time I was given my orders, and the suspense was over. My fate had been sealed pretty much the way I expected. Camp Eagle was my new home. No amount of fast-talking or finagling was going to change that.

The time had come to face my nemesis; in fact, I was eager to do so. The quickest way to get out of here was to get moving and do the job I'd been sent to do. Getting to my new digs proved to be fairly simple; one of the O-2s from nearby Hue Phu Bai had undergone repairs in Da Nang. I didn't ask how it had gotten broken—I wasn't certain I wanted to know—I just knew that it would provide a handy ticket to Phu Bai. There I hooked up with Capt. Lynn Damron, one of an exclusive group of guys who could claim to be the northernmost FACs in South Vietnam.

Well, Scoop, you always wanted to be part of the in crowd; now you're about as in as you can get: in-processed, in-country—and in trouble.

As an Army post, Camp Eagle was not set up to accommodate aircraft, at least not the kind with fixed wings. Our O-2s were kept at Hue

Phu Bai airport, an eight-mile drive from Eagle, or a five-minute heli-copter ride when the road was unsecured, which was most of the time.

"Here ya go. We can't leave Phu Bai until you're suited up." Captain Damron tossed me a bulletproof vest and a battered helmet as I climbed into the jeep. My awkward catch and puzzled look were met with a reassuring nod. "It's okay—mostly just a precaution. Security patrols swept the road this morning and didn't find anything, but you never know if one of those damned dinks is holed up in the ditch wait-ing to blow your brains out." His words trailed off and he eyed me warily, as though analyzing my fear threshold. I shrugged and nodded, then plopped the helmet on my head and pulled on the bulky vest.

Damron grinned and flopped into the seat next to me. "It's a short drive. Just hold on and enjoy the ride. Oh, just in case, there's an AR-15 behind you. You might want to throw it in your lap."

Okeydokey. Just let me know at what point the "enjoy the ride" part begins.

The road from Hue Phu Bai to Camp Eagle was only marginally passable. It had been stripped of all cover by massive earthmovers, after which erosion and heavy equipment had taken their toll. The jeep seemed to be in a constant state of swerve as it veered between pot-holes, divots, and furrows. Two ditches flanked the roadway, and an assortment of shabby little bushes fanned out on both sides. I looked around with curiosity and a creeping sense of excitement. Far from being afraid, I was grateful to finally be starting my tour.

"So, what's it like up at Camp Eagle?" I already knew the answer to that question, but it was a good starting point.

Damron shrugged. "It's pretty much of a hellhole, but you get used to it. We've got it better than the Army grunts. The Air Force gave us a water heater, a generator, and a TV. They all work some of the time, although there's not much point in turning on the TV. There aren't any stations around here."

"So, what do you do for fun?" It seemed like a silly question, but I had to believe—*needed* to believe, actually—that normal routines and activities could coexist with the anomalies of combat.

"We play foosball, we drink. There's the occasional USO show. Mostly Orientals, but every so often we get round-eyes; now *that's* a treat. After a while you start to forget what American girls look like." Damron was animated now. Women were a universal language that every pilot spoke fluently. "We have a saying here: 'When the locals start looking good, it's time to go home.' You'll understand. The Vietnamese don't wear very well, but I guess growing up in a war zone probably does that to you. And, of course, we've got the doughnut dollies; they're a nice reminder of what we left back in the world."

"Doughnut dollies?" I envisioned a two-wheeled cart that trucked breakfast pastry around the camp.

"They're Red Cross gals, mostly Americans. They come over here to raise morale and support the troops and, I dunno, maybe to check out future husband material. But most of them are here because they give a damn, which is more than I can say for about half the people back in the States." Damron chuckled to himself. "Still, ya gotta admit, if you're a single girl with limited prospects, there are worse places to be than in the middle of nowhere with five thousand lonely GIs."

I laughed, but I couldn't imagine any level of loneliness that would send me to a war zone in search of companionship. The captain's insights provided some depth and color to my new environment, and it suddenly occurred to me that I really was enjoying the ride. Except for periodic whiplash and the weight of an AR-15 across my knees, it wasn't much different from cruising Tipp City's main drag with Joe and pondering the mysteries of women.

As the main gate of Camp Eagle appeared on the horizon, my spirits briefly retreated to a darker, more unsettled place. The camp had the stark, uninviting quality of a prison, complete with guard shack and concertina wire, although in this case the point was to keep people out, not in. But I knew, even before I fully absorbed the look and feel of the place, that I was about to stand face-to-face with everything I'd been warned against by everyone I'd ever known who'd been to Vietnam.

Since leaving the continental United States, my life had bounced from one culture shock to another. Clark Air Base seemed like a hellish nightmare at first, but I soon discovered that there are worse things than having houseboys do your laundry, clean your living quarters, and fetch your wayward tennis balls. Cam Ranh Bay soon replaced the

Philippines as something south of purgatory, only to be unseated by Da Nang, which would prove to be the height of comfort and convenience when compared to Camp Eagle. It was a discouraging but intriguing descent into the underbelly of human existence.

Camp Eagle was, quite simply, the worst thing I'd ever seen. As Lynn and I rolled through the main gate, I was startled by the relentless clouds of acrid dust that powdered up around us. It didn't matter whether we were walking, driving, or standing perfectly still; any movement, any breath of air seemed to whip the loose, parched earth into a frenzied squall of sand and dirt.

Like the dry creek bed we'd driven in on, the streets of Camp Eagle were rocky, pockmarked thoroughfares that challenged the suspension system of any vehicle tough enough to navigate them. I reminded myself that this was the Army, a completely different mindset and structure from that of the Air Force. I had occasionally played with the Army when I was at Shaw, training Fort Bragg and Fort Benning ground pounders on how to communicate with airborne FACs. But it had never been the total Army immersion that this was; it had never been a hostage situation.

Actually living with the Army was yet a new level of culture shock. It occurred to me, with no small measure of irony, that after all my weaseling efforts to avoid being drafted into the Army, here I was bunking with them anyway. I had to laugh. It was just another case of my attempting to avoid something that was determined to get me in the end.

The terrain around Camp Eagle had all the visual appeal of an outpost on the moon. Flat, brown, and devoid of any vegetation, it was a dramatic departure from the miles of lush jungle that typified most of the Vietnamese landscape. Sandwiched inside the perimeter fence were acres of squat little gray-brown buildings that looked like some perverse variation of the popular Levittown-type subdivisions of the 1950s. Ours were truly "little boxes made of ticky-tacky," as the song stated. And ticky-tacky in Army terms meant sandbags, corrugated metal, and an assortment of plywood and rough-hewn lumber.

Lynn Damron brought the jeep to a screeching halt in front of one of the endless rows of cobbled-together shanties.

"There she is." He poked a finger past my nose, pointing to an unassuming plywood shack that looked as though it might have been uprooted from rural Oklahoma at the height of the dust bowl. "That's your home away from home for the next year. It's not much, but at least the Air Force makes an effort to help out FOL [forward operating location] guys like us. We've got the generator and a pretty decent little water heater and of course the TV. They've also given us paint and acoustical tile and a bunch of other crap that we have no use for, but at least they're trying. I give 'em points for that much."

I nodded and stared at the hooch. Something told me I should be horrified, but I was still locked in fascination mode. This was all so new and strange. I had the sense of being in a movie, and I felt an urgency to fast-forward to the next scene. I kind of enjoyed peeling away the layers of this new environment, as long as I didn't dwell on the length of my exposure to it.

I gathered my bags, then headed inside for a close-up look at my new digs. The plywood door hesitated as the humidity-swollen frame decided whether to loosen its grip. When it finally gave way, the door swung open quickly, clattering against the outer wall. It was a louder entrance than I had planned, but no one seemed particularly unnerved. As I stumbled into the dimly lit main living area, I got a cursory nod from a guy lounging on the battered old couch that dominated the room. I nodded in turn, and gave Lynn the lead as he directed me back toward the bedrooms.

"Hey, Clyde," Lynn called back to the guy in the front room, "this is Mike Jackson. Mike, Clyde Elmgren. . . . Anyone else here?"

"Nope." Clyde seemed singularly unimpressed with my arrival. I couldn't blame him. I didn't know how long he'd been here, but he'd probably seen plenty of people come and go for any number of reasons. I often wondered, during and after my tour, whether some of the military's morale problems in Southeast Asia weren't self-inflicted. Throughout the war, as various policies were floated and discarded, government support for the troops seemed to ebb and flow and dwindle away to nothing. People were randomly dropped into the SEA theater in a haphazard manner. You didn't arrive with the same group

↓ My parents, Edmund and Winnie Jackson on their wedding day, 1945.

← My best pal Joe (front) and I ham it up in one of those cheesy little photo booths that seemed to be everywhere in the 1950s and 60s.

← I worked as a stock boy, cashier, and "jack-of-all-trades" at Dorsey's Supermarket in Tipp City all four years of high school and my first summer in college.

→ My high school classmates in Tipp City. I'm in the front middle with my hand on my chest. Joe Catey is second from the left wearing glasses.

← Main Street in Tipp City today. It doesn't look much different than when I was growing up there in the 1950s (or than it did in the 1850s, for that matter).

← Once I headed to Ohio University, my job fortunes changed slightly and I lucked into becoming "Mike the Milkman" in one of the girls' dorms! It was a great way to meet girls and impress them with my command of the milk spiggot!

→ One of the girls I met at the milk machine was a pretty co-ed named Karen Shorts, who would later become my wife.

↑ The T-41, "the attrition machine." The airplane itself was okay but the instructor almost did me in.

↓ That's me in the left seat flying my T-37 or "Tweet."

↑ I flew fighter lead-in training in the AT-33 at Cannon AFB, New Mexico. My confidence was increasing and I enjoyed throwing ordinance at the ground.

← Preparing to fly the "white rocket," the supersonic T-38 at Laughlin AFB, Texas.

↑ My "office" for two assignments, the O-2A. It wasn't pretty and it wasn't fast, but it kept me safe through 210 combat missions and a lot of enemy fire.

→ The in-processing office at Da Nang offered a tongue-in-cheek greeting to newly arriving airmen.

↑ Signs of the times. We were treated to constant reminders that, not only didn't most Americans want us over there, but the South Vietnamese weren't thrilled with our presence either.

← The officers' latrine at Camp Eagle. Posing beside the popular rock target are (L to R) Bob Gilday, Ed O'Connor, and our ALO Dale Ullrich, great guys all.

↑ My hooch at Camp Eagle was, at least, a roof over my head, which was more than some GIs got. Note the water tank on the conex.

↓ One of the USO shows at Camp Eagle featured Miss America, Phyllis George, center, and other Miss America contestants.

→ Striking a casual pose next to one of the jeeps at Camp Eagle.

↓ Aerial view of an American firebase.

↑ Close-up of a typical firebase, which made me grateful for my accommodations at Camp Eagle. Note the wooden boat that served as a reservoir (middle right).

↓ One of the many trails we tried to interdict. The problem was, we'd bomb one path and Charlie would simply walk around the crater and create a new trail. Note the grease pencil writing on the window.

← Jessie Hicks, our mascot at Camp Eagle.

← My pal Tom O'Neill, left, found that Camp Eagle lacked most, if not all, of the creature comforts. We managed to sneak him out in a carefully orchestrated "escape."

↑ My trusty sky pig in the revetment at Phu Bai.

→ A Cobra gunship
at Camp Eagle.

← A racey little
Loach, possibly the
one in which I logged
my first —and only—
pink team mission.

↓ The helicopter guys of the Army aviation battalion were young and eager, and lived in more sparse accomodations than the Air Force guys. Note the doorless hooch and the absence of electrical wiring.

↑ After the typhoon, our helicopter pals helped us rebuild our damaged hooch. We managed to turn the repair process into a party.

← The Bilk hooch after our move to Hue Phu Bai in January 1972. A step up from Camp Eagle—but not by much.

→ Mamasan and her girls at the grand opening of the Quang Tri "steam and cream."

← My room at Hue Phu Bai. Note the liberal use of camouflage for decor (it was free) and the loaded AK-47 next to the bed.

↑ One of my VNAF student FACs with me, right, before takeoff at Da Nang.

← Karen and me on leave in Hawaii.

↓ My hooch in the 20th TASS compound at Da Nang. Concrete walls, running water, and air conditioning—things were looking up!

→ Me pointing to the location where I took an SA-2 (SAM) in the DMZ. I'm smiling here, but I sure wasn't when it happened.

← Some of the Bilks at Phu Bai—from left, Fred Barlow, Jim Crookston, Jim Petek, Conrad Pekkola, me, Art Evans, and, top, "Sandy" Sanderson.

↑ Our final Bilk party. From left, Jim Crookston, Fred Barlow, Art Evans, Conrad Pekkola, Ed O'Connor, Jim Petek, and me.

← A welcome sight. Welcome home signs at my parents' house in Tipp City, June 26, 1972. I made it!

↑ A B-52 dropping a "stick" of bombs. I think every FAC in I Corps ended up underneath at least one arc light mission by accident. "It's raining bombs!" B-52s would continue to confound me even after my tour in-country.

↑ Receiving my DFC.

← The Distinguished Flying Cross.

← My daughters, from left, Katie and Lori, with sled dogs in Alaska in 2003. Katie is a student at Ohio University; Lori graduated from Notre Dame in 2004 and is an Air Force second lieutenant.

→ My job at the National Aviation Hall of Fame has offered more than a few amazing moments. Here, I stand with astronaut Frank Borman, one of the NAHF's stellar enshrinees, who graciously wrote the foreword for this book.

← One of the highlights of my post-Vietnam career: hanging out with legendary actor Cliff Robertson, who had dinner with me at the Coldwater Cafe in Tipp City during one of his visits to Dayton for the National Aviation Hall of Fame enshrinement.

← During our 2003 Pioneers of Flight Homecoming, I got to hang around with actor/pilot Harrison Ford, who turned out to be a genuinely nice guy who loved to talk about flying.

↑ What a great honor—to be surrounded by the likes of, from left, Scott Crossfield, Wally Schirra, NAHF president Clyde Autio, Harrison Ford, Gene Cernan, Joe Engle, James Lovell, Tom Stafford, and Joe Kittinger. How do you top that?

← My co-author, Tara Dixon-Engel, poses at a NAHF enshrinement with one of her favorite enshrinees, astronaut Joe Engle.

of guys you'd trained with. You just got dumped into a shack with a bunch of strangers who, at best, viewed you as the FNG, still unproven and therefore undependable. That made it a lot tougher to forge the kind of brotherhood bond that often motivates soldiers to persevere and prevail even when the situation appears hopeless. In our hooch, everyone was at varying stages in his tour. Even if we all made it home in one piece, we'd arrive there the same way we left—alone.

Lynn shrugged at Clyde's uninspired response. "Guess they're out and about. You'll meet them soon enough. It's a decent group of guys. You'll fit in fine. Clyde's been here about seven months. He's a competent pilot, a little quieter and less rambunctious than some of us, but a good guy. You'll like him."

A door divided the living room and bathroom from the sleeping area, which was down a narrow central hallway. Our bedrooms were made out of thin plywood, and our privacy, such as it was, was protected by flimsy plywood doors.

My personal wedge of space was eight feet long by six feet wide. It bore little resemblance to the bedrooms of my youth. It was just big enough for a battered metal bed and matching gym locker. I noted a single, bare light bulb swinging freely from its electrical cord just above my bed. *My* bed. For the first time it occurred to me that I wasn't just visiting; I was here to stay. My stomach knotted momentarily, but I was still too fascinated by this strange new world to nurse any apprehension for very long. Anyway, what difference did it make now?

Whatcha gonna do, Jackson, tell the Air Force you've changed your mind? Ask for a transfer to somewhere safe, like Hawaii?

I knew that such thoughts were academic and pointless; my concerns and misgivings would remain internal. Call it honor, pride, or sheer stubbornness, I would not (not to mention *could* not) walk away from this place until the Air Force ordered me to do so. To do anything less would be to disappoint the one person whose opinion mattered most to me—*me*.

I unpacked my bags, transferring my brand-new, olive-green wardrobe onto the shelves of a rusty gym locker. I laughed out loud as I recalled OTS and the fanatical emphasis on anchoring perfectly folded underwear precisely to the four corners of a drawer. I wondered whether there were guys in Southeast Asia who had taken those lessons to heart and were currently suffering nervous breakdowns because of their inability to follow OTS training to the letter. *Cripes.* I didn't even have a drawer. I'm a pretty organized guy, but it became very clear, very quickly that Vietnam was going to be a "do the best you can with what you have" scenario.

My room was stuffy and damp, with a small, crudely screened window that offered only marginal airflow. The hooch itself was essentially a plywood box divided into multiple smaller boxes. Packed in sandbags and buried in mud, it kept us out of the elements, but, on average, it offered better accommodations to the impressive assortment of rodents, mosquitoes, cockroaches, and angry flies with fangs that shared our quarters.

The two senior FACs in our hooch lived in the true lap of luxury; their bedroom had a small but mighty air conditioner. I held out a faint hope that, as tours ended and people headed home, I might eventually inherit one side of the luxury suite.

As my first full day wore on, I met the other FACs in my hooch: Capt. Al Duty, Capt. Herb Johnson, and Maj. Karl Wheeler. Major Wheeler was the air liaison officer and senior FAC at Camp Eagle.

As Lynn had suggested, my hooch mates all seemed decent enough. My arrival had been pretty much a nonevent, as I had expected. And the first round of hellos was followed with "report to the airfield at 0500." And so my new life began, not with a bang but with a whisper. The bangs, however, would quickly follow.

My introduction to life with the Army came in the first twenty-four hours via several howitzers positioned right behind our hooch. The powerful, short-barreled cannons fired right above our heads day and night. The shells would go supersonic just as they screamed over the hooch, giving us a distinctive double blast that nearly jarred our teeth loose. Even when the howitzers were uncharacteristically silent, I heard the constant, distinctive *thud-thud* of chopper blades, which seemed to mimic heart-pounding fear.

Helipads were everywhere around us, because we were stationed with the aviation battalion.

We lived smack in the middle of the helicopter guys. In fact, we got to know them pretty well and even went up in the choppers periodically for business or pleasure. My joy riding in Loaches, however, proved to be a potent antidote to any fantasies I'd ever nursed about flying a helicopter. It also confirmed my suspicion that the Army purposely looked for young guys fresh out of high school to train on choppers. There's an "it can't happen to me" mentality among teenaged boys that was evident in the cowboy composure of the eighteen-, nineteen-, and twenty-year-old chopper pilots. They were all mostly warrant officers, a rank that was addressed as "Mr." and hovered somewhere in that no man's land between enlisted men and officers. These guys did a job that was dangerous by anyone's standards. The Army needed guys in the cockpit who thought they had all the answers and had the world by the tail to boot. Unfortunately, only youth and inexperience breed that kind of attitude.

As a fighter-trained pilot, I had a certain level of confidence—arrogance even—and I accepted a fair amount of risk, willingly facing death on behalf of my country and the Air Force. But at twenty-four, with a college degree, a wife, and high hopes for the future, I was very aware of my own mortality and very determined to avoid any exposure to it for as long as possible. The helicopter guys hadn't done the requisite "living through" yet; they were still hot rodders with fancy machines and an unquenchable thirst for pushing them to the limit. I guess, in a sense, we were too, only we understood the price of stepping past that limit. These guys didn't. Not yet. As a result, they came home with a chest full of medals or wrapped in a body bag. Sometimes both.

In the midst of the war, our helicopter buddies lived like pigs to a much greater extent than we did. I marveled that such a thing was even possible. They were pure Army, and their accommodations reeked of it. I was startled the first time I peeked into one of the helicopter hooches, which looked more like a battered old picnic pavilion than a home. I grudgingly conceded that it was probably superior to a tent, but only marginally.

Loaches, Cobras, and Hueys were the helicopters of choice at Camp Eagle. They came and went at all hours, whipping up the grainy topsoil and flinging it like a sandblaster against hooch walls and anyone unfortunate enough to be in the vicinity of the helipad.

It is said that once you've tasted combat, there will be certain triggers—not flashbacks or the lurid hallucinations that television is so fond of portraying—that take you back again. The trigger can be just a feeling, a quickening of your pulse, a knot in your stomach, or the sudden realization that the hair on the back of your neck is standing up. For me, that trigger is the distinctive sound of air being whipped by a rotary blade, especially the peculiar *whop-whop-whop* of a Huey. My time at Camp Eagle gifted me with a certain edginess that bubbles to the surface whenever my ears detect the pounding rhythm of a helicopter.

Choppers and howitzers were only two of many new sensory inputs that required a certain amount of adjustment. During the day, tanks, jeeps, and trucks trundled down the dirt roads, kicking up dust and sand. At night, even when the artillery shells were dozing, we could still hear plenty of scattered gunfire in the perimeter. Most of the time it was our guys firing out, but not always. I learned early on not to waste precious sleep time worrying about the origins of the volleys. I figured that if the bad guys actually made it past the fence, we'd know soon enough. Positioned as we were near the center of the camp, they'd have to make it past a heckuva lot of people and weapons to get to us.

After settling into bed the first night, I gazed around my room and tried to process everything that had been thrown at me in the past twenty-four hours. It was almost impossible. My eyes were heavy and my muscles ached, but my mind was racing, bouncing from thought to thought like a berserk pinball. Images and impressions darted in and out of my consciousness: my family; Karen; my buddies from Shaw—what were they doing now?—that god-awful road from Hue Phu Bai to Camp Eagle. Were little guys in black pajamas burying mines there as we nodded off in blissful ignorance? And what about tomorrow? In a few short hours I'd be airborne again, back in an O-2, not flying some carefully orchestrated simulation but hanging it out over enemy troops with real guns. I wondered whether I should be scared. I wasn't really. I was excited and agitated and anxious to get into the game and stop being the FNG.

Cripes, Jackson, go to sleep. Everything'll shake out the way it's sup-posed to shake out. The only thing you can do to control it is get enough sleep, stay on your game, and don't sweat the small stuff.

My internal discussion was interrupted by the sharp crack of automatic weapons fire somewhere to the north.

Yeah, the small stuff, like that.

I reached up and yanked the string that dangled from the light bulb above my head. The room was dark—darker than any room I'd even seen, darker than the mountains of Washington State at 1 A.M., darker than Clark Air Base when the moon was shrouded in a cloud bank—just complete and total blackness. But I grinned to myself as I twisted to find a comfortable spot between the lumps in my bunk.

Relax, Scoop. It's just like Tipp City, except for the guns and the bombs and the endless jungle and the army of cockroaches that are gonna carry your cot to Hanoi sometime during the night.

Eventually sleep came, followed in rapid succession by dawn and the arrival of my first day on the job. On my maiden voyage as a com-bat FAC, Lynn rode shotgun as I got my area checkout. It was pretty basic: I choppered to Phu Bai, climbed into an O-2, and scoped out my AO for the first time. Three hours and two air strikes later, I was no longer a combat virgin. My uneventful deflowering didn't do much to wash away the FNG stench, as far as the old heads were concerned, but it did plenty to bolster my own conviction that I knew what I was doing. I could now lay claim to a certain sense of accomplishment and control. At last I was doing what I'd been trained to do and was finally, officially, a Bilk FAC—Bilk 12 to be precise. The first number in my call sign indicated the brigade I was attached to. I had no idea what a Bilk was.

After a cursory bomb damage assessment (BDA), which included a couple of supply caches and a small secondary explosion, I yanked my O-2 back to the east and headed home—well, back to Camp Eagle. My BDA passes had not confirmed any kills, although I suspected that several NVA regulars or Viet Cong had been holed up in the slice of jungle I obliterated. Still, I couldn't confirm it, and that was almost a relief.

I'm gonna pretend you're a honeybee, Charlie. My folks used to say, "If you leave them alone, they'll leave you alone." I've got no beef with you; I'm just here to do a job. If you keep your nose out of sight and don't screw with me, then maybe we'll both walk away from this thing in one piece. Suits me fine.

Returning to Camp Eagle, I sensed the passage of a milestone. I'd flown my first mission and handled the pressures with some measure of competence and calm. Now it was just a matter of putting one foot in front of the other and maintaining that same success rate from day 1 through day 366. *Damn leap year.* It occurred to me that if I got killed on February 29, someone, somewhere was going to get an earful. The thought offered tremendous satisfaction and even brought a grin to my sweat-streaked face.

Gradually the distractions and din of Camp Eagle eroded into a dull buzz of background noises, never completely disappearing but somehow blending into the scenery as cricket chirps once had done on balmy spring nights back in the world. But what I couldn't quite adjust to was the constant filth and grime. I'm not a neat freak, but I do have an affinity for cleanliness and order. I don't know whether I relate it to godliness; it's more about not smelling bad, not itching, and not looking like the bottom of an unwashed petri dish.

I struggled awkwardly to find a balance between the life I had known and the life that now lay claim to me. The differences were staggering; yet by Camp Eagle standards, I was living high on the hog. Our hooch was arguably the model home of the whole place, with its fashionable plywood walls, complimentary claymore mine wire for electrical wiring, and crude but functional shutters. We had electricity when our generator worked, and a roof-mounted seventy-five-gallon water tank gave us the luxury of scraping off the day's filth and grime— never quite to our satisfaction but to a much greater degree than most of the guys living in the Army hovels. Almost from the moment of my arrival, my hooch mates made certain that lesson number one for the FNG was water conservation.

"This tank gets refilled once or twice a week, but it's never a sure thing, and we need to make every effort to use only as much water as it takes to get the job done," Al Duty explained, pointing to the roof as he gingerly grabbed the shower handle, allowing a brief trickle of clear liquid to splatter onto the wooden floor beneath.

I nodded and squelched a passing irritation at being lectured about the obvious. I may have been an FNG, but I'd been bathing myself for quite a few years and I understood the necessity of rationing water so that everyone got his. At least I thought I did.

Having shared my home and belongings with three brothers and a sister, I figured I was well-equipped to deal with tight quarters and disparate personalities. Of course back in Tipp we'd had the luxury of excess water as well as parental wisdom and supervision. It probably also helped that no one wanted to kill any of us, at least not enough to make the effort day in and day out.

So maybe I still had a little adjusting to do. And maybe the other guys didn't go out of their way to treat me with the kind of deference I'd come to expect as the eldest of five siblings. In retrospect, I went through a clumsy adjustment period, but everyone does. Unless you were raised in a war zone, it was inevitable. I didn't grow up in the lap of luxury by any means, but I'd had comfortable, clean surroundings, enough to eat, and the status that comes from being the eldest child. In other words, I'd had my share of people to boss around. Not so in the 'Nam, where I was currently low man on the totem pole. I barely had a name save for the familiar FNG label that grated on my nerves more and more with each passing day.

"Hey, Jackson! Man, if I had three hundred and forty-three more days in this hellhole, I'd slit my wrists. It's rough bein' the FNG, eh?"

"C'mon guys, go easy on the FNG. The poor bastard is still forty-nine weeks away from DEROS [date of expected return from overseas]. Jesus, that sounds like a lifetime."

I'd fire off a cold smile before refocusing my attention on the various discomforts and annoyances of my new lifestyle. For starters, I was always dirty, always wipping away the sweat that beaded across my forehead and trickled down my neck. My body felt as though it had been dipped in cornmeal batter and deep-fried in a vat of tropical bacon grease. I suppose I should have counted my blessings: Despite our limited water supply, I could manage to grab a quick shower every day. Anyone with any sense of cleanliness almost had to. It wasn't a case of hygiene overkill; it was absolutely necessary if you wanted to be able to stand yourself, let alone have others stand you. Returning from a mission, I'd be blinded by my own sweat as my flight suit squished with pore juice every time I took a step. It was unappetizing at best, downright disgusting at worst. I just couldn't live like that.

By day two I had my routine down pat. After each mission, I'd strip out of my sweat-drenched flight suit and toss it into a small galvanized tub beneath the shower spigot. I gingerly sprinkled soap flakes onto the soggy flight suit, then stepped into the tub after it, releasing just enough shower flow to soak my body and leave an inch or two of water in the tub. I lathered up quickly, then marched around in the tub, agitating the flight suit with my feet like a foamy, naked grape stomper. Once I'd achieved maximum lather on body and flight suit, I quickly rinsed the soap from my skin and made a half-hearted attempt to squeeze it out of my soggy clothing.

Although acquiring clean skin was considerably easier thanks to our marginal hot water heater, that small concession to civilization did little to blunt the impact of hot wind, constant moisture, and unrelenting dust. If I scoured my skin dry, I could stay reasonably clean. My flight suit, however, began attracting dirt the second I tossed it over a clothesline to dry. In the end, the only real color in my life—green—was usually visible only after I brushed away the top layer of dull, grimy brown.

I also made it a point to shave each day in tandem with my morning dental hygiene. It was during one such session that Clyde and I crossed swords, or at least razors. As conservation conscious as I was with my shower habits, I fell into my pre-combat routine when it came to shaving and brushing my teeth. Wincing at the stubbly face in the mirror, I foamed my cheeks and chin with shaving cream and began carefully stripping away twenty-four hours' worth of growth. It was a methodical process. A narrow stream of water trickled from the faucet as I dragged the razor across my skin. Shave. Rinse. Shave. Rinse. Shave.

"Hey, Jackson!" barked a voice behind me. "What the hell are you doing?"

Knitting an afghan. What the heck does it look like I'm doing?

"Uh, shaving, why?"

Clyde shouldered past me and grabbed the water faucet, twisting it closed with a flourish.

"What part of 'conserve water' did you miss?" he demanded, folding his arms and glaring at my half-foamed face.

"Sorry, man, I didn't realize that my ten-second shave would drain the entire tank," I snapped and turned back to the sink, determined to ignore my indignant shadow.

Clyde hovered behind me a moment before exhaling heavily and stalking away. I fumed as I finished my shave, but I also knew he was right. I just didn't care to have it shoved in my face. A little diplomacy would have gone a long way, but I couldn't argue with his point—only his delivery.

Water seemed to be the single biggest source of tension at Camp Eagle. There were the haves and the have-nots. The haves were split into two groups: colonels and above who bunked in trailers, and the five little Air Force guys in the second hooch past the latrine. Eventually our hot water heater became a bone of contention with the Army brass. They argued that Air Force guys living in an Army camp ought to do things "the Army way."

Our luxurious hot water, not to mention our energetic little generator, set us apart from everyone else except the guys at the top. Naturally the brass had to field regular complaints from junior Army officers who wondered why the Air Force could manage to supply hot water when *they* couldn't even enjoy the luxury of electricity. We dug in our heels and stood firm when the Army "suggested" that we might want to remove the hot water heater.

Geeze, guys, we're over here fighting the spread of communism, right? So, what's with this "redistribution of wealth" mentality? If the Air Force wants to compensate us with a few meager comforts of home, why would we refuse? If it's that big an issue, maybe you guys should improve the standard of living for your soldiers instead of insisting that we lower ours.

This was one hill the Army wouldn't take. Although everything else in our lives was Army issue, we held tight to our water heater and cherished our small slice of the real world.

Our hooch overlooked the officers' latrine, a battered plywood box with wire screens across the top and bottom. The screens provided much-needed air circulation and, theoretically at least, minimized the stench. They did not, however, protect against incoming rocks. "Rocks?" I stared at Lynn Damron in disbelief as we made our way to the structure we laughingly called an officers' club. "What do you mean, 'Watch out for rocks'? I haven't had any problem with rocks."

"You will if you're in there long enough or often enough. One of the great sports at Camp Eagle is lobbing rocks at the latrine when an officer's in there taking a crap. Now, that's annoying enough all by itself, but the real problem is those damned screens at the top. About half the time, the stupid rock rips through the mesh and whangs you on the head. So there you are minding your own business, literally, and, pow, incoming!"

I cringed. Although I had yet to experience the rock problem firsthand, I pondered whether it might be possible to reorient my bowels to some kind of late-night schedule.

"Hey, here we are." Lynn yanked on my sleeve and pointed me into a dim one-room hooch strategically positioned behind the latrine. As my eyes readjusted from sunlight to dark, I could just see the outline of a makeshift bar in one corner. Two guys were frantically twisting the foosball flippers while a few more lounged nearby nursing beers and rooting for their favorite team.

Lynn reached behind the bar and pulled a bottle of beer from a weathered old refrigerator. I shook my head as he set it in front of me.

"Nah. I don't think so. I just don't have a taste for it today. What else is back there?"

The fact is, alcohol's the last thing I want right now. I wasn't all that crazy about it back in the States, but over here I have absolutely no urge to dull my senses, even for a couple of hours. It's not like I could possibly forget where I am; but all I'd do is make myself sick and end up in the worst possible shape to handle any kind of emergency.

Searching under the counter, Lynn pulled out a rusted can of orange soda. It looked as though it had washed ashore after oxidizing under the ocean surf for about a hundred years.

"This is about it. Kinda scary."

I nodded and yanked on the metal tab. I had to brush away a thin layer of corrosion from the lip of the can. When the liquid poured into my mouth, it was not only irritatingly warm but left a strange metallic aftertaste. Still, it had a certain familiar, even soothing effect as it fizzed its way down my throat.

I nursed my rusty orange soda and watched the foosball tournament grow increasingly more combative as my mind bounced from topic to topic, as usual.

"Hey, Lynn, where the heck are the birds?"

Lynn cocked his head and looked at me strangely. "Birds? You mean chicks? You want me to introduce you to a doughnut dolly?"

I laughed and shook my head. "No. I mean real birds. I've been over here for a week and I haven't seen or heard a single bird, even when I'm flying over the jungle. Nothing. It just strikes me as strange, and I thought maybe you'd noticed it."

Lynn's quizzical look continued as he chewed the lip of his beer bottle thoughtfully. "I don't know. I guess I've never seen any either. I never thought much about it, but you're right. They're just not here."

We were quiet for a few minutes—lost, apparently, in bird musings.

"I think it must be the percussion effect from all the years of shelling," I said finally, "all the endless explosions. I think it must have shattered most of the eggs and depleted the population."

Lynn shrugged and made a dismissive gesture.

Scoop Jackson, boy naturalist.

Okay, so maybe it wasn't the most pressing issue in-country, but it struck me as odd. And then, as now, if something strikes me as odd, I am compelled to analyze it, even if I can't quite figure it out.

A couple of weeks later, I celebrated my first successful foray into combat by taking in a USO show. There is something uniquely, endearingly American about the need to ship entertainers into a combat zone so they can spend a couple of hours trying to help war-weary soldiers forget about the near-constant din of shells and trucks and choppers. Sometimes it almost worked. Other times the USO performers looked so uneasy and out of place that you wanted to take up a collection for their one-way ticket back to the States on the next transport.

I had to sympathize. Whereas our military training had painted a vivid picture of what to expect, these poor guys and gals had traveled, in one day's time, from the land of milk and honey to the land of rice and ammo. And they did it to boost the morale of our guys in uniform. Good for them! The least I could do was show up and provide an enthusiastic face in the crowd. The fact that Miss America Phyllis George would be cavorting around the stage in a miniskirt and go-go boots didn't hurt either.

Arriving late for the USO review, I was dismayed by the sea of olive drab that jockeyed for position along the railroad tie seats of Camp Eagle's makeshift amphitheater, known as the Eagle Bowl. I made my way down the gravel aisle between seating sections, then edged cautiously toward the stage. A dusty, narrow orchestra pit, guarded by large, unsmiling MPs, separated the soldiers from the performers. I crept closer to no man's land, making eye contact with a beefy black MP who was cradling an M-16 and guarding the right corner of the stage. Instinctively I grinned. It wasn't an overt effort to manipulate, but when his gaze locked on to mine I figured it was a more effective defense than looking away or glaring back at him. Much to my delight, his eyes crinkled and he grinned back.

Okay, Jackson. Progress. Hell, you're wearing an Air Force flight suit. You stand out like a sore thumb anyway; you might as well use that to your advantage.

I strolled up to the MP and nodded a hello. He nodded back, eyeing my distinctly non-Army attire.

"Hey, this is pretty neat." I pointed to the stage, where a contingent of miniskirted "round eyes" giggled nervously and made last-minute adjustments to their red, white, and blue costumes.

"Yep. Nice of them to come all the way out here," the MP agreed.

I nodded again. *Go ahead, Jackson. Go for it.*

"Here's the deal. I know I'm not s'posed to be down here, but I'm one of the Air Force guys stationed here at Camp Eagle. I'm getting ready to fly a mission—*in about eight hours*—and I just kinda wanted to grab a couple pictures of what I'm fighting for, y'know?"

The MP looked at me, then looked back where the emcee and his patriotic cuties were assembling around a microphone at center stage.

Once more a quick grin pierced the stern MP exterior. He lowered his gun and turned sideways, allowing me to slip past.

"Go ahead and grab some pictures. It's not exactly a major security breach."

I thanked him, then steadied my camera against the front plywood panel of the stage. Phyllis George swayed back and forth in the middle of the miniskirted chorus line, greeting her enthusiastic audience with a spirited version of Nancy Sinatra's "These Boots Are Made for Walkin'." The troops whistled, cheered, and clapped as I sprinted back and forth in front of the stage, snapping some impressive close-ups of good ol' American gals. As I clicked my final shots, I gave a hasty thumbs-up to my MP pal and melted back into the sea of sweat-slicked but smiling faces.

No matter how primitive Camp Eagle might be, I was determined to observe certain rituals from my life back in the real world. Always the altar boy, I was front and center for the camp's weekly Mass. Our priest was unlike any man of the cloth I'd ever run across. As we gathered around him in an open area that doubled as a basketball court, I realized that he had been one of the enthusiastic foosball players during my first visit to the officers' club. Standing before us behind a portable altar that was little more than an upright footlocker, he had an Army drill sergeant sturdiness about him; he was a stocky, jarheaded kind of guy who wore a camouflage vestment over his Army fatigues. Straight-talking to the point of roughness, yet amazingly insightful and easygoing, Father Joseph M. Manzak was one of the coolest guys I'd met in-country. Those of us who were FNGs got a casual introduction to Father Manzak's "combat religion rules." They bore little resemblance to the strict Catholic discipline of my youth, but this place didn't bear much resemblance to Tipp City.

"Some of you have inquired about confession. We don't routinely do confession here. We do general absolution, as a group, every Sunday," the rough-and-tumble Father explained. "You're not living a normal life right now; you may make some decisions and do some things that you'd never do under ordinary circumstances. You may be ordered to take actions that you find unpleasant or even reprehensible. But it's part of your job as a soldier in the United States Army . . ."

. . . or Air Force. Don't forget about us. We sin, too!

"Look, you men are living on the edge every day. You're gonna screw up. You're gonna be not as close to perfect as you might like or as God might like. But He understands, and so do I. Every Sunday I'll absolve all of you as a group. That leaves you in good standing for the week ahead. The best advice I can give at this point is try not to be absolved for the same sin every week."

We all laughed; then he went on to explain that under "combat religion rules," health and safety took precedence over church attendance.

"If you're tired, if you're hungry, you need to concentrate on doing those things that will renew your body and mind. With any luck, your soul will have plenty of time to be renovated at a later date. Don't get me wrong. I like seeing you here, but not if it's going to minimize your ability to perform your duties in a safe manner. Okay?"

We nodded in unison, appreciating the irony that God might consider going easy on us while we were busy killing and maiming.

In the end, I made it to every service. Father Manzak had a comfortable, no-BS approach to religion and life that seemed to mesh well with the craziness just beyond the perimeter fence. He assured us that we could pretty much sin for the rest of our lives after the penance and suffering we'd endure in Southeast Asia. His version of Catholicism, though indisputably different from that of my youth, was no less fulfilling and, often, downright enjoyable.

CHAPTER TEN

THE ROCKETS' RED GLARE

AS MY SKILL at putting in air strikes increased, so did the complexity and frequency of the strikes. During periods when Bilk Control had no specific targets for me, I would head out over my area of operations and scare up my own targets. It wasn't hard. There was almost always a new weapons cache, a partially obscured supply truck, or a stack of suspicious-looking crates that begged to be obliterated if no juicier targets presented themselves.

Unfortunately, the juicier targets carried an emotional price tag; they almost always involved people. I had yet to experience a genuine confirmed kill, and, truth be told, I was perfectly content to maintain the status quo. During a post–air strike bomb damage assessment, I might see sandals on the ground and conclude that someone had been hit, but I could also tell myself that they might just as easily have just run off and left their footwear behind. It was a little game I played that kept my guilt in check and allowed me to maintain my "I won't hurt you if you don't hurt me" stance.

I didn't think of myself as a pacifist, and I fully understood that part of my responsibility as an Air Force officer in combat was to engage and kill the enemy. But, like most of the soldiers in Vietnam, I had some serious reservations about the form and function of the war. The only compelling reason I could come up with for killing North Vietnamese was that they might be trying to kill me or "my people." Thus far, I hadn't seen dramatic evidence of that. And something in my earnest altar boy beginnings recoiled at the idea of blowing a man to pieces just because he lived on the wrong side of the demilitarized zone. So I was particularly unsettled as I returned from one of my early missions and listened as the pink team reconnaissance choppers radioed, "We've got four confirmed enemy KBAs on the ground."

KBA—killed by air—killed by *me*. I felt my stomach twist and my heart sink. It would have been much easier to fool myself forever, much easier and much less troubling.

That night I crawled into my bunk unable to shake off the growing depression that tightened its grip around my conscience. What happened to "live and let live," to "turn the other cheek"?

So now you've done it. You've actually killed another human being. No, make that four of them. You, Mike Jackson of Tipp City, Ohio, are personally responsible for taking four lives. One minute they're here, the next they're dead. Gone. Forever. And you're the guy who made it happen.

The weight was almost unbearable. My gut tensed, and I felt a wave of nausea sweep over me. I'd always had the ability to rationalize almost anything. As long as I could formulate a reasonable, defensible argument for my actions, I rarely if ever felt the need to grapple with guilt. Tonight, however, guilt had crept into my room and set up camp. It showed no intention of leaving, and I could find no compelling argument to discourage it. After tossing and turning for hours, I finally drifted into a fitful sleep, which offered neither rest nor respite. Even in my dreams, I could still feel the airplane banking and twisting under my hand. I could still see the smoke rocket shooting out from under my wing, and I could hear the explosion as it struck the ground beneath me.

Bam!

From somewhere in my restless fog, it occurred to me that the blast I was hearing was awfully loud, even for a vivid dream. My eyes opened and I strained to hear something in the darkness. Seconds passed. Nothing.

Then *BAM!*

The explosion was closer now and unmistakable. We were being rocketed, as the attack sirens wailed their banshee warning.

In one fluid motion, I rolled from the bed onto the floor, where I fumbled for the flak jackets and helmet I'd stashed beneath my bunk for just this occasion. I threw on the helmet and one of the jackets, tossed the other jacket over my legs, and lay wedged under the bed, rigid and silent. My muscles were taut and my ears so alert that I could hear the blood pounding in my brain.

BAM!

That one was closer still. For the first time since arriving in-country, I had the uneasy feeling that someone was specifically targeting my little hooch. The rockets seemed to be walking toward me, each one a few steps closer, a few times louder, a little more disconcerting.

BAMMM! That time I actually felt the ground shaking underneath me, or was that my heart trying to bash its way out of my chest?

Okay. This is ridiculous. I've spent all day beating myself up for trying to kill people who are trying to kill me. This is a war, Scoop. You can go to bed every night consumed by guilt, or you can do your job and assume that every guy you kill during the day is one less guy who's gonna try to kill you during the night. Right? They don't give a damn whether you feel guilty or whether you love your work. You're an American. They don't want you here, and they'd just as soon send you home in a body bag.

BOOM! That time I was sure I felt the bunk above me jump.

I didn't want to go home in a body bag. I had a family, a wife, a future. Somehow as I lay in the darkness under my bed waiting for the rocket that would split my hooch and quite possibly my head, I had an epiphany. I wasn't dealing with honeybees benignly skipping from flower to flower. I was dealing with hornets—angry, swarming hornets—and I had two choices: take a hit, or take the first swing. In a perfect world, my lack of aggression should have defused their hostility, but this world wasn't perfect. Not even close.

I grinned in the darkness. It was really pretty simple. Kill or be killed. It was something I could have told myself a hundred times and not believed it; but right now, with the background symphony of rocket explosions, it made sense. Suddenly, I didn't feel like an FNG anymore. I didn't know whether that was good or bad in the long run, but I had a feeling that it would make my job a lot easier. I stayed under the bed for what seemed like hours but was probably more like three to four minutes. Cautiously I shimmied out of my hiding place, pausing every few inches to listen for anything that might herald a new round of explosions. But I sensed that it was over. This had been my test. *Scoop's final exam in the first semester of Combat 101.* Unlike many of my past tests, this one had required some serious thought. But I knew I'd figured out the right answer, the *only* answer if I wanted to embrace both sanity and efficiency. Clumsy with a post-adrenaline hangover, I wriggled free of my flak jackets and shoved them back under the bunk with my helmet. It took a while to force both body and mind into a relaxed state, but this time when I slept, I slept soundly.

Shortly after my rocket attack epiphany, the loss of my FNG status became official. I didn't shed my title because I had dazzled people with skill and insight but because Bob Gilday showed up to claim the bunk left empty by Major Wheeler's departure.

I was pleased with Bob's arrival, not just because he took some of the heat off me but because I had run across him in survival training, in OTS, and in FAC training. Although we had not been bosom buddies, we were at least acquaintances, and there was something reassuring about having a familiar face from the States close by. Bob was a first lieutenant like me. He was pure pilot, a confident officer with a thatch of thick black hair that tickled the limits of Air Force regulations, and a bushy black mustache that outright violated them. Not that anyone in-country gave a darn; if you were a pilot and you were breathing, it didn't much matter if you looked like Fu Manchu as long as you logged your flight time and demonstrated a reasonable level of talent and competence.

Gilday had both, and he gamely stepped into my FNG role, taking the same razzing and abuse that, only days earlier, had been lobbed at me. But whatever crap he endured from his more combat-seasoned comrades, he got no such treatment from me. I didn't like the whole FNG mentality, and if I didn't like it, why would I subject someone else to it? It was tough enough trying to acclimate to the confusion and pace of a war zone without the constant reminder that your ass was on the line every minute of every day for the next 365 days.

Less than a week after Bob Gilday's arrival, yet another familiar face showed up at Camp Eagle. Tom O'Neill, my partner in crime from Shaw, had finagled a temporary assignment as a fill-in FAC at Camp Eagle.

I wasn't sure why anyone would voluntarily exchange the comparative comfort of Tan Son Nhut for the noise, confusion, and uncertainty of life near the DMZ, but I figured that Tom must have a pretty compelling reason.

I was wrong.

"So what the heck possessed you to leave Saigon?" I asked after retrieving him from the tarmac at Hue Phu Bai.

"Well, they told me there weren't any decent FACs up here, and I was worried you guys'd screw up and let the North Vietnamese through, so I said, 'Send me up there. I'll straighten them out!' " He grinned and squeezed my hand in a firm shake that quickly became an embrace.

"Uh-huh." I tossed his bags into the back of the jeep. "Well, I tell you what, next time you get a wild hair and decide to visit the edge of civilization, let's make it an exchange program. You come up to Eagle, and I'll take your place in Saigon."

"Man, Jackson, you always were a pantywaist. Whatsamatter? Can't handle roughing it a little?" Tom's broad grin taunted me good-naturedly, and I decided it was pointless to debate the issue until he had taken a close-up look at roughing it Eagle style.

The ride between Phu Bai and Eagle was pleasant and lively, but I could see Tom's eyebrows lift slightly as we rolled through the main gate of Scoop's home away from home.

"Okay, pal, here we are in the promised land." I laid my arm across the steering wheel and turned to look at him as the jeep rolled to a stop in front of our hooch. "So are you still convinced that this is where you want to be?"

"Well, sure. Hey, tomorrow's your birthday. I couldn't let my best buddy celebrate all by himself way out here in the middle of—geeze—whatever it is we're in the middle of."

"Purgatory."

Tom clapped me on the back and squeezed my shoulder. "Nope. Sorry, pal. I'm in purgatory. This. . . ." He paused, shaking his head as he scrutinized the hooch and the nearby officers' latrine. "This is definitely hell!"

Located on the northern edge of Saigon, Tan Son Nhut was just about the closest thing to western civilization that Vietnam had to offer. Soldiers and airmen slept in air-conditioned comfort. They took real showers that didn't involve sprinting through a sixty-second mist or doing double duty as a human washing machine. They lived in honest-to-god cement buildings with toilets and desks and functional television sets. They had the luxury of nearby restaurants and entertainment and shopping. It beat the heck out of Del Rio, Texas, let alone Camp Eagle.

Even during his first few minutes at Eagle, I could see an undercurrent of bemused disbelief bubbling just beneath the standard O'Neill ration of BS.

"Man, I had no idea you were living like this." He flopped down on our homemade sofa and looked around the hooch with poorly concealed disdain. This would be his new home for roughly two days, until our air liaison officer, Maj. Dale Ullrich, returned from an assignment with the ARVN. After that, Tom would find out the true meaning of substandard housing. I kept my mouth shut, but it occurred to me that if he thought my accommodations were a nightmare, he was going to be horrified by the Army hooch that would soon become "home sweet home."

Personality-wise, Tom fit in right away, but he adapted less gracefully to the inconveniences of life at Eagle. On September 8, the day after Tom's arrival, I celebrated my twenty-fifth birthday. We headed down to the outdoor theater to watch a movie and tip a few "rusty oranges." I was still unable to stare down a bottle of booze, so the celebration was pretty low-key by our historic standards. But I also sensed that Tom was grappling with his own Eagle adjustment issues. As we crouched on the railroad ties and watched a grainy version of *Patton*, he angrily swatted away the hoards of insects that were treating him like the blue-plate special.

"Dammit! These things are gonna drive me crazy. Jackson, you're a bigger pantywaist than I am. How come you're not going nuts?"

I shrugged. *I kinda thought I was; maybe it's all relative.*

"I dunno. I guess I don't have much choice. It's not like I have anywhere else to go. Plus I just keep going from bad to worse, so I guess it's kind of a gradual descent. If I'd come here straight from the Philippines or even straight from Cam Ranh Bay, it might have been more of a shock. Although this isn't exactly a picnic for me, either."

Tom swatted away another cloud of hovering gnats and heaved a sigh. He remained quietly unconvinced that anyone could learn to tolerate the disagreeable conditions at Camp Eagle. I couldn't bring myself to tell him that it would only get worse.

After the movie, Tom retreated to his room and I settled down to enjoy a box of birthday cookies that my mother and sister had baked for me half a world away. Perched on the edge of my bunk, I tore into the battered cardboard box, relishing the idea of devouring something that hadn't been dipped out of a metal can and slopped across sectioned aluminum trays. In the course of their travels, the cookies had been crushed and crumbled, but their distinctive "Mom's kitchen" aroma still managed to both tempt and reassure me. I reached in and grabbed a handful of cookie parts and shoved them in my mouth. The rich chocolatey flavor shocked my taste buds into something approaching euphoria. I grabbed another fistful and crammed it in. *Man, this is good. This is really good. But . . . what the heck is moving?* My jaw froze in midchew as I struggled to identify the strange sensation in my mouth. Although my mouth stayed rigid, the movement inside continued. Jerking the cookie box up toward the light, I could almost hear the shrieking shower music from *Psycho* as I stared into what now resembled a grade-B horror movie, wherein my mom's baked goods had transformed into a writhing sea of ants, punctuated by a few scattered cookie crumbs.

Immediately I spewed the moveable feast in my mouth as fast and as far as I could. Clawing at my tongue, I leaned over the floor and continued to spit until anything that once resembled cookies or ants had been forcibly expelled. I heaved the box across the room and tried to stifle my queasiness, but I couldn't shake the image of hundreds of little black bugs tumbling down my throat, clinging frantically to the remnants of Mom's and Deb's cookies.

Regaining some composure, I swatted ants off my legs and flicked them from the edge of the bunk, whereupon I ground them into the plywood floor with my heel. I stared at the spot where my cookie box had been stored and noticed a winding trail of ants making its way from a crack in the wall toward anything that smelled like food. I also realized that, having just spit cookies across the room, I could probably count on being overrun by tiny six-legged vermin in very short order. I sighed and began scraping the floor with any and all available tools. It was going to be a long night.

By the next morning, I had managed to remove most of the evidence of my infestation. I decided that fumigation would be the easiest way to ensure that all invaders had been dealt with. In true Jacksonian style, I tried to put a good face on the whole ordeal, reassuring myself that, first, it could have been a lot worse—spiders, silverfish, snakes—and, second, it would eventually make a funny story, just as soon as I could tell it without gagging.

After retrieving two olive drab cans of generic "bug death in a bottle," I set off the mist bombs and watched in fascination as my room disappeared under a thick white fog that smelled like a cross between paint thinner and rotten eggs. I decided that whatever was spewing out of the Army-issue spray cans was on a par with low-level chemical warfare, and it was probably a bad idea to be sucking it into my lungs. I vacated the premises until everything in my room had died or moved on to greener, less toxic, pastures.

Tom wasn't as successful at taking the rigors of Camp Eagle in stride. His transfer from Major Ullrich's room to nearby Army quarters proved to be just as unsettling as I had feared.

"Man, I can't believe the way *you* live. But these Army guys! I'm living in a damned tarpaper shack without electricity or water, or even frigging doors! I'd be more comfortable sleeping outside. At least I'd get a breeze now and then. This is insane. All the enemy has to do is offer us air conditioners and water, and people'll start surrendering by the hundreds." Tom shook his head and looked at me with an exaggerated mixture of annoyance and puzzlement.

The standard theme song for every soldier in Vietnam was "We Gotta Get Out of This Place," but I could tell that Tom was singing with considerably more gusto than some of us. He remained his usual fun-loving self, but he was obviously ill at ease with the spartan surroundings. Then, on September 14, he reported uncertainly that HQ was telling him he'd either be returning to Tan Son Nhut or heading up to Quang Tri the next day. Quang Tri, an ARVN post to the north of us, was by all accounts as bad as or worse than Camp Eagle. *But at least it's closer to the enemy.*

"You know, this place sucks, but it's probably marginally preferable to Quang Tri. Look, Jackson, I've enjoyed hanging out with you, and this little adventure into how the other half lives has been enlightening, but I'm pretty sure that Quang Tri can survive just fine without me." He ran his hand around the back of his neck and marveled at the dirt and sweat that glistened on his palm. "Yeah, I'm real sure."

I stared at him for a minute, my mind racing through a variety of scenarios and options, each with the potential to get us both court-martialed. But my buddy was unhappy and, as a loyal pal, I felt compelled to put him out of his misery. So I grabbed a couple of the AR-15s leaning against the living room wall of my hooch.

"C'mon, let's grab a jeep."

Tom shot me a puzzled look. "You're gonna take me somewhere and shoot me? I admit it's tempting, but I'm not *that* miserable. I'll let you know if it gets worse."

"Geeze. Get a grip. We're gonna drive down to Phu Bai and see what's scheduled to fly in tomorrow, and where they're headed once they leave."

Tom's face lit up. He was seeing a light at the end of the tunnel, and it looked warm and inviting.

"Yeah. If someone's headed to Tan Son Nhut, maybe I can hitch a ride. I mean, HQ did say I'd either go back to Tan Son Nhut or up to Quang Tri—"

"Huh, what's that?" I cupped my hand to my ear. "I didn't catch that last part. Quang what? All I heard was Tan Son Nhut. HQ definitely said Tan Son Nhut. I'm sure of it."

Tom grinned and followed me out the door in search of an empty jeep.

At Phu Bai we successfully nailed down phase one of Operation O'Neill Airlift. Base ops confirmed that a C-130 would be arriving the next day to drop off a fresh supply of soldiers before heading back to Tan Son Nhut. It would be a shame to send it southward empty-handed.

On September 15, I scheduled my flight for late morning, giving me ample time to load up Tom and his bags. I didn't exactly sneak him out of camp, but I also didn't call attention to his departure. I had already made up my mind that it would be best if no one was placed in the position of asking or answering questions. On a very different topic in a very different time, someone would coin the phrase "don't ask, don't tell." That was the prime objective of the Great O'Neill Airlift.

Because Tom was leaving from one of the Army hooches, he was able to avoid the ALO, who might have violated the "don't ask" portion of the equation. The "don't tell" part was easy. We just kept our mouths shut and roared out the main gate, heading toward Hue Phu Bai and Tom's deliverance. At Phu Bai we just "happened" to drop in on base ops where, lo and behold, we ran across the crew of a C-130 headed south.

"Hey, my buddy here needs to get to Tan Son Nhut." I pointed to Tom, who casually grinned and nodded. "Any chance you guys can do a favor for a fellow pilot and give him a lift?"

"Sure, if he's ready to go. We're headed out of here in about five minutes, and he's welcome to tag along."

As we had suspected, no one gave a damn about official orders. No one wanted to see signed papers or formal travel directives. If Tom said he needed to go to Tan Son Nhut, well, he must have a good reason for doing so, and no one really cared why. It wasn't as though he was hitching a ride to Hawaii.

Tom heaved an audible sigh and disappeared out the door to retrieve his bags. When he returned, dragging all his earthly belongings behind him, we stood in the base ops office and shook hands, finding ourselves oddly tongue-tied. Tom shook his head and smiled awkwardly. "Watch yourself, okay? Just—take it easy." He patted my shoulder briskly, then loped out to the C-130. He turned and lifted one bag in the air as a farewell salute before disappearing into the bowels of the aircraft.

I loitered around the edge of the tarmac, watching until the C-130 lifted into the air and lumbered southward toward the promised land of paved streets, friendly locals, and an occasional bowl of ice cream.

Alone again, I drove over to the revetment where my O-2 was stored. Tom was headed back to his world and I was heading out over mine. I was happy for Tom. But watching the C-130 fade into the dull gray sky, I felt a momentary pang of envy and isolation. Having Tom around had been a vacation of sorts, a brief reminder of a time and place that seemed suddenly distant and inaccessible.

Don't even start, Jackson. You've had your adjustment period. You've done your moping. You're okay, and you'll stay okay unless you start feeling sorry for yourself. Anyway, count your blessings. You could be one of those poor bastards holed up at some godforsaken firebase or somewhere out in the bush. No matter how bad Camp Eagle seems, there are plenty of guys in-country who have it worse.

In a few minutes I'd managed to buoy myself back to my typical happy-go-lucky attitude. It usually didn't take long. Even the inequities and inconsistencies of combat couldn't completely dispel the optimism that was equal parts Tipp City, Jackson genetics, and my own biochemical cocktail of happy juice.

After flying an uneventful mission, I returned to Camp Eagle alone, and seriously apprehensive about Tom's absence and the inevitable questions it might raise.

"Where's O'Neill this afternoon?" Major Ullrich paused at the hooch door and waited for an answer.

I had been stretched out on the sofa with a paperback, but Ullrich's question brought me upright and alert.

Okay, Jackson. Calm, cool, collected. Just play dumb.

"He went back to Saigon this morning; I thought you knew that," I said matter-of-factly, flipping the paperback pages with my thumb.

"Oh, okay." Ullrich nodded and shrugged, heading out the door. It clattered shut behind him.

That's it? "Oh, okay?" That's the final word on the Great O'Neill Airlift? Man, if I'd known it was going to be that easy, I'd have airlifted myself out too. "Orders, Major Ullrich. Gotta report to Honolulu immediately. Top-secret mission."

I shook my head and returned to my dog-eared paperback, Irving Stone's *The Agony and the Ecstasy.* Somehow, the book provided an odd kind of solace as I shared the triumph and tragedy of Michelangelo's struggles with popes, politicos, and his own inner demons. The artist's frenetic emotions and dogged determination offered me both escape and encouragement. Vietnam was a long way from the Sistine Chapel, and we sure weren't creating anything that even vaguely glorified God, but I could still identify with the political maneuvering and the short-sighted bureaucratic weenies who, like cockroaches, seem to endure across the ages and the miles.

Tom's departure left me disheartened but determined to make the best of my situation. It wasn't as though I had any options to the contrary, so I concentrated on honing my FACing skills and giving Charlie a run for his money. In fact, in late September my skill and precision in the air strike arena hit an all-time high—or low, depending on your perspective.

It was a rare morning in the 'Nam—clear, cool, and comfortable. I took off with the sun looming large and red just above the waters of the South China Sea. Back in the world, this would have been a perfect day for washing cars, mowing grass, going on a picnic, and just generally taking advantage of comfortable, between-seasons weather. But here in Southeast Asia, it was the same old, same old. I turned my back on the sun and headed west toward the A Shau Valley.

Morning, Charlie. If you had any sense, you'd stay home today and wash your ox or re-thatch your roof. And if I had any sense, I'd be back in the world doing the same thing—well, maybe not the ox washing part.

As I cruised over my AO, I launched into the gentle rolls that gave me the best view of the terrain below. Time seemed to pass slowly, and I was feeling distinctly uninspired but typically uneasy. Out of the corner of my eye, I detected movement. Not guy-with-a-gun type of movement but something out of place and yet oddly familiar.

Banking the sky pig to the left, I took a second, longer look, hardly able to believe my eyes. It looked like a deer, a plain old run-of-the-mill Ohio whitetail. I'd never been a hunter, and I sure wasn't an authority on animals of the cervine species, but I knew enough to recognize venison steaks on the hoof.

I chuckled to myself as I radioed Bilk Control to acquire the call signs and frequency of two of my chopper buddies who were out and about in the area east of my AO.

"Warrior Two Six, Bilk One Two," I radioed to the chopper. "Warrior Two Six, you're not gonna believe what I'm looking at here. There's a deer grazing about two hundred yards from the edge of the jungle. Anybody interested?"

"You're shitting me, Bilk. An honest-to-god deer? Are you sure? I can't believe there's actually a real deer in this godforsaken hellhole. Damn. I'd kill for a fresh tenderloin strap," came the energetic reply from my chopper associate. "Does he have a nice rack?"

Okay, Jackson, you can be pretty sure he's not asking about the deer's breasts. He must be talking about antlers.

I rolled the airplane and took another look at the grazing buck. I wasn't sure what constituted a nice rack, at least not on a deer. I could make out antlers, but I lacked the tools necessary to comment on their quality.

"Hard to tell from this height. I don't see anything spectacular." I thought I covered well for my absence of sportsman savvy.

"Ah, probably a puny-assed little thing, like everything else in this frigging country," the chopper pilot mused. "Still, even a puny set of tenderloins would beat the hell outta tonight's mystery meat. Stay put, Bilk. I'm gonna call for reinforcements. You think you can talk us in?"

"Hey, it's what I do for a living. As long as he stays put, I'll getcha there," I confirmed.

I upped my altitude to avoid spooking tonight's dinner. It was probably an unnecessary maneuver. This deer had grown up listening to airplane engines, trucks, and choppers; those noises were as natural to him as the sound of leaves or rain or wind.

"Bilk One Two, Warrior Two Six. Ya still there?"

"Roger, Warrior Two Six. What's up?"

"Well, it looks like we've got a deer strike in the making. I've got a Cobra gunship and a couple Loaches on the way. I just called in a Huey slick to haul out the meat once we nail him."

"Okay. Let me know when you're ready and I'll talk you in."

"You got it, Bilk. Hot damn, we're havin' tenderloin tonight!" My young chopper associate clapped his hands and whistled into the mic. I couldn't say I really cared whether we ate venison or shit on a shingle, but it was a nice change of pace to go after something that wasn't shooting back at me. In a matter of minutes, I had the entire aviation battalion closing in on me, M-16s in one hand and wild game marinade in the other.

"Hey, Bilk, we're heading about two eight zero degrees. I've got the A Shau Valley in sight. Where are ya?"

"Okay, Warrior. Do you see where the highway meets the east side of the A Shau?"

Pause. "Yep, got it."

"Okay, you're gonna want to cut a little more south and head to where the road runs parallel to a small creek. About fifty meters west of that, the creek cuts off to the east."

"Roger that, Bilk. I see the road and the creek. We're moving down the creek."

"Good. Do you see that grove of really tall trees about twenty meters south of the creek?"

"Negative, Bilk. Hold on. Okay, got it! Now what?"

"Just the other side of that grove is a clearing. Your target is on the far side of the clearing. If you come in from the east, you've got a shot at stopping him if he breaks for the jungle. I'm circling overhead to the south. Do you have the FAC in sight?"

"Tallyho, Bilk. We gotcha—we're heading toward the grove, lookin' for dinner!"

I peered out over the nose of my O-2 and watched as two Huey gunships, a Cobra, and a couple of stray Loaches buzzed into view like a cloud of large, angry mosquitoes. I glanced back at our quarry. The deer had stopped eating and was standing still and alert, its tail flicking nervously from side to side.

"Uh-oh, guys, looks like the target knows it's our guest of honor tonight. Better move fast."

"Roger, Bilk, we're closing in. He can run but he can't hide!"

I watched, fascinated, as the two Loaches peeled off and flanked the grove while the Cobra set up a slightly higher orbit to protect the "little birds." The Hueys followed in quick succession. The deer took a couple of halting steps before sticking its nose into the air and sniffing for imminent danger. His head turned suddenly in the direction of the chopper invasion, and I could almost feel his muscles tense as he sprang toward the jungle—too late. In a matter of seconds, the choppers were unloading everything they had on him. Back in the States, a well-placed deer slug would have handled the whole operation with some level of efficiency and cleanliness. But this unfortunate critter was treated to a hail of munitions that made the St. Valentine's Day Massacre look like a kindergarten snowball fight.

Okay, guys, let's not forget that we're in a free-fire zone. Charlie is all over the place, and he's probably gonna wonder what the heck we're shooting at. Or, worse yet, he won't give a damn. He'll just start shooting back.

As the carnage below me unfolded, I had to wonder whether the deer would weigh substantially less because of the body mass that had been obliterated by projectiles and explosives, or considerably more due to the inordinate amount of lead that had wedged itself between sinew and bone.

"Shit hot! We got him!" my eager chopper pal shouted into the mic. "Barney Four Three, we need the slick. Bilk One Two, can you widen your orbit and make sure Charlie's not heading out to see what the ruckus is?"

"Roger, Warrior, I'm already on it," I radioed, glancing at the jungle terrain surrounding our dead deer. It occurred to me that if Charlie popped out of nowhere and blew half of us out of the sky, those who remained would have one heck of a time trying to explain what we were doing in no man's land blowing the crap out of Bambi.

I watched warily as the chopper landed in the jungle clearing and two guys hopped out and dragged the carcass on board. My gut tensed ever so slightly. This had been an exercise in blowing off steam;

it was just plain fun, and the best-case scenario included the possibility of something new and different for dinner. But I didn't dare ponder the potential for worst-case scenarios.

Once the Huey was airborne again, I flew cover until they were well clear of the valley, at which point I resumed my lazy circles over the A Shau. The excitement of Operation Bambi left me thoroughly uninspired about the prospect of any serious engagements for the remainder of the mission. I wouldn't leave my AO unless my fuel gauge told me it was time, but I was really hoping that Charlie had been dissuaded by the assembly of Hueys and Cobras. Chuckling out loud, I tried to imagine how the whole operation must have looked to a contingent of NVA regulars tromping through the valley. I figured their radios and walkie-talkies probably lit up like Christmas trees as they tried to figure out what kind of massive covert operation was taking place at the edge of their terrain. Wouldn't they have been surprised to know that the highest-ranking U.S. official involved in the whole sordid affair was a lowly first lieutenant whose boredom had overcome his good sense? Even more ironic was the fact that the whole operation went off without a hitch.

Nobody over the age of twenty-five or the rank of 1st Louie has any inkling what the heck just happened. Well, Jackson, now you know the secret for winning the war. Ya think Westmoreland will listen?

By the time I got back to camp, my chopper pals had successfully gutted, skinned, and hung the deer. I almost laughed out loud when I took a good look at the pathetic corpse. It was riddled with dents and cavernous pits. And, sans skin and antlers, it looked like little more than a glorified house cat.

Still, the aviation battalion was abuzz, and there was a steady stream of excited soldiers peeking around the hooch for a quick appraisal of tonight's dinner. I even spied a couple of majors nonchalantly licking their chops. Of course no one would admit to any knowledge of how and where the deer was felled, but everyone was plenty happy to help consume the evidence.

By evening the kitchen crew was firing up the grills, and Operation Bambi was almost a fait accompli—at least until the camp veterinarian caught wind of the proceedings. Who knew that the stupid place even *had* a veterinarian? A better question would have been why, because we were seriously lacking any kind of four-legged companionship, unless you counted a few scattered Army guard dogs and the rats that wallowed in the garbage dump. As the kitchen crew stood with knives poised to filet and fricassee the remains of Bambi, the veterinarian shoved past the line of hopeful diners that had formed near the kitchen.

"No one is eating anything until I've had a chance to look at it," he announced, righteously miffed that his wisdom and counsel hadn't been sought from the get-go.

A moan of despair rippled through the crowd. The good doctor did not appear to have any intention of encouraging or supporting the covert venison feast. In fact, he seemed hell-bent on throwing a wet blanket over what had the makings of a pretty decent party.

After a brief inspection of the carcass, he delivered the killing blow to Operation Bambi.

"I don't know where the hell you found this deer, but it is riddled with disease and parasites. This thing is filthy rotten and completely inedible," he announced imperiously, pausing just long enough to allow an anonymous wag in the crowd to shout, "Sounds like yesterday's lunch!"

We all chuckled heartily—well, all of us but the peeved vet.

"I'm serious. You are *not* eating this deer. I forbid it. You are to dispose of the carcass immediately."

And there it was: the word from on high. Moses had come down from the mountain and crapped all over the golden calf. The veterinarian glared defiantly at the crowd before sweeping past them with something approaching a regal air.

Like angry villagers who had inadvertently stormed an empty castle, we stood at loose ends for a moment, wondering what to do with our torches and pitchforks.

"Let's burn the carcass," someone shouted gleefully.

"Yeah! Throw it in the fire!"

"Yo, Jimmy, go grab a case of beer from the officers' club. We'll pound some brews and roast tonight's mystery meat over the Bambi blaze."

The new course of action was greeted with an enthusiasm that equaled or exceeded that of the original plan. There was some satisfaction to be derived from not allowing the prickly vet to have the final word on our fun.

And so, in the end, my covert deer strike did prove to be a morale booster of sorts. Everyone got roaring drunk and reminisced about meat, potatoes, and related delectables that lay just beyond our grasp somewhere back in the world. And no one ever did ask where the deer came from.

CHAPTER ELEVEN

RATS!

MY LIFE at Camp Eagle typically ricocheted back and forth between the bizarre and the ridiculous. I was never completely sure which was which, but at least I could count on the dull moments being few and far between. That suited me fine, as long as the excitement didn't involve stark terror. Fear, adrenaline, anxiety, and uncertainty were constant companions, and most of us learned to accept, if not befriend, them. There was something to be said for staying on your guard and maintaining a healthy situational awareness.

Having always been observant and alert, this strange new culture didn't exactly leave me fumbling for unavailable tools. But every so often I was confronted with an experience so foreign and unexpected that I was forced to invent a whole new layer of coping mechanisms. One particular night would forever alter my sleeping patterns.

Theoretically our hooches were gun-free zones. Personal weapons were forbidden, which seemed ludicrous considering we lived in a war zone. Every time I flew a mission, I'd head over to the tactical operations center (TOC) and draw my .38 and an AR-15. And every time I returned, I handed my guns back to the TOC. Kinda sorta.

Beyond the theoretical absence of personal weaponry was the reality of living in a combat zone with the Army. Translation: There were more stinking guns than you could shake a stick at. In my room alone, I kept an AK-47 with one regular banana clip and a second banana clip taped to the first one. I also had my own personal arsenal of pistols and related weapons squirreled away for any emergency. And right next to my bed, set on full automatic, was yet another AK-47 assault rifle, fully loaded and cocked. And I wasn't exactly the Eagle arms dealer. In fact, my arsenal paled in comparison to some of the stashes scattered around camp. Obviously, the "no weapons" edict was more a suggestion than a commandment.

The presence of all those guns necessitated one ironclad hooch rule, and it was the one rule that nobody ever violated: You never, ever walked into anyone else's room at night. You didn't even think about it unless, of course, you'd suddenly developed a potent death wish.

There was a general consensus that the only appropriate response to a room incursion was to shoot first and ask questions later. You had to assume that anyone who didn't know the rules was either an enemy intruder or simply too stupid to live. Camp Eagle was experiencing an unsettling increase in the number of people probing the perimeter; there were rumors that sappers had worked their way into camp, and that some of them were "trusted" employees such as hooch maids, or the shit burners who had the unenviable task of emptying the latrines and disposing of their contents.

Sappers were enemy engineer types with explosives who tried to infiltrate the camp and commit sabotage, or just randomly kill people for the sheer pleasure of sending a message. As the enemy incursions intensified, we were awakened throughout the night by the sound of shots being fired through the perimeter fence, or flares going up because someone had tripped them from the outside. There was no question that the North Vietnamese were trying to get in; the only mystery was whether they'd make it—and whether we'd find them before they could do any real damage.

During daylight hours I had a comfortable sense of security, but after dark it was different. We had a saying "Charlie owns the night," and it was true. At night we didn't ever pretend we controlled anything; we just hunkered down and waited for sunlight. It was unnerving to say the least.

But none of the vague what-ifs compared to coming face-to-face with a living, breathing manifestation of every nightmare I'd ever had. It happened at the close of one of those days that had left me feeling like a limp rag. I was sweaty, exhausted, and uninspired by foosball, conversation, and the night's movie selection, so I hung it up early and crawled happily into my bunk. As had been the case throughout my life, sleep came quickly and easily.

Then something, or someone, nudged me back into consciousness. I didn't know how long I'd been asleep, or how deeply. I knew only that I was surrounded by inky blackness and that, as I came more fully awake, I wasn't alone. Someone was gently rubbing my head.

In my first moments of sleepy awareness, I was back in Tipp City. Mom was tousling my hair in an effort to wake me for school. No, wait, that wasn't it. Mom never tousled my hair; she yanked off the covers and told me to get my lazy bones moving. Ah, I was at home, my home, and Karen was gently running her fingers through my hair, pausing to tickle the top of my ear. . . .

Wait a minute, Jackson. I was coming fully awake now and, for the first time in my life, I understood what it meant to feel your blood run cold. *You're not in Tipp City, or anywhere else civilized. You're in Vietnam. There's no Mom, no Karen. So, what or who is rubbing your head?*

I knew from stories around camp that a sapper didn't just sneak in and kill you. No, that would have made sense in some odd, primitive mindset. A sapper, before he slit your throat, would make sure you were fully awake so he could savor the look of terror as you took your last breath. These grim tales crowded my mind as my nerve endings came alive with adrenaline and fear. I tried to tell myself that I was emerging from some kind of deep dream state that only *seemed* real, but I knew this was wishful thinking cozying up to denial.

Cripes, Jackson. You're awake, all right, and someone wants to make sure you stay that way, at least until he decides to slice your throat wide open.

The rubbing had intensified, and I fought to control my breathing and develop some kind of action plan. I knew if I opened my eyes, the last thing I'd feel would be the feathery sweep of a knife across my neck. The worst part was I didn't know whether the intruder was going to kill me as a message to the others, or whether everyone else in the hooch was already dead and I was the last guy to go.

Time seemed to slow down, and I could hear my pulse pounding in my ears. I was fully awake now and fighting every impulse that might signal my level of awareness. I had to buy myself some time to think, not that thinking was exactly an easy process at the moment. My mind was racing, and my muscles twitched and tensed in an effort to resist the adrenaline overload. Somehow I managed to construct a loose action plan, even as I questioned my own ability to carry it out.

Geeze, Jackson, you're just a little guy from rural Ohio. You've got no motor skills to speak of—unless you count that motor mouth of yours, and it's not gonna help you much with someone who doesn't even speak English. What the hell makes you think you can get the drop on a seasoned guerrilla fighter?

I forced the negative thoughts to the outer edge of my mind. They refused to leave altogether, but they did pipe down long enough for me to acknowledge that I had very few options.

At least no one will ever say you went down without a fight.

By this point I'd decided that everyone else in the hooch was probably dead. In my mind's eye I could see that fully loaded AK-47 leaning against the wall beside my bed. I also counted among my assets the light-bulb string that dangled just above my head at arm's length. My only other asset was a marginal element of surprise, because at the moment I appeared to be the world's soundest sleeper.

Time was running out. I could sense that the urgency of the rubbing was intensifying. I could also tell that he was crouched with his back against the wall just to one side of my head.

My plan wasn't exactly comprehensive. I'd catch him off guard by rolling over as fast as I could in his direction and knocking him off balance while yanking on the light cord to momentarily blind him. Then I'd grab the AK-47 and wheel around, spraying bullets until I was certain he was disabled—permanently.

Even in my fear-addled state, it occurred to me that my bullets would also pierce the plywood boards that separated me from my hooch mates. Although I was pretty certain that everyone else was already dead, I did resolve to try to direct my bullet spray above bed level.

Finally, as the rubbing reached a crescendo of urgency, I screwed up my courage and energy and exploded out of bed.

Okay, Scoop, it's now or never. Grab the light, get the gun. Move! My hand yanked the cord so forcefully that I sent the fixture swinging into the wall. Thankfully the bulb didn't break. As brightness flooded the room, I vaulted off the bed, seized the rifle, and spun around, ready to begin firing as soon as my barrel was trained on the headboard. The light was still dancing on its cord as my finger tickled the trigger. Then I paused.

Sitting on my pillow staring at me defiantly was the biggest rat I'd ever seen. It showed no trace of the frenzied fear that gripped me. It just gazed at me curiously and flicked its long, hairless tail against the mattress. For reasons that escaped me then, and have forever after, the damn thing had been walking back and forth on my pillow, circling my head and doing God knows what up there.

I let out a yell and threw the gun into the air—by the grace of God and a sturdy trigger, it didn't go off when it hit the floor—then tore out of my room, down the hall, and out the front door. Once outside, I stood sweaty and breathless in my underwear, sucking in the dense night air and doubling over as I fought to regain my breath and my sanity.

Admittedly, a rat—even a huge one—wasn't quite the equal of a sapper wielding a razor-sharp knife, but the rat carried its own set of dangers. Rabies, for instance. Everything in Vietnam that could crawl, run, or scuttle seemed to be infected with rabies.

Okay, Scoop, did the damn thing bite you? Would you even know if it had? It was getting pretty aggressive with your head. And what the heck was the deal with that anyway? Since when does my head look like a lady rat?

I wasn't convinced I would have noticed a bite, at least not a gentle one. As fired up as I was, the stupid rat probably could have nibbled my ears off and I would have stayed fixated on the idea of a skulking Charlie, sitting on his haunches, waiting to bleed me out like the prize pig at a county fair.

After recovering my breath and my senses—and reassuring my bleary-eyed hooch mates that I hadn't gone nuts—I headed for the bathroom and tried to perform a scalp inspection with minimal light and a battered mirror. Nothing revealed itself immediately, but I was convinced that my unwelcome guest had ample time and opportunity to scratch or bite me somewhere. I realized that if I wanted to avoid a series of painful rabies shots, I needed to find the rat for tissue analysis.

I grabbed one of the .38s stashed in the living room—one of those theoretically nonexistent guns, according to camp rules. It seemed like a marginally more efficient way of disposing of my house-guest versus blowing him to pieces with the AK-47. When I got to my room, he was still there, resting comfortably on my pillow and looking as though he owned the place. I swear he'd gotten even bigger in the minutes I'd been gone. My hand shook slightly—my body was still draining off excess adrenaline—as I leveled the pistol at my hairy roommate. A bead of perspiration slid through my hairline and down my cheek, causing me to pause and shake away the tickle. In that instant of hesitation, the monster rat leaped from his perch and disappeared between the bed and the wall.

No!

Dropping to my knees and peering across the floor, I could see that he had made his timely escape through a hole at the base of the hooch wall that he or one of his buddies had chewed. There was nothing else I could do. He was gone. Completely. I didn't even get the satisfaction of blowing him away. Worse yet, I would have to take it on faith that he hadn't bitten me, or subject myself to painful, sickening shots, which would probably render me temporarily useless as a pilot.

I paced back and forth for a few minutes before sliding the .38 under the edge of my bunk and climbing into bed. I settled uneasily into a semi-supine position and waited for a sleep that never came. Every time I started to drift off, I'd jolt back to awareness, certain that things were crawling on me.

This is crazy, Jackson—or maybe you are. It was a stupid rat, not a VC, not a vindictive shit burner, just a lousy, stinking rat. Are you really gonna let it get the better of you?

In a word? Yes.

Eventually something akin to sleep swept over me, but it was weak and pathetic, kind of how I felt. At first light, I went in search of every 2x4 I could scrounge, and nailed them securely around the entire base of the room. But it was another two weeks before I could manage to fall asleep for any length of time. Every night, just as darkness closed in around me, I'd slam back to consciousness, rattled by the sensation of things crawling on me—bugs, snakes, rats, dogs, you name it. Somehow they all managed to breach the fortress I'd built and haunt my nights.

After wandering through several days like a restless sleepwalker, I snagged a couple of sheets of mosquito netting from my Army buddies and built a little tent over my bed. My nightly ritual now included checking under the pillows, under the blankets, under the sheets, and under the bed until I was satisfied that I was completely alone. Then I'd jump into bed and tightly tuck the netting under my mattress, knowing full well that if the stupid rat had chewed through my wall, it could certainly chew through mosquito netting.

But somehow my mesh fortress gave me the sense of well-being that had been evading me. A psychologist would probably say that it was the act of taking control—not the presence of mosquito netting— that finally allowed me to sleep again, however marginally. That would probably be right. Eventually I tossed the mosquito netting; it was too big a pain in the neck.

On the positive side, I couldn't find any evidence that the rat had mauled me. And as the days passed, I noted no tendency toward foaming at the mouth or acting erratically, at least no more than usual. But in the end, the rat got the last laugh. As a kid I'd been an incredibly sound sleeper; friends and family joked that nothing ever woke me up. I could saw wood with the best of them, through thunderstorms, construction, screaming siblings, and—without question—alarm clocks. My rat encounter changed all that, and not just temporarily either. Somewhere deep in my brain, a switch had been flipped. Some primal survival instinct kicked on and never kicked back off. No amount of security or comfort would ever again allow me to "sleep the sleep of the dead."

The whole rat affair also prompted me to modify my after-hours eating habits. I became highly selective about the foodstuffs that entered my room, shying away from anything that had the potential to attract ants, roaches, or rodents. I even developed a taste for the Army's limitless supply of Lurps, an early attempt at a dehydrated meal, kind of like today's MREs (meals ready to eat) and supposedly the fare of choice for long-range reconnaissance patrols (or LRRPs, hence the nickname Lurps). Lurps were essentially Styrofoam sheets of freeze-dried food wrapped in plastic. They were labeled chili or macaroni and cheese or beef stew, but they all looked pretty much the same. And they all tasted about like you'd expect flavored Styrofoam to taste. In fact, I was the only person in my hooch who could manage to eat them, although I think I found them more intriguing than palatable.

Lurps had been designed for handy field consumption. Theoretically a soldier on patrol who was overcome by hunger could break off a chunk of Lurps and pop it in his mouth. Once the dry concoction was exposed to saliva, it would begin the slow and gooey process of reconstitution that supposedly resulted in something resembling real food. This was okay in moments of desperation, but the preferred method for consuming Lurps was to crunch them up in their bag and douse them with hot water. After a few minutes of absorption and expansion, they resembled brown paste in texture—and flavor.

When my Army pals next door decided to do a little home improvement on their hooch, they approached us for some of the paint and acoustical tile that the Air Force had generously provided. Because everything in Vietnam ran on the barter system, our first response was, "Sure, you can have anything you need, but what do we get in return?" The answer came in the form of several cases of Lurps, which inspired no one but me.

My first encounter with Lurps set the tone for a love-hate relationship that never quite gelled, although it did provide many hours of anatomically perverse entertainment.

It all started with a bag labeled chili con carne. Not wishing to minimize the whole Lurps experience, I followed the instructions carefully, crunching the brown Styrofoam into bite-sized morsels before drowning them in hot water. Then, instead of allowing them to set for five minutes, I waited a full ten. Once they were visibly rehydrated, I gobbled them down along with my ever-present can of rusty orange soda. As bad food went, it was pretty good. I chewed up mouthfuls of something that might have once been meat or chili beans, then washed down the whole mess with a sizeable gulp of soda.

But as I ate, I noticed that I was feeling quite full—much fuller, in fact, than my few mouthfuls should have warranted. Dropping my spoon, I sat back and waited for digestion to catch up with consumption—or a decent cleansing belch. But the longer the Lurps sat in my stomach, the more they seemed to expand, until I had gone from not hungry to full to extremely full to *Yikes, I think I'm going to blow up.* As I sat on the edge of the sofa, I thought I noticed the skin across my belly growing tighter and thinner with each passing minute, and the top button on my fatigue pants suddenly battled to restrain the swelling gut beneath it.

Okay, Jackson, so what happens if it doesn't stop swelling? You can stuff only so much crap into a five-pound bag before it rips open and everything spills out.

This particular mental image left me feeling nauseated as well as bloated.

I dumped out my soda, realizing that the more liquid I swallowed, the more the Lurps seemed to come to life in my belly. I developed an immediate empathy for pregnant women as I tried to ignore the sickening feeling that all my internal organs were being mashed against my spine. I paced back and forth, trying to walk off the ever-expanding discomfort. Eventually my distress began to moderate slightly, but I also discovered that Lurps were the gift that keeps on giving. For the rest of the day whenever I took a swig of water or soda, I would feel the stirrings of a sleeping giant in my belly.

Still, despite our somewhat unpleasant first encounter, I couldn't completely disavow my Lurps. I began to experiment with the Lurps-to-water ratio. If I ate four bites, then drank two cans of soda, would I be as full as if I ate ten bites but drank only half a can of soda? In a world where entertainment was where you found it, Lurps evolved into an odd game of playing with my food, then watching in fascination as it returned the favor.

I was pretty certain that Lurps were a wartime romance, not something I would ever pursue once the rigors of combat were behind me. But for now they offered a strange and compelling diversion.

By my third month in Southeast Asia, I had undergone a dramatic upheaval in hygiene standards, sleep routines, and food consumption. My bathing habits would also be further redefined, and I would never again step into a shower without pondering the potential for disaster.

CHAPTER TWELVE

NAKED IN DA NANG

THE SOUTHEASTERN United States has its hurricane season. The prairie states can lay claim to tornado alley. And, of course, the West Coast shakes, rattles, and rolls with frequent tremors and earthquakes. In Southeast Asia we dealt with the monsoon season and its occasional typhoon, which was nothing more or less than an Eastern Hemisphere hurricane.

Like everything else in Vietnam, our typhoon evacuations were perpetually backward. Whenever we had a practice evac, we'd pile into an airplane and head for Ubon, Thailand. Not a bad deal—plenty of nightlife, good food, inexpensive shopping, and no small measure of female companionship for those who were on the prowl.

But for some insane reason, when an actual typhoon threatened, we were ordered to Da Nang, positioned neatly astride the beaches of the South China Sea.

Just like a hurricane, a typhoon sweeps in from the ocean and hugs the coastline, making beachfront property an unpleasant place to ride out the storm. Even as a naive young lieutenant, I couldn't fathom the rationale of greeting an approaching typhoon with the announcement, "Hey! Let's head for the ocean!" I tried to imagine Floridians in Orlando bracing for a hurricane by packing up their worldly goods and streaming toward Daytona Beach.

On October 21, Lynn Damron came into the hooch and tossed a sheet of paper onto the makeshift end table beside the sofa. Bob looked up from a magazine, and I triumphantly played the last card in one of many games of solitaire.

"Where's Clyde?" Lynn asked. He didn't wait for an answer. "Just got this from the TOC. Typhoon evac—Supposedly, this time it's the real thing. They're calling her 'Hester,' and we've been ordered to grab the planes and head to Da Nang."

Bob shook his head and shot me a quizzical look.

"Da Nang? Why the hell would we go to Da Nang? Wouldn't we want to head inland where the storm is weaker? Why would the practice evacs send us to Thailand when they're gonna send us to Da Nang for the real thing?"

I chuckled as Lynn dismissed the question with a wave.

"Welcome to 'Nam, Gilday. Don't expect anything to make sense, least of all orders." Lynn flopped down on the edge of the sofa. "Someone needs to stay here and hold down the fort. The rest of you should head out as soon as possible."

"The rest of us—hmmmm—I wonder who's staying." I grinned at Lynn. "Are you sure you don't want to take off for Da Nang and grab a little downtime?"

Lynn shrugged and looked around. "What, and leave all this? Bite your tongue, Jackson. Anyway, if we all go, what's Jesse Hicks gonna do? Fend for himself?"

I shrugged. Lynn was referring to our newest recruit, a scraggly little black-and-white mutt that had wandered up to the hooch late one afternoon. Like Mr. Whiskers before him, I had committed the tactical error of picking him up and making friends. Now he was a permanent fixture. I couldn't complain. He was a cute little guy—just about the only dog in Southeast Asia with a straight tail. I was pretty certain that his tail said something complimentary about his breeding, but I wasn't sure what.

"Jesse Hicks is tough. He'll manage fine. Heck, Lynn, *he* can protect the hooch, defend it from rats and critters, and probably take on a whole platoon of NVA regulars," I argued.

"Nope. I hate to pull rank and force you guys to abandon the luxury of Camp Eagle, but I'm the acting ALO and it's my job to hang tight. Tomorrow I want each of you to grab a plane and take it to Da Nang. Secure it and wait out the storm in the BOQ. I know it'll be tough dealing with indoor plumbing and air conditioning, but I'm guessing you guys'll manage."

Bob sighed, twisting his magazine into a hollow tube. "It just makes absolutely no sense. It's like running into a burning building to escape a fire."

I grinned and flipped a five of clubs off my fingertips in his direction. "Aw, c'mon, Gilday, how long do you have to be here before you figure out that anything in this place that makes sense is probably against the rules?"

Al Duty had DEROSed a few days earlier, just in time to miss all the fun. So on October 22, Bob, Clyde, and I piled into our O-2s and headed south down the coast toward "safe haven." As we taxied our planes to the ramp at Da Nang, the wind kicked up and pelted our O-2s with dirt and gravel, which pinged off the spinning propeller blades like random sniper fire. The air closed in around us, heavy with humidity and the earthy smell of approaching rain.

Eyeing the ragged clouds, I was certain of one thing: Da Nang would not have been my first choice of places wherein to seek shelter. Air Force meteorologists weren't offering much detail (to a pack of lowly first lieutenants, anyway) on the path or intensity of the storm, only that it was headed toward Vietnam, and everyone along the coast should batten down the hatches.

Our accommodations in Da Nang were primitive by American standards. But based on how I'd been living for the past four months, this was pretty ritzy stuff. We stayed in a two-story concrete dorm with sparsely furnished rooms and long, dark hallways, thanks to the military's aversion to windows in a combat zone. Not that there was much of a scenic view available. In fact, the absence of windows was a definite confidence builder in a town that had earned the nickname Rocket City. In the event of an aerial assault, I might be buried under a ton of cement, but I wouldn't be sliced to ribbons by shards of glass. We were encouraged to find that our makeshift BOQ was located just down the street from the DOOM club—Da Nang Officers' Open Mess—which offered some hope for food, beverage, and entertainment.

Bob and I doubled up in a room two doors down from the second-floor community showers. I relished the prospect of unlimited water. Given the choice between a private audience with Racquel Welch and twenty minutes alone in the shower, I was almost positive the shower would win. In fact, I was so starved for a thorough cleansing that I probably would have turned down twenty minutes alone in the shower *with* Racquel Welch, simply because it would have distracted me from the pure, hedonistic pleasure of endless water.

My first night in Da Nang passed uneventfully, although I awoke several times to strange, wet swishing sounds that I drowsily likened to rolling through a car wash. In fact, what I was hearing was the sound of the storm—which I was supposedly avoiding—catching up to me full force.

By morning, the typhoon's fury had settled over Da Nang with a vengeance. Bob and I lounged around the BOQ until total boredom spurred us to action. Bob wrapped himself in an assortment of rubber ponchos and headed out toward the DOOM club in search of something to eat. I listened uneasily to the clatter of boards, trees, and sheet metal slamming against the building and decided to sit tight until the storm abated or my hunger overcame my good sense.

As the storm intensified and the day wore on, I exhausted my patience for reading and solitaire. *So, what's the one thing you've been dreaming of, Jackson? Hmmm . . . well, other than that . . . Yes! A shower! Hot and cold running water, really clean skin.*

The time had come to indulge myself. I was eager to become reacquainted with the luxury of a slow, muscle-soothing shower.

I unlaced my boots and pried them off my feet. I could hear the wind pounding against our sturdy windowless building. I smiled. For the first time in a long time, I felt reasonably comfortable and secure.

I padded down the empty hall and peeked into the narrow room that housed a row of honest-to-goodness flush toilets and a bank of shower stalls, stained reddish brown by minerals in the water. The toilets alone were so appealing that I embraced with childish glee the joy of bathroom breaks sans mosquitoes, rats, truck exhaust, and flying rocks. Who knew that indoor plumbing could lead to such ecstasy?

I ran my hands across the discolored shower tiles. The gritty film once would have repulsed me. Not today. I turned on the hot water full blast and waited for the top layer of grime to melt off the walls. When the bathroom was sufficiently bathed in humidity, I braced myself for the thrill of cleanliness.

Few events in my life have equaled pausing for long, luxurious minutes under the pounding force of an uninterrupted high-flow shower. I relished every second as I soaped up my body with slow, deliberate precision. No wham, bam, thank-you ma'am this time. No siree, I had all the time and water in the world; I could savor the lather of the gods. And then, ahhhhh, the hot water surged across my thirsty pores, making me feel as though I was dissolving into a tranquil puddle of foam.

Damn, Scoop, there's not a spa in the world that could feel this good. I stepped out of the direct flow of water to finish lathering my hair, my face, my feet, and every part in between.

You are going to be the cleanest person in Da Nang, and tonight you're going to sleep between clean sheets on a real bed in an air-conditioned room. Y'know, life could be a lot . . .

Worse.

My thoughts trailed away to nothingness as I suddenly became aware that I was standing in total darkness and the shower flow had ceased completely.

"Aw, man. What the . . . ?"

I fumbled for my towel, with no success. I slid my feet gingerly out of the shower stall and felt my way along the wall, hoping to locate a towel or a functional light switch. I briefly entertained the possibility that some smart-ass pal—*All right, Gilday, you'd better be at the DOOM club*—had flipped off the lights to confound and annoy me, but I knew better. Electricity was a casualty of the storm. The best I could hope for was a towel and the ability to stumble back to my room. Soap trickled from my hairline and into my eyes, where it tingled and burned. I was suds from head to toe, and I could feel the soapy residue hardening across my skin like varnish.

Then, as often happens to me in a moment of crisis, my analytical instincts kicked in. What are my options? How can I fix this?

Okay, think it through, Scoop. It's not nearly as challenging as an air strike. In fact, you should come out the other side of this without getting shot at or having to kill anybody. The lights probably aren't coming back on anytime soon. You're quickly turning into six feet of soap scum. If you can just rinse off, life'll be a lot better.

It occurred to me that I had seen a fire escape at either end of the hall. If I could feel my way to the fire escape, I could step out into the rain and rinse off. It wasn't as though anyone would be wandering the streets and staring up at my nudity. *Face it, Scoop, anyone with any sense is inside.* I was about to discover the wisdom of that observation.

Feeling my way out of the bathroom and into the hallway, I stubbed my toe twice. More melting lather dribbled across my forehead and into my eyes, intensifying the burning and loss of vision. Not that it mattered much; everything around me was wrapped in blackness. I stretched out my arms on either side and stumbled toward the thin square of light that I guessed was the fire escape door. I must have looked like a kid playing "airplane." The irony of that was not lost on me.

My plan was simple and foolproof: jump outside, rinse off, and get back inside.

As I neared the door, the strength of the storm startled me. I could hear the rain beating against the outer walls. Frequent thuds and bangs shook the building as it was battered by trees, boards, sheet metal, and anything else light enough to be picked up and slammed around by the winds. From the sound of it, that was anything not tethered to the ground.

I turned the door handle and pushed. Nothing. I pushed again. This time the door opened slightly, before slamming shut in my face.

Careful, Jackson. You've got loose body parts that wouldn't be real happy about getting slammed in a fire escape door. The very thought of it made me momentarily queasy.

If I hadn't been so obsessed with rinsing the soap from my eyes and my skin, it might have occurred to me that a storm powerful enough to slam a metal door in my face should probably be avoided at all costs. But, as is my tendency, I had already mentally fast-forwarded the scenario to a successful conclusion. There was no turning back now.

I gave the door a mighty shove, careful to turn my delicate parts toward the hinges and away from the gaping maw to the outside. This time I stepped quickly through the opening and onto the fire escape. The door slammed shut behind me, but I was busy reveling in my own genius. The rain was sharp, and blowing almost horizontally. It pounded my skin like birdshot, but at least I could feel the soapy residue being scoured off my body.

I jumped as a thick branch sailed past my head and smashed against the building a few feet away.

Holy cow, Jackson. Get yourself rinsed and get your ass inside.

I tried to hurry the process by rubbing my wet hands over my body. It occurred to me with a certain edge of perverse humor that I was a naked man standing on a public fire escape rubbing myself in the rain. I was pretty sure I'd be arrested for that back in Tipp City.

As tiny welts began to form on my skin from the force of the rain, I decided that I was clean enough. I turned and offered the deserted street a moon shot as I seized the door handle and tugged.

Nothing happened. In fact, the handle didn't even turn. The frigging thing was locked!

I banged frantically on the door, hoping that someone would come to the rescue. But my voice and my pounding seemed to be carried away on the shriek of the wind. After a couple of minutes, my knuckles were scuffed and red. Still no rescuers emerged. I was beginning to worry.

Okay, Jackson. Let's look at this rationally. You're a naked guy standing two stories up in a combat zone in the middle of a typhoon. It's not like things can get much worse.

A large slab of plywood slammed against the wall just below me and shattered into toothpicks.

Okay. Strike that. It could get worse. You could be a dead naked guy two stories up in a combat zone in the middle of a typhoon.

By this time, all parts of my body were being lashed and buffeted by violent wind gusts while barbs of rain tenderized every square inch of exposed flesh, which was all of it.

I craned my head back and forth for better visibility as I began a slow and awkward descent down the fire escape. I wasn't worried about spectators at this point, but I was very concerned about the untethered parts and pieces of Da Nang that were shattering against the building above and below me. Periodically I paused and clung protectively to the fire escape ladder as falling debris showered over me. Leaping to the ground, I headed around to the opposite side of the building, hoping I'd have better luck at that entrance. Once there, I resumed my pounding and yelling, again to no avail.

I made a quick circuit around the structure, yelling as I went, pausing to knock on any opening that I might conceivably be able to climb over, under, or through.

As I stumbled back around the building and into the street, my discomfort became mental as well as physical. *Okay, Jackson, you're a naked guy in a foreign country in the middle of a killer storm. What happens if something knocks you over and you die and you're lying here in the street naked? How do they find out who you are and why you were out here?* I tried to imagine what the Air Force would tell Karen in the event of my untimely demise. *"Yes, Mrs. Jackson, your husband was found naked in the street with a tree on top of him, but, boy, was he clean!"*

I'd lived a pretty straight and narrow life up to this point. How would anyone ever figure out that wandering naked in a typhoon wasn't the emergence of some latent aberrant behavior? Would the Air Force actually tell my wife that I had been found without a stitch of clothing? Would she go to her grave believing that I'd been engaging in some kind of inappropriate shenanigans?

I decided to give the door on the west side of the building one more concerted effort; at least it was marginally more sheltered from the full force of the storm. As I turned and lowered my head against the wind, I noticed that several homes outside the U.S. compound had thrown open their shutters. As I stared with a detached blend of horror and curiosity, dozens of startled Vietnamese faces stared back at me. Several women gestured frantically as children were pulled away from the window. Many more just stood there mystified, apparently not accustomed to naked Americans wandering the street in any weather, let alone a typhoon.

I diverted my eyes and turned my attention back to the BOQ. I couldn't even manage a sheepish grin for my puzzled audience. I was still too focused on my frantic game of save Scoop's ass—and all other exposed parts as well.

I ducked my head low and stumbled forward into the shadow of the building, where I was once again obscured from view. I resumed my kicking, pounding, and yelling at the west entrance. Suddenly, as though divine intervention had occurred (*yeah, God's got nothing better to do than look after naked pilots in typhoons*), the wind seemed to slack for a split second. I seized the opportunity and bashed both fists against the door, screaming until my throat was raw.

To my immense relief, the door edged open and a startled face gaped back at me. We stared at each other, the naked guy and his reluctant rescuer. Then, as the wind kicked up again, I shoved against the door and he stepped back, apparently unwilling to question the motives of a frantic, semi-crazed nude man whose body parts were, literally, twisting in the wind.

I let loose a sigh as the dark building swallowed me and the sound of the storm diminished into the background.

"You got a towel, man?" I asked into the darkness.

"Uh, no . . . ," The detached voice had retreated down the hall and was addressing me with considerable reticence.

Geeze, how dangerous can I be, buddy? It's pretty obvious I'm not armed. I resumed my naked game of blindman's bluff as I felt along the walls in search of the stairwell.

Finally, thankfully, I managed to grope my way back to my own room. At least I was reasonably certain it was my room. I tried to recall where I had left various belongings. Yep. There were my boots, tucked under the edge of the bed. And there was my crumpled flight suit. And there was. . . .

The lights flickered on. It *was* my room! I thankfully collapsed onto the bed, pausing to revel in quiet, comfort, and electricity before my instincts kicked back into gear.

Okay, idiot, what are the chances that the lights will go out again? Pretty good? Then why are you sitting here naked? Are you really interested in an encore?

I fished around in my bag for fresh underwear and anything that promised to cover most of my skin. Then I stretched out—fully clothed at last—and savored the thought of some mid-afternoon shut-eye. My brief escape from the rigors of combat had turned into its own life and death struggle. Now that it was over, I couldn't help chuckling at the hotshot pilot, ducking and covering, scrambling bare-assed and *em*barrassed, through the streets of a foreign—and only marginally hospitable—city.

Nice work, Ace—yet another tale of valor to share with the grandkids when they climb into your lap and ask all wide-eyed, "What did you do in the war, grampa?"

Then again, I had to assume that any grandchildren of mine would probably relish the humor over the valor anyway.

Admit it, Jackson, your life isn't always fun, but it's sure as heck never boring.

I slowly drifted into a well-earned slumber, secure in the knowledge that if I ever dreamed about being naked in a public place, I could smile, shrug, and say, "Yeah. So what?"

Two days later Typhoon Hester beat a hasty retreat, leaving thirty-nine dead, thirty-four wounded, and a whole bunch of twisted metal and splintered wood. Although I was thankful not to be among the dead, I was plenty disgruntled to find that one of the pieces of twisted metal was my O-2.

At some point during the height of the storm, Hester had seen fit to seize a hangar door and drop it squarely on my trusty little sky pig. The damage was such that I had to hitch a ride with Gilday back to

Camp Eagle, where we were further confronted by Hester's devastation. Clyde met me at the entrance to our hooch—at least what used to be our hooch.

"Lynn's down at Hue Phu Bai," he said, adding flatly, "in the hospital." Then he stepped out of the doorway and allowed me to peek into the living room. The place was a mess. Part of the roof was missing, and the contents of the main living area had been battered, soaked, and tossed about like kindling.

Momentarily stunned, I turned back to Clyde. "What happened to Lynn? Is he okay?"

"Well, apparently at the height of the storm, the roof started to rip off, so Lynn grabbed a ladder and climbed up to pile more sandbags on it. Bad idea. A strip of corrugated metal tore loose and sliced him across the face from his forehead down his nose and across his cheek— a real jagged slice. A hundred and forty stitches."

I winced as Clyde continued. "The good news is they're gonna let him DEROS six weeks early."

I shrugged, not certain that 140 stitches and the possibility of permanent disfigurement was worth a six-week reprieve, unless of course you happened to die during those six weeks. Happily for Lynn, the Army doc who stitched him up had just completed a specialization in plastic surgery. Thus his handiwork reflected a much more polished approach to skin stitchery than anyone could have hoped for under the circumstances.

Still chagrined by the devastation, I numbly poked my way through the hooch, stepping around soggy magazines and paperbacks, as well as parts and pieces from other hooches that had apparently blown in through the gaping hole in the roof. On the bright side, the roof had stayed put over the bedrooms, so most of our personal belongings had weathered the storm.

With Lynn headed home, there were only four of us left: Bob, Clyde, me, and Dale Ullrich, who had just returned from temporary duty. We set about renovating our storm-ravaged home. It turned out to be something akin to Vietnam's version of a good old-fashioned barn raising. The helicopter guys pitched in and helped us clear out the soggy mess, mend the walls, and lay on a new roof. We managed to turn the proceedings into an impromptu party, with copious amounts of beer, soda and anything else we could scrounge from the wind-damaged officers' club.

As I shoveled debris from the living room floor, it occurred to me that this was probably the first good overhaul the hooch ever had. Typical Jacksonian "find the silver lining in the black cloud" philosophy. But, hey, after doing battle with mildew, rats, ants, and roaches, this was a good opportunity for spring cleaning, even if it was late October.

After dumping the last pile of waterlogged garbage into a steel drum outside the hooch door, I paused to nuzzle Jesse Hicks, who had wandered up in search of food. I was grateful that he had survived the typhoon with no ill effects.

"Hey, buddy." I scooped him up and scratched his belly as I positioned myself gingerly atop a stack of corrugated metal strips, careful to avoid doing to my rear what Lynn had done to his face. Thomas Zieg, one of my aviation battalion buddies, squatted next to me and fed Jesse a piece of beef jerky.

"Cute little guy. Looks like the Border collie my neighbors used to have. I always wanted a dog, but my folks wouldn't let me have one. Made up my mind to get one once I was out on my own, but Camp Eagle turned out to be the first place I was out on my own."

I chuckled, remembering the dog craze that had briefly swept the Ohio University (OU) campus while I was there.

"Yeah. A bunch of my buddies at OU decided that dogs were the way to a girl's heart. All of a sudden everyone was walking a dog around campus, hoping that some cute co-ed would pet it and strike up a conversation. I guess it worked sometimes, but I thought the whole thing was stupid."

Thomas eyed me with a cynical twitch in the corner of his mouth.

"Okay, Jackson, what's the rest of the story? You don't suffer fools quietly. What'd you do, buy a Shetland pony and ride it around campus?"

"Not bad, but not quite. No, I decided there had to be some way to get in on the game without appearing to be part of the pack. I wanted to have some fun and maybe make a statement at the same time, so I bought a little alligator. I figured I'd buy a tiny collar and leash, and walk my alligator around campus."

Thomas burst out laughing and startled Jesse Hicks, who was intent on gnawing through his jerky.

"I'll bet that was a sight to see!"

I shrugged. "Well, it would have been, if I could have kept the stupid thing alive. I ordered one from a Woolworth's near the campus in Athens, and it arrived dead. So I ordered a second one, and darned if it didn't show up dead too. I guess alligators aren't very hardy, at least not when they're out of their element. I'm not sure how well he would have fared during an Ohio winter, but it would have been fun while it lasted."

"Tough luck," Thomas said with a laugh. "So, did you ever come up with the perfect way to meet girls?"

"Well, yeah, but I got a little help from the university. I took a job to help pay my way through school. That job turned out to be running the milk machine in the Jefferson Hall dining room, the largest girls' dorm on campus. Man, talk about a target-rich environment! I was Mike the Milkman—king of the chow hall—and if a girl said 'hi' she got rewarded with a frothy glass of cold milk. If she ignored me, she got squat. I just turned off the milk machine, folded my arms, and waited. It was great; I had total power. Ya know, I met my wife that way."

"Ah. So she said 'hi'?"

"Nah, she ignored me," I said, laughing. "There ensued a lengthy battle of wills. In the end, she got a calcium deficiency, and I got her."

Thomas shook his head and cuffed me on the shoulder. "Y'know, they call us helicopter guys nuts, but we're pretty sane compared to you, Jackson." He grinned at me, and I had to chuckle. The kid couldn't have been more than nineteen, with a swatch of freckles across his cheeks and a good-natured grin—as all-American as they came. And although I always called him Thomas, it fit him like a bad suit. He was more of a Tommy, more like the kid next door who played baseball, swilled sodas, and tried to work up the courage to invite Peggy Sue to the prom.

He broke off another hunk of jerky and fed it to Jesse Hicks.

"So, are you ever gonna take a ride with us? You can't say you've had the complete Vietnam experience until you've flown a pink team mission. It's pretty wild. You guys think you fly low and slow; hell, I'm so close to the ground I can count the pimples on Charlie's ass."

In my heart of hearts, few things sounded less appealing than skimming across the elephant grass trolling for VC. Loach pilots routinely hung it out and tempted fate in ways that made my skin crawl. The six years that separated Thomas and me were chock-full of life lessons and the growing realization that nothing is a sure thing. Thomas still lived in that place where "it can't happen to me." And he was one of the safer, saner Loach drivers.

But in true Jackson form—and leaning heavily on my ever-present luck o' the Scoop—I shrugged and said, "What the heck."

What's the worst that can happen? I forced myself to disregard possible answers to that question, at least for the moment.

On the plus side, I figured that the experience might help me be an even better FAC. Frankly, I was curious about what these guys did and how they did it. I knew they were about half nuts, and equal parts cowboy and hot dog, but I also knew they did some of the most necessary, and dangerous, work in-country.

My respect for helicopter pilots was and is unwavering. I wouldn't have traded places with them for all the rusty orange soda in Southeast Asia. But I lived with these guys, ate with them, and hung out in the club with them. I felt a certain obligation to understand what the war looked like from their perspective.

The term pink team was a tad misleading, sounding as it did like a homosexual coupling or a bridge club twosome. Actually it was the byproduct of pairing Loaches (called "white birds") and Cobras (called "red birds"). Pink teams were also known, more accurately perhaps, as hunter/killer teams. The Loach would skirt the treetops—or lower— and hunt for targets or enemy activity. When one or the other appeared, the Loach, or "little bird," would mark it with a smoke grenade, allowing the Cobra to swoop down and handle the killer part of the equation.

It was a deadly combination, but not always for the North Vietnamese. Loach drivers had one of the highest mortality rates. Of the 5,086 helicopters destroyed during the Vietnam War, 842 were

Loaches, second only to Huey losses. But those statistics spoke to the dangers inherent in scouting rather than to the durability of the aircraft itself. Loach drivers couldn't say enough good things about their little birds. The Loach, a light observation helicopter (LOH), was a surprisingly sturdy little ship, able to absorb plenty of enemy fire and keep moving. The chopper's A-frame design was reminiscent of a race car and was similarly configured to allow for impact and rollovers, which would leave occupants relatively unharmed. Unfortunately, the prospect of living through a Loach crash was overshadowed by the reality of being plucked from the wreckage by little guys in black pajamas who would happily cart you back to Hanoi. The problem with Loaches was that they were right down there for everyone to see—and shoot at. The North Vietnamese correctly assumed that, as with FACs, if they knocked out the guy closest to the ground, they'd have a better shot at escaping undetected. Perhaps that was part of the kinship I sensed with Loach pilots; we both knew what it felt like to have the entire country of North Vietnam open up on us as we tried to mark our target.

Several days after my conversation with Thomas, I made good on my promise to find out how the other half lives. Standing beside one of Camp Eagle's crude helipads, I watched Thomas finish his preflight inspection. It was heartening to see him take the process so seriously. Perhaps he was as determined to dispel the myth of the lunatic chopper pilot as I was to present FACs as something other than suicidal hotshots.

Thomas motioned me to the left side and introduced James Zimmerlin, the door gunner. James nodded to me, then squeezed his beefy frame behind the right seat. He sat crossed-legged on the floor, positioned near an M-60 that peered out of the cockpit behind the pilot. I climbed into the little bird, marveling at its form and function. The teardrop body gave it the look of a large, bug-eyed insect, an illusion magnified by the Loach's ability to dart around the sky with bumblebee precision.

Thomas adjusted his helmet and tossed me mine.

"You get to play observer today. I reckon you're used to that role. James will take care of the bad guys from this side. If we end up in a hot zone, I'll use the minigun and you can use the M-16. Just remember to take the safety off, set it for rock 'n' roll, and smile. The cool thing about the minigun is every time I fire it, I have to stomp on the right pedal just to keep on target. Friggin' high deadly torque, man! Ya ready, new guy?"

I swallowed hard, nodded, and looked around the cockpit. The interior reminded me of my wife's Volkswagen Bug sans the nominal luxury. Although James had managed to fold himself into an awkwardly comfortable position, his stocky build overwhelmed the rear of the chopper. He grinned good-naturedly and shrugged as I shot him a sympathetic glance.

"I'm used to it," he said, fiddling with ammunition and several metal containers. "I'd rather fly than eat, so at least this gets me into the air, even if I get there kinda squished up."

I nodded, my attention focused on a wire that stretched behind the pilot's seat and attached to either side of the bird. The wire sagged from the weight of a dozen or so hand grenades that dangled from it, looking for all the world like a perverse assortment of armored fruit.

"So, what's up with the grenades?"

Thomas glanced over his shoulder. "Smoke grenades. The wire's threaded through each pin. When we see a target, James yanks one off and throws it. Saves time. Takes one motion instead of having to pick one up and pull the pin."

I nodded again as Thomas set the throttle and hit the ignitor switch. The engine fired up and the blades jumped to life, swatting the air above me. They admitted a chattering hum, thanks to the Loach's flexible four-blade configuration.

I buckled my four-point harness, patted my helmet, and gave Thomas a thumbs-up.

He let out a war whoop as the Loach tipped forward and lifted into the air. Puffs of dry ground powdered up under the force of the down wash as pebbles and sticks skittered across the dirt and smacked the metal drums that banked the helicopter revetment.

"This is the only way to fly," Thomas shouted into his boom mic, grinning from ear to ear.

I smiled and nodded. *Personally, I'll take a little more distance between me and the bad guys. And some fixed wings would be kinda nice too.*

Although I had willingly agreed to participate in this mission, I didn't intend to leave everything to chance. Nestled between my feet on the floor was a bag of hand grenades. Beside me—tucked into a convenient metal holder—was an M-16. Additionally, the pistol in my pocket was flanked by extra rounds, and I'd filled every available spot in my flight suit with bottled water.

The prospect of ending up alone in the jungle was bad enough. I tried not to ponder what the North Vietnamese would think if they yanked me out of the Loach and demanded Army intelligence.

I wondered whether they would even believe that I was an Air Force guy out for a joy ride in an Army chopper. Let's face it, who in their right mind finishes his own grueling mission and says to himself, "Hey! I didn't get killed today, maybe I'll hitch a ride with someone who flies even lower and slower than I do." Who? Well, me, of course—which pretty much negated the question of a "right mind." I may not have been smart, but I was rarely bored. I finally decided that the North Vietnamese would probably kill me no matter what. They weren't real fond of FACs for a variety of reasons. In fact, there was a persistent rumor that FACs had a bounty on their heads. A FAC masquerading as an Army guy would just be too confusing to bother with.

Nice policy, Scoop. Always embark on new adventures by visualizing the worst-case scenario. That way, if you come back alive and reasonably intact, the whole thing can be called a success.

The chopper climbed up over the shantytown of Camp Eagle and lurched toward the jungle beyond.

"So, are we on our own?" I asked, trying to subdue creeping apprehension. I was pretty sure a pink team needed more than one chopper. But so far, we were it.

"Nah. We're doing 'heavy pink' today," said Thomas. "That's one Loach and two Cobras. They're coming up from Phu Bai."

Thomas switched to the UHF frequency and radioed the rest of our team.

"Renegade One Two and Renegade Three Six, this is Comanche Two Nine. You guys in the air yet?"

I settled back in my seat and looked around the aircraft. I'd been in Loaches before and even handled the controls once or twice. I decided I probably ought to reacquaint myself with how they operated. If Thomas somehow became incapacitated, I'd need to figure out the lay of the land pretty quick.

Chances are you couldn't land this thing in a million years, Scoop. But, hey, just get it to the ground and jump. Beats the heck out of riding it into a fiery explosion. And if it falls on you, well, at least you gave it the old college try.

"So, explain this thing to me," I said as Thomas pulled a lever with his left hand and urged the Loach forward by pushing on the stick in his right.

"It's a piece of cake, really. It's a turbine engine; once you get it up to full throttle, the governor takes over and keeps the engine and rotor in the green. The throttle's over here on the collective. Works just like a motorcycle throttle."

Great. Good news for someone whose only encounter with a motorcycle involved "borrowing" his brother Steve's and wrecking it—sailing over the handlebars and onto the asphalt some twenty feet away.

"The stick works pretty much like the stick in an airplane—turns you left or right, points you up or down," Thomas continued, ignoring the fact that I had fixated on the motorcycle throttle concept. "The torque pedals on the floor control the tail rotor. You could pretty much get rid of the right pedal. 'Bout the only time I need it is when I fire the minigun. The rest of the time I'm riding the left pedal to counteract the high torque."

He paused for a moment. "When you're hovering above the trees, make sure you keep your nose into the wind, for two reasons. First, there's lower torque on the engine, and second, for smellin' Charlie up ahead."

His enthusiasm was admirable, if a little disconcerting.

A faint noise to the south caught my attention over the chattering Loach blades. I leaned out the door as our Cobra escorts buzzed into view. They took up their positions—one trailing us about 300 feet above, the other about 1,000 feet above him. Thomas hailed them on the UHF frequency and began briefing them on the mission. We were headed about five nautical miles east of the A Shau Valley in search of reported activity along a new trail that Charlie was blazing through the jungle. The A Shau was my terrain and I was comfortable with it, but I had a sudden fierce desire for the familiar trappings of my trusty Oscar Duck.

So there you go, Scoop. It's the old story of why fish and birds don't mate: Neither one can live in the other's world.

As Thomas wrapped up his briefing, I watched the Cobras tracking us overhead.

"Man, those are pretty nimble gunships, but they move like Studebakers compared to this little sports car," I said, laughing. With its size, speed, and maneuverability, the Loach did have a certain casual sportiness about it.

As we moved closer to the jungle that crept up the side of the A Shau, the little bird skimmed lower and lower over the treetops. I leaned out the door again and scanned the ground as best I could.

"This triple canopy jungle sucks," I shouted. "Charlie could be hunkered down under a bush or branch and be almost completely hidden."

Thomas grinned and raised his eyebrows.

"That's where you and I are different. This bird has a few tricks your O-2 doesn't have. Hold on."

"Hey, Renegade, hold fast. We're gonna check things out down under," Thomas radioed to the Cobra.

Down under? We're flying to Australia? Kay, I'll trade Viet Cong and swamp rot for sheep and Aborigines any day of the week.

Although I figured that Australia was a long shot, I wasn't sure I wanted to know what "down under" really meant. In one fluid motion, the helicopter made a diving turn that brought us almost to ground level facing a dense cluster of jungle vegetation with a tiny opening. Very tiny.

The chopper hovered just above the elephant grass for a few minutes as Thomas eyed the vegetation and knitted his brows in thought.

"Whaddya think, door number one or door number two?" He pointed to the tiny clearing and, about fifty yards away, an even tinier one.

Door number nothing. Tell Monty Hall I'll take the box on the floor. Or, better yet, give me the lovely Carol Merrill as a parting gift and send me home.

I cringed inside and motioned to the lesser of the two evils.

"Can you really fly through that?" I asked with all the bravado I could muster, which wasn't much.

"Do it all the time. How else are we gonna find Charlie in his element?"

You're assuming, of course, that I have any interest in finding him.

The helicopter sped forward. My gut tensed as we entered the clearing about ten feet off the ground. The trees crowded around us. Foliage and branches whipped through the whirling blades and fell to the ground.

"Shit." Thomas gently nudged the chopper toward the center of the narrow trail. "My crew chief hates it when I come back with green on the blades, doncha, James?"

The door gunner casually extended a middle finger in Thomas's direction. It was an interesting Army policy that tapped crew chiefs for double duty as gunners. The practice rightly assumed that the guy overseeing maintenance would be extra thorough if he depended on that same ship to bring him home safe and sound.

As the jungle closed in, we found ourselves wrapped in darkness and unbearable humidity. The air weighed heavy with the pungent smell of fungus, moist dirt, and rotting vegetation.

"Keep a lookout for footprints, ammo boxes, or movement back in the trees," Thomas yelled as his hands and feet worked in tandem to guide the chopper down the narrow trail.

Somewhere above us, the "high birds" hovered and waited. I squinted and tried to see through the vegetation, which blocked out the blue sky and sunlight. It was a lost cause.

"Can they see us from up there?" I shouted to Thomas.

"Nah. But it's okay. We have a radio."

A radio? So if we smack into a tree and hit the dirt, we can do . . . what? Call the Cobras and say, "We're down here. We'll give you another call just before Charlie drags our sorry asses to Hanoi?" Yeah, that'll work.

I looked at Thomas, who was perspiring as he skillfully jockeyed the tiny aircraft around the undergrowth. Behind him James crouched in silence, absently tracing the rivets on the M-60 with his thumb. We were all intent on scanning the jungle for signs that Charlie was in residence. The precision of the Loach amazed me. It could stop on a dime, pivot, and dance about like a hummingbird. I had to admit that

Thomas was masterful in handling the machine. He made it look easy, although I got a certain queasy feeling every time I glanced at the right seat and realized that he looked all of twelve and, in fact, wasn't that far removed from such a tender age.

"Anything?" he asked without taking his eyes off the landscape beyond the chopper bubble.

I shook my head vigorously and said a silent thank-you that our recon mission was proving to be uneventful, unless you count the sheer terror of flitting wildly through a rain forest at ground level.

We flew on in silence as I craned my neck and scanned the shadowy landscape around me.

"Aw, dammit." Thomas reined the little bird to a hover and glanced around, shaking his head.

What? VC? NVA regulars? Tigers? A herd of angry baboons? What?

I followed Thomas's gaze, seeing nothing but trees and heavy air that shimmered with heat and moisture.

"We've gone as far as we can go here. The trail pretty much ends. I guess Charlie screwed us this time."

"So, what do we do now?" I tried to sound casual, but our options seemed limited.

Thomas shrugged and adjusted his grip on the cyclic stick.

"We'll back it out. I need you to stick your head out and help guide me. Watch the tail rotor and the main blades. The last thing I want to do is slap this son of a bitch into one of those bamboo trees, or whatever the hell they are. James, you know the drill: Watch the rotor, and keep half an eye peeled for Charlie."

Suddenly, the forest seemed to close in even more. I hadn't been thrilled with the concept of zipping in here facing forward. The idea of trying to back our way out was unthinkable, except that we had no other choice.

I leaned out the door as far as I could and shook the river of sweat off my face.

"You've got about six feet of clearance on this side," I said.

"Clearance from the main blades?"

"Yep."

"Okay. I'm a little skinny on this side. I'm gonna scoot your way just a bit. Give me a yell if I get too close."

Too close? Six feet was too close, and now we were going to press the envelope further?

My heart pounded in a way that it rarely did on one of my missions. I had a definite comfort level in my O-2. I knew what to do, and I was confident of my ability to follow through. Here I was just a passenger, completely out of my element. I knew that Thomas was more than competent as a Loach driver, but now I was asking myself whether he had gotten in over his head. Was he trying to show off for me? Did he underestimate the density of the jungle and overestimate his aircraft's capabilities?

I pondered these questions as I hung out the door and shouted directions. We'd long since given up looking for signs of the enemy. In fact, it occurred to me that the entire North Vietnamese Army could probably sneak through the trees and yank us down by the skids and we wouldn't know what was happening until it was too late.

"Watch it!" I shouted. "You've got trees behind you. You need to make a turn to the . . . uh . . . right. Yeah, turn your tail right." I felt far more flustered than any great warrior should admit to.

The whole process of backing up in the air was foreign to me. I didn't realize how foreign until just this moment.

Thomas and James, on the other hand, seemed focused but reasonably at ease with the situation. Maybe they really did do this all the time.

The radio crackled and our Cobra escort checked in.

"Comanche Two Nine, this is Renegade One Two. Are you guys okay down there? You've been gone a while. What's up?"

"We're fine. Just hit a dead end. I'm backing out, and with any luck we'll be visible again in about two minutes," Thomas responded, poking his head out of the cockpit and moving it back and forth and up and down like a dog on a joy ride. "Hold tight, Renegade. We didn't see diddly shit down here, but I think our Air Force pal had fun."

I couldn't decide whether the jaunt through the undergrowth had been custom-made to unnerve the fixed-wing guy or was a typical pink team mission. Didn't care. Just wanted to see the sky again.

We broke out of the woods ass end first. Then Thomas spun the helicopter around and gained altitude.

He seemed genuinely disappointed that our trip "down under" had been fruitless. I still wondered whether he was playing to his audience. What I was certain of was that this was my last pink team mission. I'd done my bit for interservice harmony. The Army could keep its hunter/killer teams. I'd do my own hunting and killing but from a slightly higher vantage point.

Back at the hooch, Bob Gilday chided me for safeguarding my bod in such a cavalier manner.

"Those guys are nuts, Jackson. You probably came closer to getting killed today than any time so far. If you've really got a death wish, there are cleaner ways to get it done."

I grinned. "Yeah. I could volunteer to go to Southeast Asia."

I figured it was a matter of perspective. The fighter jocks thought FACs were crazy and dangerously exposed; the FACs thought the chopper drivers were crazy and dangerously exposed. But none of us would have traded places with the guys on the ground for any amount of money.

I reminded Bob that I had passed up an opportunity to participate in a Navy exchange program that would have placed me on an aircraft carrier in the backseat of an F-4. If helicopters pressed my comfort zone to its limit, the idea of flying onto or off a carrier dramatically exceeded it. Although I might razz my Navy cohorts mercilessly about joining an inferior branch of the armed services, I would never minimize the difficulty of landing an airplane on a bouncing Band-Aid in the middle of the ocean chop.

"So, ya see? I don't exactly have a death wish, more like a serious-wound wish."

But Gilday was probably right. I had taken an unnecessary risk. Then again, every day here was a risk. It wasn't as though I ever really felt safe. In fact, constantly feeling unsafe provided an odd sense of detachment.

By and large I didn't waste a lot of energy overthinking my situation. I believed, both then and now, that a little bit of analysis goes a long way. If guys went crazy in the face of combat, it was probably from thinking too hard about what was happening to them or, worse yet, what might happen.

Me? I was content to whistle in the graveyard and hope for the best. Like everyone else in Southeast Asia, my life hung in the balance about 90 percent of the time. I knew if I let myself dwell on that unfortunate truth, I'd twist my psyche into a knot that would leave me useless to everyone.

If the specter of combat sometimes threatened to overtake my resolve, that's when being a pilot provided a strange kind of refuge from reality. Of course, pilots got killed, shot, or banged up on a regular basis, but an eighth inch of plexiglass and a cushion of air offered just enough separation from some of the harshest realities of war.

Face it, Scoop, you've got it better than the ground pounders by anyone's definition. You never really get a close-up view of what's happening down there. No blood spurting, no body parts flying, no turning to talk to your buddy and discovering that his face has been blown off. It all looks different from here. Not better necessarily, just different.

It was never a matter of making a conscious effort to separate myself from the starkness of the jungle warfare below me; it just happened. In the thick of an air strike, I was 100 percent engaged, nerves taut, adrenaline pumping. I made the decisions, sweated the results, cleaned up the mess, then left it all behind me and flew on to the next thing. As events unfolded, they were frantic and immediate and real. But, suddenly, it was over and it wasn't real anymore, at least not the kind of real that gets under your skin and lies there twitching.

Plexiglass and distance protected me, gave me the sense that I was in the action but not completely part of it. However, there were the occasional defining moments when distance fell away and reality stared me straight in eyes. I was never quite prepared for it but always oddly intrigued when it happened.

Two days after my harrowing flight with the pink team, I had the opportunity to view my chopper pals from yet another perspective, one that reminded me that I didn't always have as much detachment from the world around me as I might have liked.

The cool of the morning had burned off more quickly than usual. By noon the sun was blazing and the air shimmered with moist tropical heat. I casually mopped up my third air strike of the day, eyeing the dropping fuel gauge that urged me homeward. My replacement on station, Clyde—Bilk 13—would be airborne shortly.

"Banshee Three Two, Bilk One Two. Here's the BDA on your mission: three dead, two automatic rifles, two secondaries. Six minutes time on target, 100 percent of ordnance on target, 100 percent of target covered, no duds."

I flicked out my tongue and caught a trickle of sweat as it rolled down my cheek. Not exactly the refreshment I needed at the moment. An orange soda and a box of crackers took on the aura of a gourmet meal, and a couple of hours of shuteye also tickled my fancy.

Okay, Charlie. It wasn't exactly a red-letter day for the good guys, but you're down a few men and machine guns now, so I guess I did my job.

I rolled the sky pig into a steep bank and gave the ragged land below a final scan before pointing my nose eastward. Then my radio crackled to life.

"Bilk One Two, we have a pink team Loach down. Need you to head over there and help with the SAR."

Bilk Control provided coordinates that placed the downed chopper roughly five klicks west of Firebase Bastogne.

Great. Right there between Camp Eagle and the A Shau—a really crappy place to drop your bird, guys. I could imagine them squatting nervously on Charlie's welcome mat like a couple of terrified Fuller Brush salesmen. *Hold tight, fellas. If you made it through the crash, we're sure as heck not gonna let Charlie get his hands on you.*

My stomach tightened as my mind wound back into high gear. *Crap.* Events were not unfolding according to plan. I was about to launch my fourth air strike of the day, approaching minimum fuel in my aircraft, not to mention the fuel that had leaked from my psyche. Rusty orange and shuteye would have to wait.

"Roger, Bilk Control. I'm on my way."

It wasn't tough to find the spot. Unfortunately, if *I* could make a beeline to the downed Loach, so could Charlie. Two Cobra gunships hovered over the site, providing cover and suppression fire while additional Cobras and Hueys converged on the area, rallying to the defense of their downed comrades. When an American pilot hit the dirt, the war ground to a stop. Any priorities that had existed in the moments preceding impact were frantically reshuffled as we each focused our rescue efforts with an urgency we hoped would be repeated should Charlie ever succeed in knocking *us* out of the sky.

Bilk Control radioed the Cobra call signs and radio frequencies, and provided a situational update. This wasn't my search and rescue (SAR), and I knew better than to take the lead. The Army would be all over this one. My job was to put in air strikes that would distract or dissuade Charlie from trying to reach the stranded chopper pilots.

"Raptor Zero Six, this is Bilk One Two approaching from the south at four thousand feet."

"Roger, Bilk. Archer One Nine is down from ground fire and has been on the ground about ten minutes. The pilot and gunner are within twenty-five yards of the Loach. They're alive, but hurt. A slick's on the way, but so's Charlie. We're looking at heavy ground fire west of the crash site. Looks like around twenty-five NVA, maybe more. Probably more. If you can put an air strike to the north and west, that'll take some of the heat off."

I immediately recognized the radio voice as that of my partner in crime on the infamous deer strike. I was sure he recognized me as well, but in the midst of a SAR there was no time for our typical casual banter; we were all business with one shared objective: getting our guys out alive.

"Roger, Raptor. I've got two fully loaded F-4s and a couple A-4s on the way. Is the enemy far enough away that I can put in a 500-pound bomb?"

"Affirmative, Bilk. Bombs away."

"Do me a favor, Raptor. You got a pretty good idea where Charlie's at?"

"Roger, Bilk. He's not being shy."

"How about you go ahead and mark the target, so I'll know exactly where to put my smoke when the fighters get here."

"Roger. Hold on."

The Cobra shot off a high-explosive rocket, which arced into the jungle about 300 meters from the downed Loach. I took a mental photograph of the rocket's impact point, then turned my attention to the approaching fighters. Meanwhile, the gunships worked over the area near the rocket hit.

"Thanks, Raptor. That's exactly what I needed. I'll check in with my fighters and come back up on this frequency prior to putting in the F-4s."

I watched as more Hueys and Cobras converged on the scene and set up orbits above the crash site. There was no stealth to a SAR. It was a free-for-all airborne traffic jam that made precision an absolute must.

Let's see, whaddya got out there, Jackson? Four fighters inbound. Three . . . no four Cobras, three Hueys, one . . . two Loaches. Okay, guys, let's all pay attention and try to keep from plowing into one another.

All four radios were screaming at me, a situation made more unnerving by the fact that I recognized many of the voices. These weren't a bunch of anonymous ARVN soldiers or even some nameless, faceless Americans. These were my guys, my pals from the 101st, and I was none too pleased at the prospect of losing them to a swarm of VC.

I flashed back to Sunday's harrowing ride with the pink team. Who's down there on the ground? I wondered. Is it Thomas and James? Chances are, whoever it was, I knew them. I looked down at the crumpled Loach, swallowing hard as I realized that the crash site was no more than a mile from Sunday's pink team outing.

Two days, Scoop—forty-eight hours. Charlie was MIA two days ago and today he's knocking people out of the sky. A chill shot up my spine. I shook it off and radioed my Cobra contact.

"Raptor Zero Six, the fighters are five minutes out. I'm going to bring them in from the north to the south. I need your guys to stay clear off to the east. I'll start with 500-pound bombs, napalm, and guns. That oughta push Charlie back far enough for the slick to set down and pull the Loach guys out."

"Roger, Bilk. I'll keep my guys out of the line of fire. Be advised you're taking some ground fire from the southwest. I think my rocket pushed 'em back to the south a bit."

"Heck, if they weren't shooting at me, I'd think they didn't love me anymore."

"Roger that!" the Cobra pilot said with a chuckle.

I jerked the yoke and twisted my O-2 back toward the east. *Just keep firing, Charlie. Let's me know right where to stick my smoke.*

In short order my F-4s checked in, and we began the awkward dance of trying to blow up the bad guys without taking out a chopper or two, or the FAC.

Six passes later, Charlie was beginning to question the wisdom of pursuing his Loach quarry any further.

"Bilk One Two, the slick is headed down to the crash site. So far it looks clear."

The gunships moved in to cover the downed Loach as the Huey made its way toward the ground. My attention was focused on enemy movement, which had diminished dramatically, and on my Navy A-4s, which had just checked in, but I was relieved when my radios erupted into a series of cheers and whistles.

"The slick is up! We got 'em!" someone shouted.

"Hey, Bilk, we got our guys and we're heading back," my Cobra buddy radioed. "Nice work. We appreciate your help."

"No problem. Hope everybody's okay." I was genuinely pleased that everyone was safely out, but the thought was overcome by events as I shifted into cleanup mode. The A-4s showed up in time to take out the stragglers who hadn't been killed or dispersed by the first set of fighters. Having completed four passes with the Navy jets, I tacked on one final assignment.

"Osprey Two Eight, we're going to take out the Loach so Charlie doesn't have any toys to play with."

I pulled the O-2 around and fired a Willie Pete about twenty-five feet from the little bird's tail rotor. I had deliberately walked the A-4s toward the crash site anyway, hoping to catch any die-hard NVA intent on ransacking the chopper for radios or weapons. I watched the lead fighter swing around and head in on the desired course.

"Lead's in. Tallyho on the FAC."

"Osprey Two Eight, you're cleared hot. Hit my smoke."

The bomb dropped straight and true, but I decided to bring in the second A-4 for a parting shot. Afterward I surveyed the charred landscape with satisfaction. Billows of thick black smoke plumed up from the Loach. Its shell was no longer visible as the flames around it devoured the remaining fuel, cooked the weapons on board, and fed off the towering sprigs of elephant grass.

There ya go, Charlie. If you can find anything salvageable in that mess, take it with my blessing.

For the first time since the beginning of the air strike, I nervously eyed my fuel gauge, which had dipped way below my comfort zone.

Okay, guys. This BDA is gonna set some speed records.

"Osprey Two Eight, your BDA is as follows: ten minutes on target, 100 percent of ordnance on target, no duds, and one United States Army helicopter completely destroyed. Not exactly a claim to fame, but necessary. And if I don't get my tail back to Phu Bai in the next ten minutes, you'll be doing a SAR for me."

"Roger, Bilk. One SAR a day is one too many."

I turned my nose east, as I had done an hour ago when I thought I was calling it a day. This time there was no choice.

I gained altitude and trimmed the airplane for cruising speed. I could feel my brain ease into that comfortable transition from rapid-fire synapses to autopilot. My respiration steadied, and I became suddenly aware that my flight suit was drenched in sweat. As the runway at Phu Bai filled my windscreen, my stomach muscles unclenched and I began plotting my next few hours.

Okay, Scoop. You're done for the day. Since you're already in Phu Bai, you might as well head over to the hospital and say hi to Lynn Damron before he DEROSes. Then it's back to Eagle for that long-awaited rusty orange and a few hours of R&R.

The morning's air strikes were receding into the darkest corner of my mind, where even I hesitated to go. In typical fashion I had already moved past the events of the last couple of hours and was thinking ahead. All in all, it was a pretty good place to be.

The hospital at Phu Bai bore no resemblance to even the most primitive stateside facility. It was a typical in-country structure, pieced together with plywood and metal and featuring two long rows of cots that hugged either wall. The aisle down the middle was packed with loitering visitors or medical staff; it was tough to tell the difference, because everyone was swathed in olive drab. There were no crisp white smocks or gleaming stethoscopes in Phu Bai. Back in the States, Americans were flocking to a new movie called *M•A•S•H*, which featured combat medical facilities only slightly more primitive.

I casually whistled to myself as I headed toward the hospital. It would be good to see Lynn one more time before he went home. I wondered how distracted I would be by the scar on his face. A hundred and forty stitches sounded pretty substantial, and I hoped that I could look him in the eyes without showing my discomfort.

Truth is, for a mighty warrior, you're really not especially at ease with the sight of blood. And sick people make you, well, sick. Guess it's a good thing you're a combat pilot and not a doctor.

I was chuckling as I pushed through the hospital door and into the narrow, crowded wardroom. The door latched behind me, and I was suddenly aware of a strange sensation, a feeling I couldn't quite identify. It was as though every nerve ending in my body had suddenly and inexplicably switched on. My senses were briefly overwhelmed as I tried to understand what I was feeling and why. I looked around the room and noticed an unusual amount of activity. People were moving quickly. Doctors, nurses, orderlies—I couldn't tell who was who, but I gradually became aware of familiar faces at the far end of the room, a cluster of men in Army flight suits pressed close to the back wall, speaking in hushed tones and glancing awkwardly at the medical staff rushing past them. A side door opened and a gurney was hauled past me and down the long aisle toward the anxious group of soldiers. The young man on the gurney also looked vaguely familiar, although I couldn't be certain because half his face was hidden beneath a heavy gauze bandage. His pants had been ripped up to the thigh, and another bandage was wrapped around his knee. Although secured with a leather belt, it sagged to one side under the weight of the blood that saturated the bandage and dripped onto the gray-green gurney cloth. I drew a sharp breath as I realized I had stumbled into the arrival of the Loach crew I had just helped rescue.

I was perversely fascinated by the activity around me, and mildly troubled by the thoughts that bounced through my mind.

So this is all real. It's really happening. People on the ground are getting hurt; people are dying.

I rarely if ever came face-to-face with the aftermath of my missions. At most, I would get a hasty radio "thank-you" from ground troops or from the fighter jocks above me. If I never actually saw or touched the action below, then I could almost believe that it didn't really happen. Perhaps because I was a pilot or maybe because I'd honed an ability to think past the moment, I had been reasonably successful in shutting out or disengaging from much of what went on around me. I understood the realities of combat but stubbornly refused to dwell on them.

Of course they're pretty hard to ignore when they're being wheeled past you on a gurney. Geeze. Admit it, Jackson, on some level you really don't want to know what's going on down here on the ground. You're still hanging on to that altar boy belief that the world is an orderly place. If you can keep your emotions in check, if you can distance yourself from some of the harsher truths, then maybe you can get out of this place with a few of your illusions intact. Maybe.

My uneasy reverie was broken by a shout from halfway down the row of cots. "Hey, Jackson, did you come to visit me or are you just sightseeing?" Lynn Damron was grinning and waving.

I shook off my discomfort and greeted my pal. The moment was gone and I was back into autopilot, and glad of it. But I knew that later, as my eyes closed for that long-awaited afternoon nap, I would revisit this place and these thoughts, and realize that my precious eighth inch of plexiglass couldn't completely shield me. And maybe that wasn't always such a bad thing.

Somehow transportation, except for the O-2 kind, usually managed to get me in trouble. There wasn't a whole lot of entertainment at Camp Eagle, so activities such as my pink team excursion always seemed like good ideas at the time. So did the occasional jeep ride. I enjoyed having the run of the camp and occasionally venturing out to visit more exotic locales. In fact, I made a couple of interesting but seriously unauthorized visits inside the walled fortress of Hue City. I wasn't supposed to be there, and probably could have gotten myself killed without a lot of effort. But it was good to engage in mundane activities such as driving and sightseeing, even with an AR-15 by my side.

When it came to transportation, we Air Force guys had it knocked. If we had access to a jeep, we could drive it whenever we wanted. The Army, on the other hand, required that officers have an enlisted driver.

Of course, just because we had a jeep handy didn't mean we were necessarily authorized to use it. We were reminded of this as our ALO, Maj. Dale Ullrich, prepared for another one-week TDY assignment.

"I'm not asking you guys, I'm *telling* you to leave my jeep right where it is. There are two other jeeps you can use. Just leave mine alone. I mean it. If you want to continue to have transportation privileges, I strongly suggest that you keep your mitts off while I'm gone."

We all nodded soberly and agreed that we would not mess with Major Ullrich's jeep—until he was safely beyond the confines of Camp Eagle. After that, it was "take a number and enjoy your ride." And enjoy we did, right up until two days before the major's anticipated return. Bob came into the hooch one afternoon looking unusually despondent.

"I think there might be something wrong with Major Ullrich's jeep," he muttered as he flopped onto the sofa and swatted a mosquito off his neck.

I looked up from my solitaire game and glanced at Clyde, who grimaced and shook his head.

"What makes you think there's something wrong with it?" I asked, hoping for news of a small tick or burble that could be easily ignored.

"It won't run," Bob said glumly.

Well, yeah, that's always a good sign that it might be broken.

We all trooped out to investigate, and each in turn said our own private last rites over the lifeless pile of metal and bolts. Several of our more mechanically minded radio operator associates performed a postmortem and declared that the jeep's U-joint had been broken

Discussion turned toward how best to hide our transgression.

"We could just leave it here and pretend we never used it," I suggested.

Pappy, the senior radio operator, tapped on the odometer and raised an eyebrow. "That'll work fine if you know how to roll this thing back. Otherwise he's gonna know someone's been driving it."

None of us would lie about the incident if asked a direct question. We just wanted to avoid volunteering any more than necessary.

After an uninspired round of brainstorming, we had to face the inevitable: We would have to steal a jeep from the Army, sand off the Army numbers, and stencil on the Air Force ID that currently resided on Ullrich's dead vehicle.

"How the hell do we get the new numbers painted on?" Bob asked.

"Well, heck, we've got plenty of paint," I volunteered. "It's out back with the acoustical tiles. But I'm not sure where we get a stencil, especially one with the same numbers as Dale's jeep."

Pappy dismissed the question with a wave of his hand. "We can cut out our own stencil. That's not a big deal. We just need to get hold of a jeep without anyone figuring out what we're doing."

So that was it. We agreed to keep our eyes open and take advantage of the first unattended jeep that one of us stumbled across. It didn't take long, especially when we enlisted the assistance of two of Gilday's Army buddies who were looking for a little fun and excitement. Less than twelve hours later we had reconvened at the hooch and were sizing up our new set of wheels.

Someone pointed out that the pilfered jeep wasn't identical to Major Ullrich's. Different seats. Slightly different shade of olive drab. But, hey, it was a jeep, and it ran. First things first.

"Can we steal some seats?" I asked uncertainly.

Rather than expanding our list of larcenous activities, we decided that we could probably remove the existing seats and replace them with the seats from Ullrich's jeep.

The first order of business, however, was to make sure we could successfully sand and re-stencil the identifying numerals. We each took a turn at gingerly removing the paint that established our guilt.

"Well, what the shit?" Bob was the first one to notice. The rest of us crowded around and watched as he blew the paint flecks off the hood and wiped his sleeve across the work area. "I'll be damned, take a look at that." He stepped back and we all gazed in shock and disbelief at a new set of numbers peeking through the sanded surface.

'Hey! Those are Marine Corps numbers," one of the radio operators said, puzzled. "How do you like that?"

"The nerve of those Army guys!" I said. "Where do they get off stealing a jarhead jeep?" Everyone turned and stared at me, so I shrugged and shut up.

"So, what do we do now?" Bob asked.

No one could answer that question, but somehow the additional layer of numbers took the wind out of our sails. We wondered aloud whether we would find even more numbers under the Marine digits. With the additional challenge of having to remove and replace new seats, we finally decided that we were singularly unprepared for a career in grand theft auto. It was more trouble than it was worth. Sheepishly we returned the jeep to its original resting place and prepared for a good soul-cleansing session with Major Ullrich.

The years have erased all memory of any dramatic retribution for the great jeep escapade. I recall that Major Ullrich was unhappy, but not completely surprised, because we had been "borrowing" his jeep for months. We did eventually repair it, possibly by "salvaging" parts from other jeeps and certainly with the mechanical assistance of our crew chiefs at Phu Bai.

As the weeks rolled on, we completed our hooch repairs and forgot about typhoons and U-joints as life around Camp Eagle resumed its normal—if you could call it that—pace. Aside from the specter of death or capture, our biggest headache came from the United States Postal Service.

Mail delivery was a persistent and far-reaching problem in Southeast Asia. For many of us, it was a more disturbing private hell than any of our encounters with the enemy. At least in combat we had the illusion of some small sense of control over our physical well-being. But when it came to communication with our families, nothing seemed adequate.

In early November I discovered that Karen and my parents had gone almost two weeks with no mail from me, despite the fact that I had been writing almost every day. Karen had even attempted to track me down via the highly undependable MARS network. This Rube Goldberg system, staffed entirely by volunteers, patched phone calls to and from our loved ones through a series of links that included actual phone lines, ham radio operators, and, probably, little kids with tin cans and string. It was far from ideal, but for better or worse, mostly worse, it was all we had.

Karen's efforts to find me were unsuccessful, but when I got a letter trying to confirm my whereabouts and physical status, I attempted to calm everyone's nerves with my own MARS call. Also unsuccessful. Seems as though bad weather, sunspots, and planetary misalignment constantly plagued the MARS efforts.

The mail delivery situation was so bad that *Stars & Stripes* ran news articles chronicling all the complaints at Camp Eagle. The problem was that our mail was considered free and was mass-transported to major postal centers in San Francisco or Portland, Oregon. Apparently the free status meant that we got what we paid for.

For those of us in-country, the mail delivery situation was painful and frustrating. For those who waited at home with absolutely no control and no knowledge of situations and circumstances, it was excruciating.

Some guys found themselves on the ragged edge of divorce court, thanks to the comedy of errors that resulted from delayed and out-of-sequence mail delivery. When no word from home was forthcoming, it was easy to feel alone and abandoned. For some guys the only way to tackle that emotion was to sit down and dash off a nasty-gram to hearth and home. Some of them emphasized the nasty part.

"So, what the hell's going on back home?" one of my pals wrote his wife. "I'm getting shot at every day, standing a very real chance of coming home in a body bag, and you can't find the frigging time to write me a 'hi honey, go to hell' letter? If I'm that much trouble now, maybe you need to decide whether you even give a damn if I come home."

Back in the States, his young wife had been dutifully sending letters every day and agonizing about his whereabouts and condition.

Two days after posting his letter, a whole flood of out-of-sequence mail arrived on this guy's doorstep. Man, did he feel like a jackass. However, by this time his sweet, patient wife had more terse words to describe him. While he was frantically drafting a "fall on my sword and beg forgiveness letter," she was squeezing the last drop of vitriol from her pen and sealing the envelope with arsenic.

The two letters crossed en route, whereupon she was overcome with guilt at having jumped to conclusions about his missive, and he, well, he got mad all over again after receiving her letter. So the circle of angst grew wider and more pervasive.

There was never any real solution for it; e-mail came years too late. Those of us in-country had to take it on faith that our loved ones were writing us and hoping for our safe return. Those back in the States often had to grit their teeth and hope for the best, even when the worst seemed to be splashed across their TV screens on a nightly basis.

Sometimes the stress of not knowing what was going on was made even worse by America's volatile and peculiar political climate. Years after my tour in Vietnam, I was almost moved to tears by my sister's recollection of a confrontation that was typical of the antiwar movement's blind assertion that the real enemy was the American military.

OTHER VOICES: Debbie Jackson Becher

I was in my early teens when Mike was in Vietnam. And, like most girls that age, I was shy and awkward, hardly someone who hungered for confrontation. The stress on our family of having a loved one in combat was constant, but there were times when it was almost unbearable, like when the mail wasn't getting through and we had no way of knowing where and how Mike was.

One of my teachers during this period was a young man who was very much a flower child; he embraced all the tenets of the liberal, anti-war movement and he made it a point to share his "enlightened" beliefs with as many impressionable young people as he could. Even then, I remember thinking that he was taking way too many liberties with his position of authority. Of course I didn't say anything. At least not until the day he announced in class that all the American soldiers fighting in Vietnam were "baby killers."

The words hit me like a rock and I was furious and hurt and terrified. But I stood up in class—shaking like a leaf, as much from anger as from fear—and said with as much authority as my 13 years could muster, "My big brother happens to be fighting over there right now. We haven't heard from him in almost two weeks and we don't know whether he's dead or alive, but what we do know is that he is not over there to kill babies. He's over there to save them. And I'll thank you to keep your opinions to yourself."

Feeling nauseous and awkward, I scooped up my books and left the room, hurrying to the girls' restroom, where I collapsed and cried my eyes out. After the initial adrenaline rush wore off, I began to worry about being suspended or, worse yet, expelled for my outburst. Interestingly, however, nothing was ever said about the incident, and the teacher in question never made a statement like that in class again.

The sad truth was that while we were fighting the North Vietnamese, our families were sometimes fighting their friends and neighbors, desperately trying to counter the popular belief that the military somehow made the war happen and, worse, that we were enjoying it.

Enjoy it we didn't, though we made every effort to entertain ourselves and pass the time as quickly and efficiently as possible. Sometimes the entertainment came from within our ranks. An entire volume of Camp Eagle lore grew out of the exploits of one of the young helicopter pilots, a personable fellow we dubbed Short George. He wasn't short and he wasn't named George, but with the surname of Tallmitch, it was an inevitable nickname; at least we thought so.

Barely nineteen and just this side of peach fuzz, Short George was one of those aviation battalion guys who was certain he would live forever. He tested that theory daily. If there was an unsavory mission or a hot location, Short George wanted in on the action. The problem was that George's miscalculations were nearly equal to his enthusiasm. It was said that he had actually managed to shoot himself down four times, either by misplacing hand grenades or accidentally shooting off necessary parts of his helicopter. The brass reportedly planned to court-martial him if he racked up a fifth loss, but they would blunt the impact somewhat by also declaring him an "Ace."

Short George had managed to get away with the first four losses because of the nature of the Army structure. Unlike the Air Force, where we had maintenance officers who were typically ground pounders, the Army's aviation battalion was made up of helicopter pilots, so Short George might have doubled as maintenance officer in addition to flying a chopper. As a result, the chopper drivers were in a much better position to cover their own asses, and did so to the extent that it was possible.

I never knew for certain whether the whole Short George scenario was true, but he did manage to make it to the end of his tour without destroying a fifth chopper. The Army no doubt breathed a collective sigh of relief when George's eager but accident-prone feet were firmly back on American soil.

There were other less credible but equally entertaining tales of combat weirdness, including the story of Robin Hood, an early FAC who was either highly dramatic or certifiably insane (it helped if you were both). Robin Hood, so the story went, took to dressing all in green, including a green-feathered cap, and carrying a bow and arrow on his daily missions. I never understood whether he used the bow as a prop or an actual weapon. I tried to imagine him radioing to the fighters, "Okay, guys, hit my arrow," and was forced to assume that he probably used it to take random potshots at the enemy, although drawing back a bowstring in the cramped cockpit of an O-2 would require a certain skill at contortionism, not to mention a fairly potent death wish. At best, it was unorthodox, but probably about as effective as firing an AR-15 in such close quarters. I came to that realization after nearly being blinded by spent shell casings when I fired from my foul weather window at enemy troops below. Eventually I managed to secure a couple of grenade launchers, which proved to be much safer and more effective.

Theoretically we weren't supposed to be shooting at anyone, except with the Willie-Pete rockets, but we took whatever opportunity we could get. I discovered that I could point the grenade launcher—which functioned like a large shotgun—out the window much more effectively than I could the AR-15, which offered far less control and didn't allow me to position myself behind it in order to fire accurately. I'd heard stories about guys actually shooting themselves down by accidentally firing through the strut, which housed the fuel lines and control cables.

Then there were the peanut butter bombs, ingenious little devices that enhanced the efficiency of hand grenades lobbed from the cockpit. Grenades offered a desirable level of explosive power, but timing was an issue. Unless you were very close to the ground—too close—you could count on witnessing a midair explosion that damaged little more than treetops and passing bugs.

An innovative pilot had come up with the idea of dropping the grenade into a peanut butter jar. You could pull the pin and toss the jar out the window, and the grenade spoon would stay snug until the glass shattered on impact.

I cringed at a story about one of my fellow FACs who didn't fare so well with his customized bombs. Supposedly at the beginning of a mission he carefully set the peanut butter bomb on the floor of his O-2, well within arm's reach. But during a typical round of jinking and clear air turbulence, the jar tipped over and rolled to the back of the plane. When the hapless FAC crawled back to retrieve it, he threw the plane's center of gravity out of kilter. The plane began seesawing back and forth, creating some tense moments as he gingerly fought to keep from blowing himself out of the sky. Eventually the rolling jar came to rest near his foot, and he was able to grab it and chuck it neatly out the window. He promptly did likewise with the entire box of additional peanut butter bombs that he'd stashed in front of the right seat.

I never got confirmation on the identity of the unfortunate peanut butter bomber, but it sounded like a plausible scenario. I had briefly tried the PB bomb approach, but I never got used to the idea of potentially exploding jars of hand grenades rattling around my airplane, not to mention that it was just plain difficult to use them effectively. It is tough enough to hit a street sign with a banana while driving a car about forty-five miles an hour (I've tried it), but it's darned near impossible to accurately toss a hand grenade out an airplane window from 1,500 feet.

I adopted the grenade launcher as my weapon of choice. It wasn't as though we could use our smoke rockets as weapons, although every so often it worked out that way.

During one air strike setup, I happened to notice a brazen little guy blasting away at me from beneath a tree. I eyeballed his position and rolled in, intending to mark the tree and have the fighters blast the whole area.

I guess my eager opponent figured there was no way I was going to hit him—that certainly wasn't my main objective—so he failed to duck and cover. It was the last thing he ever failed to do. It was one of those blind luck things. Yeah, I was aiming in his direction—probably even aiming at him—but the gun sights were imprecise and the chance of hitting a five-foot person with a Willie Pete was slim to none. But darned if I didn't take him out completely. I turned and looked back at the smoke, noting that it was an unusual color: bright pink at the center and lighter as it billowed upward. As I rolled back around and eyed the fighters, I glanced at the ground and noted two unattached legs lying where my dedicated shooter had been standing.

I can't say it bothered me particularly. He was hell-bent on killing me; I just beat him at his own game. Maybe his buddies in the nearby woods would think twice about firing at forward air controllers in the future. I hoped it served as positive PR for those of us flying low and slow; let these guys know we can play rough too.

I'd probably managed to kill someone with a rocket before: a Willie Pete has about a ten-foot kill radius from the white phosphorus. But I had never hit anybody dead-on that I knew of. It was an interesting exercise, and the pink smoke was pretty in a macabre kind of way.

There were other less gruesome diversions and forms of entertainment. The Air Force, being well-intentioned but periodically misguided, would send us stuff for which we frequently had no earthly need. They gave us a television, but there were no stations to pick up. They gave us paint and acoustical tile, for which we had no use other than to trade to the Army for Lurps, and I was the only one who liked them. They did send us a water heater, which we appreciated, and paperback books—boxes full of them. My attention span never lent itself to wading through book after book, but Vietnam was a different kind of environment. There wasn't much else to do. Maybe because I was so adrenalized and intense during the day, it was easy to relax and lose myself in a book come nightfall. So that's what I did, to the tune of two or three books a week. It wasn't lightweight stuff either; it was Updike and Chekhov and Stone—outside the realm of my limited experiences. Above all else, it was a temporary escape from the "surreality" that surrounded me.

As Clyde Elmgren's days dwindled, we began to speculate about his replacement. We were a cohesive group, and nobody wanted to see a hot dog or a slacker show up and muddy the waters. We were relieved when the Air Force handed us Ed O'Connor, yet another first lieutenant. Ed was tall and lanky, with an easy smile and a distinctively Jacksonian sense of humor. I liked him right away, and the continuity of our little group was thus preserved.

OTHER VOICES: Ed O'Connor

Mike and I hit it off immediately. He was friendly, quick-witted, and extremely competent as a FAC. He was also willing to take pity on the FNG and share some of his expertise with me. This worked better with some topics than others. One of our requirements was to maintain a certain level of night FAC competency. Although it was true that "Charlie owned the night," this didn't stop us from at least trying to put a crimp in his style or, at a minimum, provide a little harassment. None of us really enjoyed the night sorties, but we resolved to make the best of it. Since Mike already had some night missions under his belt, it fell to him to show me the ropes.

Normally a FAC mission was a one-pilot operation, but the cover of darkness required two of us. One pilot flew while the other opened the co-pilot window and scanned the ground through an Army M-16 starlight night-viewing scope. The scope magnified available light (moon or star) and (theoretically at least) made it possible to see objects on the ground. There were FACs in SEA who did this kind of flying for a living; they, apparently, became quite skilled at it. We were not among them!

The starlight scope was not designed for use from a moving platform at 3,500 feet. Fortunately for Charlie, those of us who typically flew day missions were pretty useless at night. For us, the starlight scope was like searching the ground in a green haze through a straw.

We experimented with parachute flares to provide additional light, but this proved to be overkill and the starlight scope remained useless. Fed up with the futility of our impossible mission, Mike came up with what seemed like a brilliant idea for passing the time. Why not drop a parachute flare and try to hit it with the rockets we carried on the O-2?

Sounded good to me, so we spent the rest of the night dropping flares and shooting our Willy Petes at them for no particularly good reason, save frustration and boredom. It was really something to watch our rockets streak across the night sky like roman candles, although I don't recall that either of us ever came close to hitting one of the airborne flares.

Given the nature of the technology available at the time, and our seriously limited exposure to it, there was no way we would ever become proficient night FACs. It was just one of those things you jotted down in your memory bank as "this is crazy and I hope I never have to do it for real!"

Time passed. Slowly.

Every night before checking my bedroom for ants, roaches, snakes, and rats, I'd mark another day off the calendar. In the beginning it was almost painful. By November, the marked and unmarked days were starting to even out, and I began to believe that maybe I'd actually see Tipp City again.

Of course I took nothing for granted. There was still plenty of "living through" to be done. Every mission carried its own set of risks; every successful return to Phu Bai was its own reward. Most missions brought the typical set of hazards and tense moments. I learned to take them in stride, at least to the degree that anyone can adapt to being shot at and missed (which, of course, beats the heck out of the alternative). Occasionally, however, the weather would conspire to present its own unique set of challenges.

Cruising atop an undercast, I would wait for the clouds to either clear or stack themselves into something threatening that would send me scurrying for shelter. I could handle the clearing, which allowed me to call in air strikes, or the threatening, which gave me an excuse to head home. But I wasn't especially pleased with the uneasy boredom of poking around the sky waiting for Mother Nature to decide on her course of action. One particular day I putted along warily, splitting my attention between the fluffy gray cloud cover and a recent copy of *Stars & Stripes* newspaper. Every time I finished reading four pages of the military tabloid, I'd yank out that section and toss it through the window. Then I'd chase the floating newsprint across the sky, trying to chew it up in my propeller. As entertainment, it ranked up there with my moonlit efforts to target parachute flares with a Willie Pete, although this was marginally more successful.

Easy does it, Jackson. Thar she blows. That's it: execute a smooth 180, lose about fifty feet, watch it, watch it. Yow! Perfect shot! You are the master!

I grinned as bits of newspaper shot out from the prop and drifted lazily into the clouds below.

There y'are, Charlie. If you've got enough time and tape, you can piece it all together and find out what the capitalist running dogs are up to.

I rolled back and forth, glancing at my fuel gauge, then back toward the ragged mountains that flanked the A Shau Valley. I was none too pleased with the churning dull gray sky that filled my windscreen. Mother Nature had made her choice. She'd apparently decided that if Charlie wasn't going to give me a run for my money today, she'd fill the void. With a growing sense of urgency, I pointed my nose back toward the coast, shoved the throttles up, and started the climb that would take me over the mountains and "home" to Hue Phu Bai.

The roiling bundle of clouds had begun to spill over the peaks and into the valley. I'd lost all visual reference to the mountaintops, but I knew that some of them shot up past 3,000 feet. My O-2 collided with the creeping cloud bank, and I was alone in the darkness. Rain pelted me from all sides at once, and I fought back a strange claustrophobic feeling mingled with the unsettling knowledge that somewhere in those big, puffy clouds were several big, not-so-puffy mountains.

Well, this stinks. But I guess it could be worse. At least no one can find me to shoot at me. The thought had barely left my head when I was suddenly aware that my flight suit was wet. *What the heck? I'm scared, but I'm not that scared.*

As I ran my hand under my rear end and thigh, I noticed that the edge of the seat was also soaked. Then my eyes caught the glitter of water droplets trickling in beside and above me. Whatever positive qualities this particular O-2 may have had, being watertight was not among them. Tiny streams dribbled across the dash and sprinkled down from the observation window above me. I flicked off the water as best I could and flew deeper into the weather, wondering whether I could outfly it or maybe just climb above it. Nah, I'd been watching these clouds build; they topped out at 30,000 to 35,000 feet. There was no way my O-2 was climbing out of anything except, I hoped, mountain peak range.

It occurred to me, as I watched the rain pound its way into the cockpit from every possible seam and opening, that water and electrical devices have a natural antipathy toward each other. In a battle of wills, water usually wins. Of course even before the full impact of that thought took hold, the cockpit suddenly went dark. The lights, the gauges, everything just died.

I exhaled sharply, a noise that hovered somewhere between a chuckle and a sob.

Easy does it, Jackson. Keep your head and your wits, and assess the situation. What do we have? We have no instruments, no light, no visibility, and no idea where the hell we are, and I'm soaking wet and low on fuel.

I reset the master switch and the circuit breakers and tapped on the instruments in an effort to prompt some magical fix, which I knew wouldn't happen. My mind began to race, though not out of panic. I had the uncanny ability to sort through options and outcomes in the time it took most people to say "oh shit." I was keenly aware that my options were limited and my outcomes were not at all assured.

I couldn't go backward, because the weather had closed in on the valley as I was flying out. My landing fields were limited by my dwindling fuel supply and the inconveniences of being in a war zone. I decided that my best option was to head through the storm and out over the ocean.

I began picking my way through the clouds and—I hoped—over the mountains that flanked the A Shau Valley. My mind raced through a variety of scenarios and came to rest on the one where my plane smashed into a mountain peak and no trace of me or the O-2 was ever found. Somehow that was less palatable than being shot down in combat. If I just disappeared off the Earth, no one would ever know for certain what happened. My family would remain in limbo forever. The very thought made me queasy.

Don't do this, Scoop. You're taking a bad situation and making it worse. Just get this sucker across the mountains and over the water and you'll be home free. Concentrate, stupid. And stop thinking so much!

After what seemed like hours, the clouds in front of me began to dissolve and separate, and I could make out a thin strip of water on the horizon. The South China Sea had never looked better. Just the sight of it told me that I had managed to evade the mountains. I lost altitude and headed toward the water. From there I turned south and followed the coast toward Hue Phu Bai. My heart pounded and my knuckles grew whiter as I nudged the O-2 toward home, descending steadily to stay below the clouds. When Phu Bai finally appeared in my windscreen, I was cruising at only 200 feet above the ground. I let loose the breath I'd been holding for forty minutes and turned the soggy O-2 westward, hoping that Mother Nature and I would never again confront each other in this manner—or that, at a minimum, I could come up with some way to insulate the sky pig against future downpours of this magnitude.

OTHER VOICES: Ed O'Connor

Weather played a defining role in much of what happened in Southeast Asia. I arrived at Camp Eagle during monsoon season and quickly learned that Mother Nature could be a more potent foe than Charlie.

Sometimes, however, her tantrums provided an ironclad excuse for delaying combat activities in favor of some much-needed R&R.

Evenings in Southeast Asia were typically long and boring, with little to do but talk of home, family, and future aspirations. Recreation came from a small Army O-Club, to which we had gained a standing invitation from our Loach buddies. Mike was a skilled foosball player; I was distinctly mediocre. But we both enjoyed few things more than an energetic evening of "challenge foosball" between Army and Air Force.

During our spirited tournaments we were ever mindful that someone from our small detachment would have to alert the chopper schedulers as to our transportation needs the following morning. Whoever had early take-off would need to hop a Loach to Phu Bai since the roads would not yet have been swept for mines. Takeoff, of course, was predicated on favorable weather, so we often found ourselves playing amateur weatherman late in the evening as we tried to predict the conditions at dawn.

I recall Mike and me standing outside the O-Club in the dark mist of the monsoon season discussing whether we should go ahead and cancel the morning Loach. This decision directly affected whether we— and the Loach pilots—could continue to play foosball and enjoy the spirit of the evening, or return to our hooches for a brief bit of shuteye.

I remember thinking, here we are, two lieutenants using our casual observations from the door of the O-Club to determine whether our part of the war will go off as scheduled tomorrow. The irony was that this weighty decision was often heavily influenced by whether we were winning at foosball.

By mid-November my flight time was piling up so fast that I found myself pulling duty officer in the TOC to let the other guys play catch-up. The buildup of flight time was mostly a fluke. Storms would roll in with the midday heat, and because I typically flew morning missions, I'd often head out just ahead of the weather. By the time my mission was over, it would be too crummy to send out anyone else.

The Air Force wanted to keep everything balanced, so the ALO sent me to cool my heels in the TOC while everyone else caught up.

As duty officer, it was my job to keep track of the other FACs who were up and about. I'd stay close with frequent radio checks to confirm their location and position. That way, if someone disappeared, we'd have a vague notion of where to start our search-and-rescue efforts. The FACs, in turn, would call in their targets, and I'd request air strikes for them from further up the chain of command. It was something different from—and a darned site safer than—my standard airborne missions. But all things being equal, I was happier in the air. It fed my need for challenge and excitement and it gave me a certain sense of order and control, not to mention it being a lot less boring than sitting in an underground control center for hours. I'd been sent to Vietnam to fly missions in an O-2. When I wasn't doing that, I wasn't fully engaged, I wasn't wholly serving my purpose. It was that simple.

CHAPTER THIRTEEN

HEAVEN AND HELL

THE PROMISE of Christmas leave in Oahu with Karen was keeping me sane and motivated, but such things never come with guarantees. I figured at best I had a 50-50 shot at actually making it to Hawaii. Our newly acquired air liaison officer had the option of scuttling everyone's plans if the spirit moved him. As unpredictable as an ALO could be, Charlie was an even bigger question mark. We knew things were heating up, but we still weren't sure why. If Charlie staged a big offensive, all bets—and travel plans—were off. So I nervously counted the weeks, the days, and, finally, the hours until I could actually revel in the real world once again.

Not that Hawaii was much like the real world. It was a whole lot better, in fact, especially for a guy who had been living like a pig for six months.

After a pit stop to visit O'Neill at Tan Son Nhut, I flew out of Saigon on December 20, 1971, with a quick layover in Hong Kong, then back in the air again that same day.

By morning I was watching the sun rise behind Diamond Head. Oahu was a paradise made all the more alluring by my months of deprivation. I'd lived without water, without civilian clothing, without female companionship, without anything but subsistence food, not to mention the absence of comfort, peace of mind, or anything that smacked of luxury.

The past six months had left me with a definite sense of my own mortality. I had already made up my mind that this trip would not be filtered through any austerity plan. I still had six months left on my tour; and who knew whether I'd make it home in one piece. This was one time that little Mikey Jackson was gonna live like there was no tomorrow, especially because I had no idea whether there would be. Karen and I spent money like bandits, we ate like royalty, and we virtually lived on the beach. I didn't worry about saving for a rainy day; I paid attention to the sand and the sun and the surf, and I reveled in the moment.

But despite my commitment to unabashed hedonism, the war still managed to intrude like clockwork. I spent every spare moment riveted to the evening news, watching for familiar places and names. It felt peculiar to leave it all behind physically yet be unable to fully detach mentally. I was awkwardly poised with one foot in heaven and the other in hell.

I always knew what day it was and how many days of comfort and freedom remained before I got tossed back into the blender. I reveled in the moment, but I could never completely forget that the moment was fleeting and made all the more precious by my knowledge of what lay just beyond.

So it was a taste of the good life with a persistent black cloud hanging just overhead. I had looked forward to this trip for months and, suddenly, here it was. But the shadow of what lay ahead never quite left my side.

OTHER VOICES: Karen Jackson

Somehow Mike managed to time his two-week leave with my Christmas break from teaching. We converged from opposite sides of the Earth on Honolulu, Hawaii. We crammed all the memorable times we could fit into those two weeks. We walked and relaxed on the beach, strolled around the International Marketplace, partied at a luau, visited Pearl Harbor, watched fireworks from our hotel balcony on New Year's Eve, and toured the pineapple fields and coastline in a red MGB.

Although we never voiced our fears, we both never forgot the possibility that these could be our last days together. We wanted to make sure there were no regrets.

On January 3, in the dawning hours of 1972, I kissed Karen good-bye and left for an overnight stay in downtown Hong Kong.

My first clue that maybe I wasn't holed up in the high rent district was when I noted that the guys who greeted me out front weren't bell-hops or doormen; they were security guards with shotguns. It was a bit surreal, especially having come from the warmth and hospitality of sunny Hawaii. I retreated to my room and stretched out on the bed for a few minutes before heading down to the restaurant to get a bite to eat.

It felt strange to be by myself after two weeks of female compan-ionship. I tried not to wallow in the emptiness, but it was tough to find any argument in favor of optimism. I was alone. I didn't even speak the language, and I was twenty-four hours away from combat.

Yippee.

With the possible exception of Christmas at OTS, I wasn't sure I'd ever felt as lonely or as uncertain of where my life was headed.

On January 4 I rolled into Saigon, where I immediately ran into one of my chopper buddies from Eagle.

"Hey, Jackson! You just getting back from leave? Oh, man, you were lucky. You missed the worst part! There's not much left. As a mat-ter of fact, we spent yesterday burning ponchos and supplies, anything we couldn't take with us. I guess your hooch mates packed up your stuff, huh?"

I stared at him as though he was speaking Swahili. Nothing he said had any context. It just plain made no sense. After a minute he stopped talking and cocked his head like the Jack Russell peering into the Victorola.

"You have no idea what the hell I'm talking about, do you?"

I shook my head mutely and awaited an explanation.

"Camp Eagle. It's gone! Well, actually, it's still there I guess, but we're gone. The 1st Brigade of the 101st stood down, and the FACs moved to Phu Bai. Nothing's left at Eagle now but dirt and dust and sappers—pretty much everything that was there before." He laughed at his own joke and chatted happily as I raced ahead of the conversation, wondering what had happened to all my stuff and whether I'd get last choice on accommodations at Phu Bai. I suddenly had a vision of Camp Eagle as a ghost town, except that all my worldly possessions were being pilfered by a bunch of tiny Vietnamese people in black pajamas.

Welcome back, Scoop. Here's your reward for having so much fun in Hawaii.

Later that day I headed for Da Nang, where Bob Gilday shuttled me back to Phu Bai in his O-2. He reassured me that they had packed up my belongings and lovingly trucked them to our new home.

"Man, Jackson, I'm disappointed in you. Do you really think we would have allowed the enemy to overrun the place and get their hands on your stash of canned crackers? What kind of pals do you think we are?" He grinned at me, his teeth barely peeking out from under his bushy black mustache that would have made Groucho Marx sigh with envy. "Seriously, man, Ed and I were very careful. All your stuff is perfectly safe."

The three FACs at Eagle suddenly mushroomed to nine, pooled from the 1st, 2nd, and 3rd Brigades of the 101st Airborne Division. Now that we were working with the 2nd Brigade, the first digit of our call signs changed from one to two. With Bilk 21, 22, and 23 already in use, I became Bilk 24, whatever a "Bilk" was.

Our new ALO, Maj. Art Evans, was a sharp-witted, tough little bantam rooster of a man. I liked him immediately. In fact, I liked all the FACs, many of whom I had already met at OTS, in survival school at Fairchild, or at Clark Air Base. But the sudden convergence of so many FACs posed a few logistical problems, especially when we were confronted with our Phu Bai accommodations.

The new place was a disaster area. Apparently the previous occupants had bailed out in a hurry, leaving battered furniture, ratty clothing, and garbage. It was one thing to be forced to live like a pig; it was something else entirely to become one. I had the distinct impression that the previous tenants had succumbed to the barnyard mentality in a big way.

This new building may have been marginally sturdier than our Camp Eagle digs. Although it offered the same plywood walls, sandbags, and corrugated steel reinforcements, it seemed slightly more stable, at least on the outside. Inside it offered no individual privacy, just a big common room where everyone lived and slept. None of us found that prospect appealing. We liked one another, but a certain amount of personal decompression time was essential to our sanity.

So after devoting several days to shoveling garbage and unpacking our own belongings, we began measuring, cutting, and constructing the plywood sectionals that would give us some meager sense of privacy.

Fortunately, Ed had an industrial arts background, which offset my carpentry ineptitude. Somehow we managed to cobble together an interior that was suitable enough for our purposes.

Once we had scraped the top layer of grime off the hooch, and I had determined that all or most of my belongings were accounted for, I turned my attention to my furry pal Jesse Hicks. Had he made it safely out of Eagle? Did someone find a nice home for him? Had he made the trek to Phu Bai?

Ed looked awkward and glanced at Bob uneasily. Bob's mustache twitched as he explained that one of the hooch maids from Eagle had reported Jesse's absence shortly before the stand-down.

"She admitted that one of the other hooch maids had . . . ah . . . had taken Jesse home for dinner."

I shook my head, and wondered aloud why they couldn't have fed him at the camp.

"Uh, Mike, they didn't take him home to *feed* him dinner. They took him home to *be* dinner. Jesse Hicks got eaten."

I just stared at my pals for a minute, my jaw dangling as I pondered the unpleasant reality that yet another of my furry friends had fallen victim to someone's appetite. Unlike the Mr. Whiskers debacle, nobody offered me a drumstick, but I was unnerved nonetheless. I couldn't fully understand a country that would turn man's best friend into a midnight snack. And Jesse Hicks couldn't have been much more than that; he was on the lesser side of slight, and as sweet a puppy as you'd find anywhere in the world. Now he was leftovers. Well, just one more reason to count the days till I could shake the dust of this place off my boots forever.

We had barely completed our hooch renovation project when rumors began circulating that we'd be standing down from Phu Bai. Although such rumors were a constant in Vietnam, these carried a greater sense of urgency than the previous speculation. It was partly because, having stood down once, it now seemed possible, and partly because we suddenly had the uncomfortable sense that Charlie was breathing down our necks.

The North Vietnamese seemed to be getting closer and more audacious. Bilk and Covey FACs who flew the northernmost AOs knew that something was going on. We were finding fresh highways that hadn't existed before, and things seemed to be picking up in pace. It was obvious that, as the Americans were moving out, the North Vietnamese and Viet Cong were pouring into the void and increasing their activity. This persistent feeling of approaching doom was augmented by a sudden spate of training sessions, where we were instructed on where to go and how to defend the air base in the event of an enemy overrun.

When they sat me down in front of a .50-caliber machine gun and said, "Here's how you load it" and "Here's how you fire it," I knew we were in trouble.

Uh, guys, I'm a pilot, and a skinny, uncoordinated one at that. I don't know how to go hand to hand with seasoned guerrillas. I know how to fly an airplane and pound the bad guys from the sky, but if Phu Bai is depending on me for its salvation, we'd better lay in a supply of black pajamas and conical hats.

Thankfully for me—and the entire American presence in Phu Bai—it never fell to Lieutenant Jackson to defend the base, mostly because we got out less than a month after I returned from Hawaii.

By mid-January we were packing up and preparing to leave for Da Nang. From my perspective, the move was a good thing. My typically optimistic demeanor had taken a beating during my transition back to in-country mode. The weeks that followed my Christmas leave were bleak and depressing. The six months remaining in my tour suddenly felt like an eternity. I had gotten a potent reminder of what life was like back in the world, and I found myself taking a couple of swift gut punches from the days that stretched out ahead of me.

In fact, it was much worse than my arrival. When I had headed off to Vietnam in June, everything was new and different; it had the quality of an unexplored wilderness, an adventure waiting to unfold. Also, I had been allowed to ease into the Vietnam experience, graduating from the Philippines to Cam Ranh Bay to Da Nang and finally to Camp Eagle. My descent into hell had been in degrees. This time they just opened the hole and threw me back in; it was a hard landing.

My mood was further tarnished by the knowledge that my post-Vietnam Air Force assignment would be handed down soon. What if I hated the assignment? You'd think that after I'd spent a year in combat, they'd say, "So tell us, Scoop, what is it you'd like to do now?" But I knew that the Air Force would send me wherever it damn well pleased. For the first time, I began to seriously consider other lines of work.

Just before our move to Da Nang, we got word that another typhoon evacuation drill was in the offing, and it was my turn to make the trip. Naturally, because there was no real typhoon on the way, we headed for Thailand. I flew over with our ALO, Art Evans, who was proving himself not only a skillful leader but a lot of fun as well.

Thailand was a seedy paradise that offered something for everyone, whether your proclivities ran toward animal, vegetable, or mineral. I opted for material pursuits, spending much of the trip acquiring jewelry, custom-made shoes, and three flawlessly tailored suits for the incredible price of $100.

The suits came courtesy of Rajah's Wolf Pack Tailors, a little hole-in-the-wall shop that catered to servicemen and was named for Ubon's legendary triple nickel 555th Fighter Group, which had gained a renewed luster of legend while under the leadership of the colorful and outspoken Col. Robin Olds.

Rajah himself was somewhat of a military groupie, and who could blame him? Even at his outrageously affordable prices, he probably made a mint off battle-weary Americans eager for a smart set of civvies that induced visions of life after war. Anxious to please his newest customers, Rajah made a point of wining and dining us, introducing my palate to an exotic array of Thai cuisine the likes of which I had never before sampled—and fervently hoped I never would again.

Art Evans and the rest of our group reveled in the many cultural wonders of Thailand, from Kobe steak to the "no-hands cafe"—"where the girls do everything for you," Art chortled. I contented myself with cheap suits and fashionable trinkets for the female Jacksons back home. But I remained both irritated and bemused by the irony of retreating to Thailand for a typhoon drill when, during the real thing, we had high-tailed it right into the eye of the storm. Where was the logic in that? *Give it up, Jackson. There is no Vietnamese word for logic.*

When we left Thailand a few days later, we were no better prepared for a typhoon, but we were at least rested and ready to shake the dust of Phu Bai off our boots and focus on our next step up the food chain, toward better living in Da Nang.

Da Nang proved to be a move in the right direction, both in geography and quality of life. Our new hooch was in the Covey FAC compound, though we retained our Bilk call signs. For the first time in Vietnam, I found myself living in something that loosely resembled comfort. We now had air conditioning, cement walls, hot and cold running water, flush toilets, and the luxury of being a little farther away from the enemy—sort of. Da Nang's nickname, Rocket City, reflected the unfortunate reality that we were a frequent target for nighttime aerial assaults. We could count on being rocketed at least once or twice a week—and a lot more than that after the Easter Offensive kicked off in April. It also sometimes depended on what aircraft were parked on base. We had a B-52 that had diverted to Da Nang for repairs after taking a hit. The presence of a BUFF (Big Ugly Fat F---er) created quite an uproar; we got rocketed every night, and one of the hooch maids was caught sneaking out with maps showing where the massive aircraft was located on the ramp.

Shortly after our arrival in Da Nang, I got word that my last FNG vestiges were being erased: I had been promoted to captain. In fact, seven of us in the Covey compound made the transition from young turk to old head in the same day, having all been members of the same OTS class three years before.

It felt good to graduate to captain's bars. The promotion carried a small pay raise; more important, it offered a new level of respect. When you're a lieutenant, everyone assumes that you have no idea what you're doing, because—well—you usually don't. The very presence of the title "lieutenant"—second or first is a minor distinction—conveys newness and, by association, incompetence.

Although making captain didn't endow me with a sudden wealth of wisdom, it did prompt strangers to credit me with a certain level of experience. Lieutenants are always newbies; you can be a captain forever. There are people who retire as captains.

Whether anyone else thought so or not, Captain Jackson was a slightly more confident and credible officer than Lieutenant Jackson had been. At the very least, becoming a captain granted me a little more breathing room in the eyes of those who measured competence by rank.

And you earned it honestly, Scoop. I recalled a buddy I had run into at the Da Nang BX back in January. We'd graduated OTS together and I knew we were due to be promoted at the same time, but there he was, sucking on a grape soda and wearing captain's bars.

"Hey, what's the deal?" I griped. "How'd you get promoted early?"

"Did it myself. I just woke up one day and decided I was sick of being a lieutenant, so I promoted myself 'below the zone,' " he said casually, using the phrase that indicated a promotion ahead of its time.

Back in the States he'd have never gotten away with it. But here in 'Nam no one paid much attention. He probably could have promoted himself to general and changed his name to Westmoreland as long as he showed up for his missions and didn't blow up any friendlies.

I don't know whether gaining my captain's bars actually enhanced my competence, but it was shortly thereafter that Art Evans pulled me aside to tell me I'd been tapped to oversee an experimental training program for Vietnamese forward air controllers.

"It's all part of Nixon's Vietnamization program," he explained. "The more responsibility the South Vietnamese can shoulder, the fewer of us need to be over here getting our asses shot at. You'll be putting together a test program that teaches VNAF [Vietnamese Air Force] FACs how to put in air strikes with American fighters. It's never been done before, so you're not gonna get much guidance. Just set it up the way you think works best."

Seeing my puzzled expression, Art shrugged and slapped my shoulder. "You'll do fine. And if you don't, probably no one'll notice."

I was never sure how my name came up to be the VNAF FAC trainer, although we'd had several group discussions about training programs when I mentioned having a teaching degree and being certified to teach driver's education.

I also had the advantage of an unusually high number of O-2 hours for a newly minted captain, thanks to the combination of my in-country experience and my stateside assignment at Shaw. So I suspect that someone just flipped a coin and decided that Jackson would be the new—hell, the only—Vietnamese FAC training officer.

Naturally the assignment was accompanied by a rumor that once we got these guys fully trained, we might stand down. It was a nice incentive at least.

OTHER VOICES: Colonel Arthur C. Evans, USAF (Ret.)

"The only way to get Jackson to behave is to throw him an impossible task." That was the gist of a conversation I had with my boss, Lt. Col. Abe Kardong. So, we gave him one: a peach of a deal.

Vietnamization was a concept that envisioned the slow, incremental withdrawal of U.S. forces as the Army and Air Force of the Republic of Viet Nam became able to take over their own defenses. The last thing the U.S. planned on withdrawing was USAF air power operating from Thailand and U.S. Navy carriers in the South China Sea. To properly employ these air resources, the VNAF needed FACs. General Nguyen Kao Ki and 7th AF approved a program whereby Vietnamese FACs would be trained to talk to, control, and employ American fighters. The

20th TASS (Kardong's baby) was tasked to set up the requisite training program—and our choice to lead it was Mike. Surely this mild-mannered, patient, nonaggressive, articulate, combat-experienced officer could write and design a training program, develop a syllabus, and train a cadre of really smooth Vietnamese FACs. Surely he could easily deal with a couple of minor problems: like, fer instance, the Vietnamese pilots could neither speak or understand English; like, fer instance, the entire training staff would be Mike; like, fer instance, he'd have to regularly brief the brass in Saigon; like, fer instance, he wouldn't be out in the AO nuking Charlie anymore—for starters. So, with tongue in cheek, I hauled Mike into the comfort of my elegant office and informed him that he had volunteered to head up the new Vietnam FAC Training Program. Kardong, Napoli, Ullrich, and myself suppressed our grins as Mike took the bait. Damned if he didn't pull it off—with class. Once Mike convinced his charges to quit trying to bail out on him (Yankee humor and all that), they developed a real camaraderie. I know Mike remembers them fondly.

Long after General Tarple and the Screaming Eagles had furled their flags and left I Corps—and General Lam and the 3rd ARVN had taken over—and with the NVA pouring across the DMZ on their special version of an Easter Egg Hunt, those FACs Mike trained were able to get the job done. I don't know if any of them survived the war, but I'll bet there are some American fighter pilots who recall delivering weapons on targets controlled by Mike's guys during the final, dark months of 1972.

The VNAF FAC training program had been handed to me on a silver platter, albeit a badly tarnished one. It was my baby to make or break, and I liked that. I relished the challenge of doing something that wasn't pure reaction and adrenaline. This demanded thought and analysis, and despite my abbreviated attention span, I thrived in situations that cultivated flexibility, creativity, and a dash of pure bullshit. This program would require heavy doses of all three. It was a clear case of "Here, Jackson, take this pile of sand and turn it into gold." I was just game and stubborn enough to give it a shot. If I screwed up, it would be my mistake and no one else's. I found that a lot more palatable than failing because some weenie somewhere down the line didn't follow through.

But I didn't intend to fail.

Now, however, I had to figure out not only what to teach them and how to structure the training, I had to overcome language and cultural barriers. After more than six months in-country, I couldn't remember ever having a conversation with a Vietnamese pilot. I knew nothing about their training process and even less about their social structure and customs.

I burned the midnight oil for a several days, drafting a syllabus and thinking through the teaching process. Despite having a teaching degree, I was not overly endowed with the skills that are the hallmark of good teachers, such as patience. But at least I would be dealing with pilots. There had to be universal character traits that all pilots share. No doubt at some point in history, some earnest Air Force psychologist determined that there exists a typical "pilot personality." I hoped this was true and that such a thing would help bridge the gap between countries and cultures, because I was not convinced that I was savvy enough to do it on my own.

My first four students were somewhat less than star pupils. Their English was even worse than I had feared. They understood little of what I said, and I understood even less of what they said. But I told myself that it was not a case of starting completely from scratch. These guys had been flying O-1s forever, and all their flight time was combat time—all of it. In fact, some of these pilots had been flying combat for five to six years. They obviously knew how to put in an air strike, because they'd been doing it for the VNAF. Now it was just a matter of clarifying terminology and procedures—phrases such as "cleared hot," "hit my smoke," and "do you have the FAC in sight?" My initial feeling was that it might take ten flights to get them proficient in the American approach. That's about how it ended up, but there were a few snags along the way.

I put together a good program, worked out a solid syllabus, and kept a notebook on techniques and tactics for improving the process. I factored in ground instruction time—including guidance on different types of American airplanes and assorted ordnance such as bombs, napalm, and guns. Fortunately, everyone pretty much left me alone. No one asked for progress reports. No one wanted to approve my methods. No one requested a detailed analysis of the program's success.

My biggest challenge was overcoming the language barrier. These guys were supposed to be proficient enough to take part in the program, but they weren't—not even close. They had gone to some kind of ten-day school on how to speak English. If the only thing they had been required to say or understand was "please" or "thank you" or "where's the bathroom," we'd have scored 100 percent right out of the box. Unfortunately, my instruction was a tad more complex and demanding than that. A lot more, actually.

They couldn't understand me and I couldn't understand them—on the ground, let alone garbled through a headset and the intensity of combat. These guys didn't stand a chance of guiding a group of American fighter pilots who were stoked on adrenaline, obscured from view, and talking a mile a minute. Plus, as a forward air controller on a real, live mission, you could be flying for maybe four to five hours and you might do nothing but run from one fire to another, or you might not put in a single air strike. It ran the gamut from sublime to ridiculous, and I was never sure which was which.

One major problem was that these guys had a threshold for excitement that was far higher than the situation warranted. In fact, they didn't just get bored; on slow days, they'd fall asleep in the airplane. I'd be in the left seat rambling on (I never stopped talking, even if things were quiet) about "this is how you would describe this terrain to one of our fighters" and "if you put in an air strike at these coordinates, you'd want to bring in the jets from the south so you don't overfly the friendlies," and I'd notice that my student was blissfully unconscious.

At first, I was puzzled by their tendency to nod off in mid-flight. The material probably wasn't the most exciting ever, but it was critical to their survival and to the survival of ARVN troops and American pilots. Then it occurred to me that my VNAF students had never known anything but combat flying. The long, sometimes tedious hours aloft didn't generate the level of intensity these guys were used to.

I resorted to feathering the front prop just to shock them back to reality. They were used to single-engine O-1s, and they'd forget that the O-2 was a push-me, pull-you. In one particular instance, I almost outsmarted myself.

I had noticed my pupil drowsing quietly as I explained the proper method of setting up fighters on the wheel. My standard operating procedure was to deliver a sharp punch to the arm, or to yank the guy's parachute harness as hard as I could. This time, however, I was too irritated. I suppressed a grin as I pulled the throttle governing the front engine, then feathered the front prop and hit the starter so the prop was sitting in a vertical—and very visible—position right in front of his face. Then I shook him violently and pointed to the static propeller.

"Nguyen! Nguyen!" I barked. "We've lost an engine! What do we do?"

Well, Nguyen couldn't care less what *I* did, but he knew exactly what *he* was going to do. With eyes the size of saucers, he clawed at the handle that jettisons the cabin door. Fortunately, his panic prevented him from cleanly completing the jettison procedure. So for a few moments at least, the door remained in place. Unfortunately, Nguyen had also yanked the D ring on his parachute, deploying it inside the cockpit. Thankfully the shroud lines didn't extend far enough to activate the emergency parachute beeper.

Okay, Scoop, let's rethink this whole "scare the crap out of Nguyen" ploy. It's not going quite the way I intended.

I dropped my voice to a more soothing tone and grabbed his left parachute harness strap with my right hand to keep him seated and inside the plane. "It's okay. I've got it back—we're fine; we've got two engines. Life is good. Just stay cool and don't do anything stupid." Well, maybe that ship had already sailed.

Nguyen's eyes darted back and forth nervously as he gaped at the now-spinning prop, the loosely tethered door, and the billows of parachute that spilled off the seat behind him. But at least he now seemed committed to staying put.

Just sit tight and let me try to nudge us in without losing the door. Easy. This is not the time for showmanship or steep turns. No G's. Treat her gently.

I tried to decide how I would explain a missing door, a deployed chute, and a terrified student. With any luck, I'd have to explain only the chute.

Nguyen seemed to be relaxing as he perched on the edge of his seat, courtesy of the chute deployment that had shoved him forward about three inches. I eased the O-2 into the traffic pattern and greased it onto the runway with a precision that surprised even me. It beat having to explain why my student had attempted to exit the aircraft in transit.

To my credit, Nguyen never fell asleep in the airplane again. And I returned to punching and shouting as a means of awakening my drowsy charges. The chute deployment episode was impossible to conceal, so we dragged the popped chute back to life support and simply explained that we had accidentally snagged the D ring while reaching for something in the cockpit. I also managed to convince the crew chief that my VNAF student had mistakenly yanked the jettison handle while reaching for another switch. I don't know what anyone said behind my back, but to my face they simply nodded and remained silent.

The training was going well—except for those periodic fits of sleeping, punctuated by stark terror—and we were all getting along famously. A few weeks into the program, my Vietnamese charges saw fit to honor me with a new title—*dinky dao di wee*. I even noted that it had made its way onto the door of my O-2, carefully painted in Vietnamese script just below my American name and rank. I was confident that my new moniker reflected their love and respect for the dashing and talented young Captain Jackson. Perhaps I was even a bit over-confident, assuming as I did that the term meant something akin to "warrior who is like a god" or "conquering hero of the air."

Occasionally I would notice a VNAF pilot chuckle and wave as he wandered past the revetment where my aircraft was kept. *Maybe reduced to nervous giggles by passing so close to the mighty warrior? Yeah. Uh-huh. That's a little tough to swallow, Scoop, even for you. Maybe you oughta ask for a translation, just to be sure.*

Next day, as my newest student pre-flighted the airplane, I pulled him up short and pointed him toward the words on the door. "There— under my name—what's that say?"

He eyed me tentatively and flashed a clumsy smile. "Ah, *dinky dao di wee*," he said quickly, stepping past me to continue his inspection.

I tugged on his sleeve and brought him back to the door. "Okay, Slick, I know what it says in Vietnamese, but what does that mean in American?"

My charge shifted his weight awkwardly and threw me a stupid grin. "Uh, *dinky dao di wee* mean . . . ah . . . the crazy captain." He scuffed the ground with his foot and pointed back to the airplane. "I finish now?"

"Yeah, go ahead."

The crazy captain? The crazy captain? Geeze, not even close to "the warrior who is like a god." Nope, not even a little.

I pondered my title for a minute. It didn't exactly reflect the level of respect and admiration I had anticipated. Of course I didn't really care if they revered me, as long as they learned something.

After all, Scoop, you've spent most of your life trying to catch people off guard, trying to keep them from figuring you out. Maybe being tagged "the crazy captain" is a tribute after all. Obviously these guys think you're out there on the edge somewhere. I grinned. *The edge. Yeah, I like it.*

Despite the occasional hiccups, the VNAF FAC training program evolved and improved. I was essentially making it up as I went along, but there were periodic flashes of brilliance. One aspect of the training gave my VNAF charges an opportunity to experience the energy and pace of an air strike without incurring the wrath of adrenalized fighter jocks. After securing permission from our operations officer, Lt. Col. Dave Napoli, I enlisted several FAC buddies to help develop an air strike simulation. Fellow Bilk FACs Bob Gilday, Jim Petek, Fred Barlow, John Downs, Jim Crookston, and Ed O'Connor alternated single ship and formation flights over to an island—we called it "the rock"—just off the coast of Da Nang, where they played fighter pilot so that my Vietnamese charges could gain insight into the American approach to air strikes. It was helpful, and it sure beat ticking off a bunch of fighter pilots who had ten minutes of fuel and a hot target below.

With the approach of the Vietnamese holiday Tet, my flying time seemed to increase exponentially. Since the Tet Offensive of 1968, there was always a certain level of apprehension that surrounded the holiday. The year 1972 was no different; we'd been noticing an increase in activity, and there was a natural tendency to brace for some kind of Tet-related action. As a result, I was spending about nine hours a day in the air, flying both combat and training sorties. Although I wasn't being shot at the entire time, there was more than enough intensity to leave me mentally and physically drained.

The flying and waiting grated on my nerves. The flying and fighting stoked me up like a coal furnace ready to blow. I'd head back to the base with every muscle fiber and every nerve ending standing at full alert. I didn't equate it with stress or fear or anxiety; it was just life in combat—a natural byproduct of people shooting at you on a daily, if not hourly, basis. If someone had inquired about my emotional state (and no one ever did), I'd have shrugged and said, "I'm dealing with it just fine. What's the problem? I go out and do my job; I come back and get ready to do it again. It's no big deal."

I would soon discover that I wasn't handling things quite as gracefully as I thought. For now, however, I toughed it out and tried to take it all in stride. But somewhere deep in my gut, tiny, gnashing teeth were starting to gnaw their way through.

As the northern AOs continued to heat up, Da Nang was suddenly overrun with journalists. They seemed to creep out of the woodwork, eager to get a story, jockeying for a chance to ride with us and gain some first-person perspective on the air war. I was happy to oblige. I couldn't figure out where they'd been the first seven months of my tour, but now they swarmed into town like locusts. Maybe it was because we had evolved into something more significant than lieutenants, or maybe it was just a geographical thing. Perhaps reporters, like REMFs (rear echelon mother-f—-ers), made a point of staying away from poor living conditions like those at Camp Eagle, Phu Bai, and the DMZ, as well as anything that might have demanded courage under fire. REMFs were middle- or upper-level weenies with an aversion to anything that smelled, sounded, or looked like combat. REMFs hid in the shadows and issued their unintelligible orders from fortresses of concrete and steel.

My journalist tagalong, however, was not a REMF or even some stateside weenie looking for an exposé on military incompetence. Rather he was a master sergeant in search of some insight into the challenges and demands placed on a typical guy in the trenches, even if the trenches happened to be cradled between cloud banks. Although MSgt. Dave McElroy Jr. found more romance in my work than I did, he wrote a balanced article that made its way into the *Tipp City Herald* on Flag Day 1972. He painted a fairly realistic picture of the long hours of boredom punctuated by the brief moments of panic and intensity. He even got the chance to witness a typical troops-in-contact situation. All in all, he got his money's worth, and he got to go home in one piece at the end of the day. I momentarily envied the idea of flying one mission and calling it a day.

It was interesting having people around who actually wanted to know what we were doing and why. At Camp Eagle and Phu Bai, no one came to see us, especially when they found out where we were. Da Nang was different. People would come to Da Nang; it felt more like a city and less like a target, during the day at least.

Two days before Tet, I attended a Tet party over in the VNAF compound. The invitation came to me courtesy of my VNAF FAC training program. Although I was honored to be invited, I did not approach the event with an excess of enthusiasm. Except for my Vietnamese trainees, I'd had next to no contact with the indigenous population. I'd crossed paths only with hooch maids and shit burners, so the potential for an in-depth discussion with either was severely curtailed by language and topic limitations.

My VNAF hosts encouraged me to bring a guest, no doubt expecting that I might be more comfortable if someone of my own language and culture was also in attendance. I asked Bob Gilday, who wasn't overly impressed.

"I dunno. It sounds like it'll be a pain. I don't know anyone, and I sure as hell don't speak the language. What am I going to do?"

"Well, I guess you could talk to me. That's kind of why I invited you." I shook my head and glared at my roommate. "It's not exactly my idea of a great time either, but they might be insulted if I don't go. And the last thing I need to do is tick off the South Vietnamese. I've got enough trouble with the northerners, ya know?"

Gilday snorted and tossed a pair of socks into his laundry bag. "Well, it's not like you're a minority; they aren't exactly fond of me either. Stop your bellyaching, I'll go." He shot me a smug smile and disappeared down the hall. *Wise guy.* But I was glad he was going.

At 7 P.M. we arrived at the VNAF dining hall on base, just down the road from Gunfighter Village, where the American F-4 pilots hung their hats. From the moment we entered the hall, it was obvious that we were the guests of honor. A Vietnamese colonel greeted me, shook my hand, and led me to the head table. Gilday managed a bemused grin as high-ranking VNAF officers welcomed us warmly and offered beaucoup thank-yous for our support and guidance.

Hail the conquering heroes. As dinner began, we were the subject of toasts and energetic speeches. I had rarely felt so welcome in my own military let alone someone else's. And I was more than a little startled when a VNAF general rose to his feet and solemnly addressed the crowd.

"Captain Jackson is putting in beaucoup time and effort to make VNAF FAC program finally success. He works much hours and shows patience and understanding. His work helps the war effort, help save many Vietnamese lives. We wish to show him gratitude with these two medals. Captain Jackson?" the general turned to me and motioned me to his side. I mechanically rose to my feet.

Geeze, guys, I'm just some goofy little brand-new captain. I'm not used to being feted and honored, by anyone. And this training program you're thanking me for hasn't even turned out its first graduate yet.

I was moved and grateful but also a tad intimidated by their obvious high expectations. I swallowed my misgivings and thanked my hosts warmly, feeling a genuine sense of pride and accomplishment as they pinned the Vietnamese Honor Medal and the Civic Action Medal on my flight suit. Years later I would realize that I should have also been handed accompanying documentation for the medals, but that's another story.

All in all, it was a thoroughly satisfying evening. We were wined, dined, and celebrated. Best of all, the meal consisted of what I hoped and assumed was simply beef and chicken—nothing exotic, just meat and vegetables, and beer. Even Bob had to admit that the whole affair had turned out to be a pretty decent way to pass the time. And it probably didn't hurt to have some friends in high places within the South Vietnamese military.

Tet itself was a day of monumental frustration. The North Vietnamese were very much aware that the United States had declared a twenty-four-hour cease-fire in honor of the holiday. Charlie responded in a manner appropriate to the stupidity of a cease-fire: He stuck his thumb to his nose, wiggled his fingers, and gave us a good old-fashioned Bronx cheer. And all we could do was watch and sweat.

Despite the cessation of hostilities, we were airborne by late afternoon, cruising our AOs and warily eyeing the terrain below. We couldn't put in air strikes, but we could let the bad guys know we were watching. It probably frustrated us more than it scared them, but we saw no value in letting them think we were lying down on the job.

The president and his weenies can take any action they want. You've still gotta deal with me, Charlie.

I cruised my O-2 up and down the Green Alpine Highway, marveling at the brazenness of the NVA and the Viet Cong. The road was relatively thick with men on bicycles and on foot. Everybody was hauling boxes and crates. It was a foregone conclusion that every single box carried a gun or a missile that would promptly be used against me or my buddies.

By 5:30 in the afternoon I was stacking up fighters overhead and itching for some action. Charlie knew what I was up to, but he also knew that my hands were tied until the cease-fire ended at 6 P.M. Charlie counted heavily on the American soldier's sense of duty and honor, not to mention a fear of being court-martialed. He knew that the odds weighed strongly against any American violating the cease-fire. And he had learned through keen observation that the American political system often unwittingly used that very commitment to duty and honor against its own troops. If it was good enough for American politicians, it was sure as hell good enough for Uncle Ho's minions.

I circled above the narrow dirt road, my muscles tensing as I fought the urge to lay a couple of smoke rockets into the snaking line of men and bicycles. I wondered where they all came from, whether they missed their homes and families as much as I missed mine. I felt sorry for them, and I hated them.

At least you're in your own stinking country, Charlie. You could theoretically turn and run home. Then again, I suppose I could turn around and fly home, assuming they'd let me refuel in Burma.

I glanced at my watch: 5:35 P.M. *Twenty-five minutes, Charlie, and then your ass is mine.* The thought had no sooner formed in my head than the line of men and supplies ground to a stop. At the southern tip of the longest column, the officer in charge gestured forcefully to the men around him, before pausing to take a long swig from his canteen. His subordinates glanced skyward occasionally as they steadied their crates and backpacks and began rolling their bicycles off the dirt path. At 5:40, the commander shielded his eyes and gazed deliberately at my O-2. I rolled the aircraft into a gentle right bank and stared back.

My binoculars offered a vague outline of his features. I could see his expression as he squinted against the sun. Maybe I imagined it, but I could almost sense something pass between us. Some strange kind of recognition or, dare I say it, grudging respect.

I was oddly reminded of the 1966 holiday ditty "Snoopy's Christmas," where Snoopy and the Red Baron cross paths behind enemy lines on Christmas Day. When the Red Baron finally gets his chance to shoot down his beagle nemesis, he defers and instead offers a gallant salute and a promise to fight again on a more secular day.

As I continued to circle and observe, the NVA commander looked at his watch and broke into a broad grin. Perhaps, like the Red Baron, he was about to offer me a show of respect from one warrior to another. He lifted his right arm skyward and extended his middle finger rigidly in my direction. *Yeah, well, it was kind of a salute, minus four fingers.* So much for a moment of mutual respect between worthy opponents.

Screw you, too, Charlie, and the bicycle you rode in on. Just stand there a couple more minutes and Snoopy's gonna blow your ass into little itty-bitty pieces.

The commander made another gesture, this time directed at the troops in front of him. In the blink of an eye, the remaining men and materials scattered and melted into the line of trees flanking the road-way, probably hightailing it into the network of tunnels that crisscrossed the nether regions of my AO.

5:45 P.M. The landscape beneath me was empty. *Shit.*

I sighed and continued my lazy circles until 6 P.M., when I could finally direct my fighters against the now-unseen and probably long-gone enemy. Just another day at the office.

Two days later I was in the 20th TASS compound when a famil-iar voice caught my ear. There stood Kraig Lofquist, my buddy from OTS and pilot training. He was a little leaner than in his post-football pilot-training days, but he was still Kraig, still had that roguish glint in his eyes that seemed to turn women to jelly.

He threw his arm over my shoulder and gave me a quick squeeze. "What the hell have you been up to, Jackson?"

I gave him the highlights of my in-country pedigree, and he explained that he was only a couple of days away from DEROSing. Kraig had been flying what we lovingly labeled "bullshit bombers," O-2Bs that had been outfitted as propaganda machines. But he had lucked out, get-ting into the propaganda game at a time when the powers that be were starting to say, "Hey, we don't think this is working."

Kraig's whole squadron had been deactivated and was heading home. But he was heading home to a Strategic Air Command (SAC) assignment, which was almost worse than remaining in combat. I swal-lowed hard as Kraig detailed his new assignment flying KC-135s. Kraig's fate didn't bode well for the rest of us, although my ace in the hole was that Tactical Air Command (TAC) officials at Shaw Air Force Base had promised to return me to TAC and put me in fighters if I volunteered for Vietnam. The Air Force wouldn't go back on its word to some poor guy playing dodge 'ems with SA-2s, would they? I didn't take the question any further. I wasn't sure I wanted to.

My visit with Kraig was followed almost immediately by a sur-prising announcement from Gilday. He stalked into the hooch one afternoon and tossed a sheet of paper across the table at me.

"New orders. They're moving me to NKP [Nakhon Phanom, Thailand] to some desk job. What the hell did I do to deserve that?" He flopped down on the edge of the sofa and fiddled with its frayed edges. "This really sucks. I know they're trying to clear us all out of here, but if they're not gonna send us home, they oughta leave us here and let us do what we were trained for. My mother didn't raise a frigging REMF!"

I was startled by the news of Bob's transfer. He was as good a pilot as we had, and I didn't see much logic in bouncing him to Thailand and into some pencil-pushing role. In addition to losing flight time, he'd be giving up combat pay and R&R eligibility. Then there was the deeper level, the responsibility we all felt to finish the job we'd been sent to do. None of us relished getting shot at, and no one liked to think about the possibility of being killed or permanently disabled, but we'd come here to fly and fight. If we weren't doing that, what good were we?

But the needs—or the whims—of the Air Force came first. A week later, Bob packed his bags and headed west to NKP, and I said good-bye to another chum.

In March I pulled duty officer for three days at Quang Tri. There was every reason in the world to hate the place. It was an ARVN base with few Americans, it hugged the DMZ, and its living conditions were comparable to or worse than those at Camp Eagle. But despite its obvious deficiencies, it offered a much-needed escape from the structure and bureaucracy of Da Nang.

I had spent the first half of my tour pretty much controlling my own destiny, first at Eagle, then, to a certain extent, at Phu Bai. But at Da Nang there were many more layers of command and control. At Eagle and Phu Bai, REMF-related decisions often confounded our efforts and prompted us to bitch loud and long, but the REMFs themselves never ventured out of their comfort zones and into our world of rats, roaches, and water by the thimble full.

Quang Tri, being similarly hellish in form and function, was virtually REMF-free. This gave it a certain odd appeal for those of us who didn't suffer fools gladly. There were days (most of them, in fact) when I much preferred going head-to-head with the enemy versus crossing swords with a rear-echelon dipshit. The enemy just wanted to kill me— *that* I could understand. But try as I might, I never managed to decipher or comprehend most of the politically motivated decrees that flowed from the very people who were supposed to be supporting my efforts.

I savored my visit to Quang Tri, even pausing to attend the grand opening of the facility's newest steam bath, better known as the "steam and cream." It was a chance to socialize and enjoy some good old American coffee and doughnuts. I was amused by the arrival of an Army chaplain, who earnestly blessed the new structure as mamasan and her girls loitered in the doorway awaiting their chance to provide comfort and distraction to lonely GIs. I cringed and made do with the doughnuts.

I was in my final day serving as duty officer, just completing a morning of radio time in the TOC and looking forward to sacking out for a while, when an Army private raced in and collared me.

"Captain Jackson, you've got to come with me. They're sending a plane from Da Nang. You're heading back there, where they want you to pick up your 1505s and fly to Saigon. Tomorrow morning you'll be briefing the brass—a bunch of colonels and some generals."

I stopped in my tracks and stared at the flushed private.

Briefing? Generals? Holy crap. I've been a captain for all of a month. What the heck do a bunch of generals want to hear from me?

Plenty, as it turned out. They were looking for a success story, a nugget of promise that could be gleaned from all the lumps of coal they swallowed daily. Somehow, somebody had decided that my VNAF training program had the potential to be just such a nugget. I was as pleased as I was terrified. Fortunately, there was little time to second-guess myself. A quick stop in Da Nang, where I grabbed my 1505 uniform and my syllabus, and it was into my O-2 and on to Saigon. I had to admit, it felt good to head *away* from the DMZ for a change.

Next morning found me patiently waiting to be ushered into one of the offices at Tan Son Nhut. I fiddled with my syllabus pages and reminded myself that colonels and generals put their pants on one leg at a time, just like me. *Yeah, maybe, but their pants are made of a much higher grade fabric than mine.*

Up to this point, my training program had been exclusive to I Corps. As I expounded on my techniques and challenges, the generals and colonels nodded, harrumphed, and, finally, declared that the program was solid enough to warrant participation by all four corps of South Vietnam. I was dumbfounded.

I returned to Da Nang feeling rather pleased with myself. It wasn't arrogance—I was too uncertain for that—but a pleasant sense of achievement, a feeling that I might possibly write a postscript to my year in-country that didn't include killing people and breaking things. Perhaps in some small way, I would contribute to a country's ability to maintain its own sovereignty instead of just killing the guys who were trying to take it away.

It was a nice thought anyway.

Newly energized, I threw myself into the training program. It was as rewarding as it was frustrating. As March drew to a close, I was beginning to really hit my stride. New students were being funneled to me from all four sectors of South Vietnam.

Look, ma, your kid is actually a leader of men! Okay, small foreign men who think I'm insane, but men nonetheless.

Then, almost as counterbalance to my growing sense of accomplishment and control, I was handed my postwar assignment orders. I'd nursed an uneasy feeling about my future assignment, but I tried to avoid agonizing over things that couldn't be managed or repaired. Still, it gnawed at me as I watched the guys ahead of me draw SAC assignments and head off to large, hulking bombers. Sending a fighter-trained pilot to SAC was like asking an Indy 500 driver to ferry semi trucks cross-country, then arguing to him that it's pretty much the same thing because both vehicles have tires and a steering wheel.

I soon learned that my next assignment would have me piloting B-52s. This was a worst-case scenario as far as I was concerned. I had no ax to grind with SAC pilots in general. I knew that bomber pilots were necessary and that some guys genuinely relished large crews, a big plane, and a heavy dose of weeklong alert tours, sitting in an underground bunker day after day waiting for the Cold War to erupt into a nuclear conflict. I simply wasn't one of them. I was especially indignant because the Air Force had done an unanticipated about-face on me.

Welcome to reality, Scoop. While you're trying to make a career of the Air Force, the Air Force is making a career of sending you everywhere you don't want to be.

The more I thought about it, the angrier I got. Unfair I could handle. But this exceeded the boundaries of unfairness; this bordered on criminal. I was over here getting my ass shot off, living like a pig, and dreaming of a future in fighters while, deep in the bowels of Air Force middle management, some REMF pencil pusher was changing the rules midstream, and expecting me to accept them and be happy. *Fat chance.*

After a day of fuming, I decided to at least make it known that I didn't appreciate the old bait and switch maneuver. I called the Military Personnel Center, where I was informed that whatever nameless TAC official had promised me fighters simply did not have the authority to do so, as if that wasn't glaringly obvious. In an effort to alter the hand that fate had dealt me, I offered to "extend" at the end of my tour and join the Steve Canyon program, a covert out-country FACing operation. I was told that they'd be happy to release me to Steve Canyon, but it wouldn't change the B-52 assignment. I withdrew my offer, figuring I wasn't going to risk my ass for another six months only to find myself being carted off to SAC anyway.

At that moment I made myself a solemn vow: If I stayed in the Air Force, I would never again let the assignment process take its course. I did not intend to spend my life like a clump of seaweed being buffeted between swells and ending up in some godforsaken deserted wasteland. In the days and years ahead, I would make good on my vow, learning not only how to play the system but how to play it like a finely tuned Stradivarius. In fact, I became a virtuoso.

But in the here and now, I not only sweated the "what" of my assignment, it dawned on me that I'd traditionally had problems in the "where" department as well.

Man, it's bad enough that I'll be in SAC—worse yet that I'll be flying B-52s—but what stateside equivalent of Camp Eagle will they stick me in now?

My weasel mode kicked into high gear as I shifted from crisis avoidance to damage control. If I couldn't alter *all* of my fate, I might just be able to sway parts and pieces in the right direction. So I got on the phone to SAC headquarters and explained how pleased I was to be joining SAC. That was one thing they didn't hear every day. In fact, they were so grateful—or mystified—that they happily granted my request to go to Wright-Patterson Air Force Base in Dayton, Ohio—just a stone's throw from good old Tipp City.

If the Air Force was hell-bent on keeping me in SAC, this would be my last hitch. Being stationed in my hometown would give me a chance to make preparations and go job hunting as my military career wound down. In the end, my finagling skills would become so finely tuned that I would not have to turn my back on the military. And the Air Force would never again let me down, mostly because I would never again give them the opportunity to do so.

On the heels of my SAC scheming came my orders to return to Quang Tri and blow the hell out of it.

It was a strange assignment. I had just been there a couple of weeks prior, during my abbreviated stint as duty officer. Now, suddenly, as the North Vietnamese forces mounted a full-scale assault, the ARVN troops defending the city were beating a hasty and none-too-subtle retreat. Quang Tri sat on the edge of the DMZ a scant ten miles shy of North Vietnam, and the whole province was clearly a major jumping-off point for Charlie's grand plan.

NVA forces were shelling the hell out of the place and showing no indication of slowing their assault. With the ARVN troops heading southward at a record pace, the first order of business was to extract the American advisers who were now being overrun by the advancing enemy. Once they were out of the line of fire, we turned our attention to the multitude of tanks and weapons that were sitting exposed and abandoned, just waiting for Charlie's loving caress. The last thing we needed was to have the dinks use our weapons against us; they were doing just fine with their own arsenal.

So I was ordered to head north and blow up anything that might hurt us if it was pointed in our direction.

It felt odd to direct air strikes against American equipment, especially because it signaled a defeat. They were the biggest air strikes I'd ever lead—lots of secondary explosions, all kinds of pyrotechnics. The irony did not escape me. I imagined taking my children on my knee many years hence and hearing them ask, "What was your biggest air strike of the war, Daddy?" *Ah yes, kids, I remember it well, blowing the crap out of your tax dollars.*

We were being pushed back even farther, and it left me with the uncomfortable but accurate impression that we were being caught with our pants down, despite the best efforts of every FAC in I Corps to convey the growing urgency of the situation.

Charlie hosed us good as we directed our strikes. He knew full well what we were doing, and it was in his best interest to prevent it. FACs throughout Vietnam, and especially in I Corps, were being knocked out of the sky with alarming frequency. There was no question that the North Vietnamese were rapidly gaining the upper hand. There was also no question in my mind that it didn't have to be that way. The military had the power and the resolve; if only we had been turned loose to run an actual military campaign, it could have been over in a matter of weeks—if not in 1972, then certainly a few years prior. But like everything else in this comedy of errors, it was a case of too little, too late. Even with full knowledge and understanding of the futility of our situation, we forged ahead and did what we were trained to do.

CHAPTER FOURTEEN

SPRING FORWARD, FALL BACK

FOR MONTHS we'd been watching helplessly as our northern areas of operation underwent a gradual but significant evolution. What began as subtle changes—recognizable only to those who flew the terrain day in and day out—quickly became explicit and unsettling. Visible supply caches tripled in number and size, and new roads, including one we christened Bilk Boulevard, appeared weekly—sometimes daily—meandering southward from the DMZ or eastward out of Laos. Men, equipment, and weapons were springing up all over.

North Vietnam had big plans, and I was watching them unfold step by step, day by day on the pockmarked land beneath me. At each intelligence briefing following our missions, we would attempt to convey the urgency of the situation. Charlie was squatting on the edge of the DMZ. He was poised at the brink of the A Shau Valley. Every day he nudged his toe a little closer to South Vietnam. Those of us FACing in the northern AOs did our best to clearly chart the intensity and magnitude of the buildup. Our commanding officers appeared to listen, appeared to understand. Yet nothing changed. It was like screaming into a wind tunnel. You knew the power of your own voice, you understood just how loud you were yelling, but the minute the sound left your mouth, it dissipated and died.

"This is a pile of shit," Ed O'Connor groused as we sat around after dinner one night. "We're watching this thing blow up in our faces and there's not a thing we can do about it. The way this is unfolding, we'll be lucky if they don't overrun Da Nang in a matter of weeks."

We eyed one another nervously. None of us ever forgot we were in a war zone, but now we were feeling a different kind of heat. The whole shape of our combat experience was changing, and changing quickly. Suddenly we were square-dancing with a centipede. We didn't have time to learn the steps; we were just struggling to keep up.

"Well, Charlie's up to something big," I agreed, "no question about it. But I'm not sure he's got the guts to launch a full-scale invasion. And if he does, what the hell are we gonna do? It's not like anyone's listening to us, at least no one with any political clout. And you know as well as I do that this thing isn't being fought by the military. It's being fought by the politicians, and they're plenty comfortable while they're doing it."

"And they're welcome to it, so long as it's *their* sorry asses getting shot at," Ed agreed.

Unfortunately, the politicians stayed conspicuously absent in-country, and the "phone-it-in" battle plans continued to confound and confuse us at every turn.

In late March, I got a firsthand look at the political and military second-guessing when I spotted a huge supply and weapons cache that rambled forever along the banks of a small tributary about halfway down the A Shau Valley. I knew this called for something more substantial than a standard FAC-lead air strike. This screamed for an arc light.

Arc light was the code name for a B-52 bombing mission. The B-52 could carry firepower unequaled by smaller aircraft. A fully loaded BUFF hauled eighty-four 500-pound and forty-two 750-pound bombs internally and an additional twenty-four 750-pound bombs externally. B-52s flew in formations called cells, which included one airplane in front flanked by two more flying side by side on either side of the tail. Flying in that configuration, the planes dropped what was called a "stick" of bombs for hundreds of yards. The effect was to blanket the landscape with explosions, leaving nothing but telltale BUFF tracks. No matter how you sliced it, an arc light was a force to be reckoned with. FACs didn't control a BUFF raid; they just tried to stay out of the way.

But sooner or later, most FACs found themselves uncomfortably close to—as in directly beneath—an arc light mission. It wasn't something we planned. No one relished becoming a friendly fire statistic. But our good intentions were sometimes overcome by events or, at a minimum, negligence. Whose negligence is yet another topic for discussion.

I was never convinced that all the arc light missions were announced in advance. And that kind of made sense. After all, we knew that the dinks had our radios, and if they were listening, did we really want to say, "Hey, Charlie, we're going to blow the crap out of your supply cache located at the following coordinates . . ."?

Perhaps Uncle Sam did indeed telegraph his intentions each and every time. But we weren't always listening. Notice of pending arc lights came over the Guard channel. Guard was the emergency frequency. If someone was shot down and bailed out, the steady *beep–beep–beep* of their parachute homing device would help us find and retrieve them. In the heat of war, there was always plenty of activity on Guard. In fact, if we were busy doing battle ourselves, we'd simply shut off the irritating Guard distraction. Four radios yelling at us were more than enough. Ignoring the Guard channel for a while might have been okay, if we remembered to turn it back on once our situation was under control. But we rarely did.

As a result, on more than one occasion I found myself suddenly aware that the whole world was blowing up around me. There wasn't a darn thing I could do about it. I was a mosquito being crapped on by a flight of Canada geese. All I could do was adjust my direction and try to fly perpendicular to the explosions instead of parallel. Obviously I was successful. I suspect there were some who weren't as lucky. Being arc lighted served one purpose: It reminded you to monitor the Guard channel, for a while at least.

However inconvenient an arc light could occasionally be, it was handy when you needed to obliterate something. The sprawling weapons and supply cache I had spotted today was tailor-made for the maximum coverage of a BUFF run. That afternoon, I sat down with the 20th TASS intelligence officer and laid out coordinates, observations, and my take on the situation.

"It's obvious that they're floating this stuff down the river at night and pulling it onto the shore for later distribution," I explained. "It's a massive cache, bigger than anything I've ever seen over here. Too big, I think, for fighters. We probably need an arc light for this one." The officer took notes and listened intently as I explained the necessary course of action.

"The river runs north and south. You need to run the B-52 cell up the river and trash everything from top to bottom," I told him, sliding my finger down the meandering blue line on the sectional map.

Confident that I had laid the groundwork for the total destruction of half the NVA's weapons and ammunition, I headed back to my hooch, feeling unusually satisfied. The sense of accomplishment faded rapidly as I returned to the coordinates the next morning and discovered that, somewhere up the chain of command, my directions had been lost in translation. Or, more likely, some staff puke or REMF who didn't have a clue what I was talking about or what I'd been seeing every day for nine months decided he knew better, so he ran the strike from east to west. Three B-52s, hundreds of bombs, total coverage, total devastation—and not one single inch of the weapons cache was hit. Not even one crate was damaged. But at least the North Vietnamese knew we were out to get them, and it was obvious that the NVA was already in the process of clearing out the site. After I launched a sadly incomplete air strike with the only two F-4s I could get, Charlie finished the job and floated the whole kit 'n' kaboodle down the river and I never saw it again. Well, actually, I probably did see it—whizzing by my cockpit window or lighting up the ground beneath me.

For me, the whole B-52 incident was a microcosm of everything that was wrong about the war in Vietnam. The guys coordinating the war were a bunch of civilian intellectual elitists who thought they knew more about combat than the guys in the trenches who were doing the fighting. It was a mentality that had been fostered by Lyndon Johnson, who, although far from an intellectual, seemed to view the military as his own personal set of toy soldiers. Not surprising from a guy who liked to brag that the military couldn't bomb an outhouse in North Vietnam without his prior seal of approval.

Nice work, Mr. President. Go ahead and build a monument to your ego. Just don't build it out of the bodies of American soldiers. Oops, too late.

There was little value in recriminations now. Johnson was out; Nixon was in. And the muck and mire of Vietnam just grew deeper and thicker.

Then, on March 30, 1972, the thing we'd feared most happened. The floodgates opened: From the north and the west, hordes of North Vietnamese poured into the country; and men and trucks and tanks—and big guns—rolled southward.

Early in the war, Ho Chi Minh had laid out the formula for victory: He declared that America would simply lose its taste for war if North Vietnam never tired of sending men to die. They didn't. And we did. The patient and pragmatic NVA leaders had watched for months as American troops dwindled in numbers, courtesy of the Nixon administration's Vietnamization policies.

Those of us left guarding the doors felt outgunned and most definitely outmanned. We could see, hear, and sense the progressive southward roll. But all we could do was hang on and hope it would right itself. It would, eventually, sort of, but things would get messy in the process.

Communist troops poured across the DMZ and into the A Shau Valley from Laos. Fourteen regular divisions, twenty-six regiments, and a whole lot of tanks, all converging on my little piece of the world, all hoping to send me home, preferably in a zippered black plastic bag. But as unnerving as the men and the tanks were, the real threat to us came from a dramatic infusion of artillery and antiaircraft weapons the likes of which our little O-2s had never seen. Now we were faced with 23-millimeter and 37-millimeter antiaircraft fire, and the huge SA-2 surface-to-air missiles. Scarier still, for us little guys in slow airplanes, were the heat-seeking Strela SA-7s, which forced us to seek higher ground by a couple of thousand feet. If one of those locked in on us, we might as well say our prayers and make our peace with the world, because there wouldn't be time for much else.

In the confusion that followed the invasion, any routine we had come to know vanished completely. Life dissolved into mission after mission, interrupted by uneasy sleep. Missions consisted of trying to hold back the approaching hordes or provide cover for the thousands of refugees fleeing southward on Route 1. Search and rescues increased dramatically as Strelas and SAMs claimed more and more of our guys, FACs included.

On April 2, I was in the air wrapping up a run-of-the-mill air strike when the call came through launching one of the biggest SARs of the entire war. An EB-66, an electronic warfare aircraft designed to jam SAM site guidance systems, took a direct hit from a SAM and went down near the DMZ. The EB-66, code-named Bat 21, had a crew of six; only the navigator, Air Force lieutenant colonel Iceal Hambleton, managed to make it out alive. The problem was, he jumped out of a crippled aircraft and right smack into the middle of what we were now calling the Easter Offensive. The American war effort ground to a halt as we threw every available resource at getting this guy out alive. Unfortunately, the more resources we threw at the escalating situation, the more people needed to be rescued. Hambleton, at age fifty-three, was not a prime candidate for an energetic E&E in the sweltering jungles of Southeast Asia.

The American rescue apparatus swung into gear almost immediately as FACs from throughout I Corps and beyond initiated a round-the-clock effort to guide the disoriented navigator to safety. The Army, Coast Guard, Navy SEALs, and the South Vietnamese all marshaled their forces to implement a successful rescue.

A lot of good men were lost in the process, including crew members from a UH-1 Huey, call sign Blueghost 39; two OV-10 Broncos; and the entire crew of Jolly Green 67. From April 2 to April 13, eleven men were killed and more than 800 air strikes were completed in what would become the largest sustained SAR of the war.

Colonel Hambleton was indeed successfully rescued. I guess you could call it a testament to our determination to never leave a man behind. But it was a gut-wrenching eleven days that took a lasting toll on anyone who was involved at any level.

Somehow in the midst of all the insanity and chaos, the week of R&R I had scheduled many months prior arrived, and they actually let me go. I had stopped counting on it several weeks before, because I sensed that the playing field was undergoing a serious overhaul. Not that my R&R was anything to look forward to; I was headed back to Hawaii, but I would be there alone. Karen was teaching school and did not have any vacation time left.

To make matters worse, I was staying at the same hotel where we had stayed at Christmas. I thought I could handle it. I'd take in some of the sights and sounds of the islands, just kick back and revel in not being shot at.

After all, Scoop, you've managed to survive spending 98 percent of the last nine months without female companionship. Who's to say that a week alone in Hawaii won't be kind of refreshing? Yeah, right.

Arriving in Honolulu was like getting a swift kick in the gut, or lower. I was about the only person on the plane not greeted by hugs and kisses at the airport. As I retrieved my bags and headed for the Outrigger Hotel, I was seized by a sinking feeling that slowly overwhelmed me. Everywhere I looked, I was reminded of the previous trip. Every place I went, there were happy couples chatting and nuzzling and doing all those "happy couple things" that I desperately longed for. My emotional state was further complicated by the realization that my buddies in-country were getting the shit kicked out of them while I was sipping mai tais in a tropical paradise.

Having thoroughly depressed myself beyond all hope of redemption, I finally surrendered to my agony and placed a long-distance call to Karen.

I poured out my angst and loneliness. It must have been convincing, because she immediately packed her bags and told her principal she'd be gone for a week. He told her to let the superintendent know, so Karen headed to his office and repeated her intentions. Being a Navy man from World War II, the guy took pity on us and sent Karen off on her mission of mercy.

The remaining five days of R&R were a joyous re-creation of my Christmas leave, although the cloud looming over me this time was darker, thicker, and considerably more distracting. I was obsessed by the events unfolding back in Vietnam. The efforts to rescue Colonel Hambleton were extracting a high price. Not only did I feel that I had deserted my buddies in their moment of need, I felt a creeping and consuming dread about returning to combat: something far more unsettling than I had ever experienced before.

I was on the downhill slide toward the end of my tour—only a couple of months to go—and the way things were unfolding, the worst was yet to come. Every time I said to Karen, "When I come home . . . ," a nagging voice in my head corrected, "*If* you come home. . . ." For the first time, the latter seemed like a distinct possibility.

My farewells this time had a darker, more permanent edge to them. Neither of us verbalized our fears, but they were there nonetheless, perched between us like Poe's raven. So I returned to the fire, deeply troubled and not at all sure I'd ever see Tipp City, Karen, or my family again.

I arrived back in Da Nang to find everything in an uproar—pretty much the way I had left it. The pre-March 30 trend of letting guys head home prior to their anticipated end of tour had reversed itself with a vengeance. People were suddenly being extended. I found out that Tom O'Neill and Lyndle Price, who'd been expecting to DEROS on April 7, had been extended to the end of the month. I wondered what all this backpedaling would mean for my late June DEROS. The idea of getting killed in combat was bad enough, but the thought of getting killed when you weren't even supposed to be in-country anymore was the ultimate act of adding insult to injury. I was sure it had happened before and would certainly happen again. I just selfishly hoped it didn't happen to me, or anyone I knew.

On the positive side, by late April the United States was beginning to bomb the hell out of North Vietnam in an effort to stem the tide of the invasion. It was a prelude to Operation Linebacker, a concentrated and highly effective assault on the enemy's infrastructure and access routes. It worked because Nixon gave his military leaders the authority to select the targets, the tactics, and the weapons. Thankfully this president didn't seem quite as concerned about whether outhouses were demolished without his permission. The net effect for those of us in Da Nang was a dramatic decrease in the number of rockets raining down on our heads. It was a substantial relief to have a slightly stronger sense of protection from being blown up while lying in our beds at night.

Of course back in the States the liberal political leaders were pounding their chests and agonizing over the impact of stepped-up bombings on the poor, downtrodden people of North Vietnam. Those of us sitting amid the debris of NVA rocket attacks were mystified and infuriated by American politicians who tacitly endorsed spitting on returning troops but were quick to defend the rights of the enemy. If it wasn't treason, it was dishearteningly close for those of us who were supposedly doing the bidding of our nation's leaders. Any use I'd ever had for Democrats had been badly compromised by Lyndon Johnson; these guys and their bleeding-heart angst over the enemy pretty much finished it off.

As the North Vietnamese pushed southward, ARVN troops were abandoning their positions and running for their lives. I can't say I cared for the idea of being the first line of defense, when the guys whose country we were defending were hoofing it south just as fast as their legs would carry them.

The whole complexion of the war shifted at this point. We would remain in a defensive crouch for the rest of my tour, and well beyond. We started taking big losses. Not only were the Bilks and Coveys getting battered; all kinds of aircraft were facing a renewed and relentless enemy. Our time was evenly divided between air strikes and search-and-rescue missions. Frequently we found ourselves embarking on search-and-rescue missions to recover a search-and-rescue mission. It was as though one disaster led to another. Bill Jankowski, Bilk 34—one of many heroes in the recovery of Bat 21—was shot down twice in two days, leaving us all with the realization that it could happen to anyone at any moment. It was unnerving to say the least. The day Jankowski was shot down, I walked through our hooch and paused by the door to his room. My stomach tightened as I wondered whether I'd ever see him in there again. It wasn't a fear I gave into willingly, but when it hit that close to home, it was tough to ignore.

Meanwhile, as the FACs and fighters navigated the unfriendly skies, we had guys on the ground—ARVN troops and their American advisers—who were getting cut off by the onslaught.

Sleep became a precious commodity as our missions grew to two or three each day, which meant eight to twelve hours of combat flying. We were constantly adrenalized, always spring-loaded and ready for anything. Charlie wasn't playing nice anymore. He was using all kinds of nasty crap to make his point, stuff that those of us below the DMZ had never seen till now, stuff that did more than rattle our cages and make us fly higher.

I got my own personal wake-up call from Charlie during one of the endless air strikes that seemed to flow continuously one into the other. I had rendezvoused with my fighters, a couple of Navy A-4s, and was preparing to blow up a huge weapons cache along the Green Alpine Highway just inside the DMZ.

"Baton Three Two, Bilk Two Four is ready for your—"

My throat locked up, although I could vaguely sense some strange guttural sound; maybe it came out of my mouth, maybe it just bounced around in my head. I had no time to ponder its origins, because I was suddenly staring *up* at the ground where the sky had been only seconds before.

My little sky pig had gone completely nuts. I was upside down, twisting, spinning, and writhing like a cobra in heat. Instinct slowly kicked in, although not before a few seconds of sheer terror.

Okay, Jackson. You're a month away from DEROS. Die now and you'll look like an idiot, and be dead to boot! Relax, don't fight the plane. Ease everything into place. You've got plenty of room . . . maybe 500 feet. Sure, plenty of room.

The words didn't fully form in my head. They didn't have time to. Later on, I would remember the sensation of thinking my way through the process, but I could never really re-create my thoughts. Except maybe one: *Holy crap!*

I struggled against the wildly gyrating O-2, trying to get her righted before nudging her in some direction that didn't fill my windscreen with rapidly approaching trees.

Somewhere behind the groaning engines and the blood pounding through my ears, I could hear anxious fighter jocks shouting at me.

"FAC, are you okay?"

"Bilk, you still with us?"

As I pulled back on the yoke and slowly brought the airplane under control, I made a sharp turn to the south. If I'd been hit by something nasty, I wanted to make damn sure I didn't drop the plane right in the middle of Charlie's living room.

The O-2 regained some measure of stability, and I was finally in a position to vaguely understand what had just happened, or almost happened.

My heart pounded against my sternum. I couldn't imagine any body part working that hard and not exploding in the process. I took a couple of quick gulps of air to chase away an unsteady, lightheaded feeling. When I felt as though I could talk again, I pressed the mic button.

"Bilk Two Four is heading feet wet, guys. What the hell happened?"

"You took a SAM! Well, almost."

"What?" The lightheaded feeling returned suddenly, and my breath caught in my chest.

It was inconceivable to me that Charlie would waste a multimillion dollar SAM missile against a little O-2, which cost maybe $50,000.

Before exiting the area, I asked the A-4s if they had a visual on the SAM site.

"Roger, Bilk. It had been camouflaged, but it's right out there now."

There was no wheel, no orbit, no "hit my smoke." Just a final, urgent report from the frazzled FAC.

"You're cleared hot!" I radioed sharply as I turned my back on the Green Alpine Highway and everyone above and below it.

My unorchestrated air strike violated every rule known to FACs, but I was too rattled to care. My concentration was completely shattered; I wanted only three things: water, altitude, and the Da Nang runway in my windscreen.

I never found out whether the A-4s hit the site or aborted the effort. I didn't really care, except in the context of hoping that neither I nor any of my fellow FACs would fall prey to that same site again. I did, however, radio the SAM site location into Covey Control once I had gained sufficient altitude.

I did a controllability check as I limped down the coastline. The sky pig responded favorably to my efforts, and I began to believe that I was actually going to make it back to Da Nang in one piece.

After an uneventful landing, I climbed out of the airplane, expecting to see half the tail blown off or part of one wing missing. She looked surprisingly whole, and I counted my blessings as I tried to breathe normally once again. After hearing my story, even the maintenance supervisor was overjoyed that my trusty Oscar Deuce apparently suffered little more than a write-up for being over-G'd.

In the end, I had to surmise that the concussion from a SAM explosion just above me had pushed down the O-2 and flipped it. Amazingly, whatever shrapnel resulted must have missed me as it continued skyward. Years later, a Ph.D. tried to explain to me some vague concept about a radial debris pattern, which supposedly illustrated how I narrowly escaped death. I'm sure there is some rational scientific explanation, but dumb luck works just fine for me.

"Damn, Jackson, you are one lucky son of a bitch." Ed whistled and shook his head as I told my story back at the hooch. "Do you know how many guys get that close to a SAM and live to talk about it? Take a peek in the mirror over there. You're lookin' at him."

My blood ran cold as I realized the truth in Ed's words. If the O-2 had been only a few feet to one side or the other, my family would have been on the receiving end of the worst kind of telegram.

An old wives' tale says that when you sense a sudden chill, it means someone is walking on your grave. I fought off a shiver and the uneasy feeling that I had stumbled across my own grave.

"Man, somebody up there sure likes you," Ed added, absently flipping the pages of a dog-eared magazine.

I wondered whether he might be right. Several hours later, Ed snapped a picture of me pointing to the spot on the map where the SAM and I almost collided. Many years later that photo remains in my collection, and I still ponder the whims of fate.

The next morning, I was back in the sky with no visible side effects from the whole SAM incident, at least none related to physical injury. But the event had a lasting impact, one that I would not fully understand until much later.

It began as a twinge in my gut, an occasional gurgle or knot when a situation was tense, but nothing that ever exceeded the range of mildly irritating. The SAM incident added a whole new dimension to my intestinal irritation. Occasional gurgles evolved into urgent cramps—so bad, in fact, that on one occasion I was forced to land my plane at Hue Phu Bai, even though it was no longer one of our active air bases, and race for a men's room. I felt like a tourist in Mexico who had violated the "don't drink the water" rules. Only Montezuma played no role in my ailment; I was a victim of "Uncle Ho's Revenge."

The whole thing embarrassed the heck out of me and annoyed me even more. It came on without warning and left me doubled over in pain. How could I not control this? What was my body doing to me?

In the years that followed the war, the symptoms intensified, plaguing me to the point that I would down an entire bottle of Kaopectate the night before a B-52 flight, only to get hit again the next day with as much discomfort and urgency as ever. I never talked about it to anyone. Aside from being a poor dinner topic, it wasn't something I wanted to acknowledge. At a minimum, it was disgusting. At worst, it was evidence of some fundamental flaw in my mental or physical fortitude.

But flaw or not, it proved to be one of the few negative situations in my life that I could not manage to avoid. For the next twenty-five years, it became a steady companion, predictable only by its unpredictability. It was one of two Vietnam legacies that would complicate, although by no means destroy, my postwar life.

The second of those legacies came on just as suddenly but was much less vague in terms of cause and effect.

The cause was hunger—well, sort of. I had flown an abnormally uneventful morning mission and found that I had the luxury of a whole afternoon to myself. By evening I had played all the solitaire I could play and had thumbed through every magazine in the hooch. I'd become so acclimated to multiple missions per day that I found myself almost bored with an afternoon of freedom.

Okay, Scoop. What else can you do to pass the time until the next crisis? A nap, you say? Brilliant idea!

I stretched out on my bunk and drifted into something that resembled peaceful slumber. By midnight I'd managed to rack up a full night's sleep and awoke to a familiar rumbling in my empty stomach.

Maybe the TASS Hole is still open and I can snag a handful of cookies and a soft drink.

I headed out the door and down the path to the local watering hole. Half an hour later, my appetite sated, I wandered back to the hooch. It was a steamy, cloudless night, like so many nights before. I could hear voices punctuated by occasional bursts of distant gunfire, but for Vietnam it was surprisingly quiet. So quiet, in fact, that my ears caught a sudden strange wailing sound as I opened the door to my hooch. Then the world exploded.

Well, maybe it wasn't the world, but it *was* the hooch next to mine. I didn't hear the rocket at all, but in the split second before it hit, I *did* hear the sirens. *Better late than never.*

The rocket blast filled my eyes and ears and threw me backward. I landed upside down against a wall with the full weight of my body crushing painfully against my neck and head. Dazed and puzzled, I lay there for a minute, staring numbly at the inverted landscape.

Okay, Scoop, what the hell just happened? Am I dead? Nah, if I were dead I wouldn't be in so much pain. Okay, so I'm not dead. Am I bleeding? Are any important parts missing?

I gingerly walked my legs down the wall and crumpled sideways into a heap on the floor. I didn't see any excessive blood flow, although my face felt pretty scuffed up. My jaw felt funny too; as I tried to open my mouth, I was sure I'd broken or dislocated it. I propped myself up on one arm and came to a sitting position—and felt an odd, spongy grinding in my neck. Moving my head slowly from side to side, I was relieved to find a fairly normal range of motion; more unnerving was the symphony of cracks and pops that echoed through my skull as though someone had filled my ears with Rice Krispies, and added milk.

At the moment, however, my jaw was claiming center stage. I couldn't fully open my mouth without the painful sensation of a bubble getting ready to burst somewhere deep in my jawbone. A dull, throbbing ache radiated up one side of my face and into my ear. The discomfort gave me an indistinct, all-over sick feeling as I struggled to my feet, steadying myself against the wall. Instinctively I ran my hands all over my body feeling for protruding shrapnel or blood flow above and beyond what was streaming down my face. I was relieved to find neither but was troubled by the pain I felt from the shoulders up.

Only then did I glance through the front door of my hooch and realize that I had been thrown backward about twenty feet and that a smoldering crater now marred the walkway between my hooch and the field-grade hooch next door.

I hobbled toward the door, feeling older than my years. I could hear voices from inside the damaged hooch. Majors Dale Ullrich and Art Evans stumbled out the door, shaking their heads and muttering profanities. Lieutenant Colonel Napoli followed them out and surveyed the front of the building.

"Man, Art, that sucker hit right next to your bedroom. You think Charlie's trying to tell you something?" Napoli's voice disappeared around the corner. The majors followed and were soon joined by a handful of guys from neighboring hooches. I mopped the blood off my upper lip and stood by—in a wobbly kind of way—to see if I could help, but my own rocket-induced aches were beginning to intensify. Once I had determined that my assistance was not needed, I shuffled back to my bunk and tried to find a position that minimized my growing discomfort. I also tried to decide whether I was exceedingly unlucky in selecting the most inopportune time to go for carryout or incredibly fortunate that I was still essentially ambulatory. I preferred to think of it as the latter, although it briefly occurred to me that my life was a series of near misses; I always walked away shaken but unharmed. Jackson-related adventures might involve fear, anxiety, and damage to private property, but they had never marred my person to any medically discernible degree.

Until now.

The rocket attack probably classified as a close call. Had I been a few seconds later in returning from my snack, I might be dead or at least missing a variety of useful parts. But I also had the nagging feeling that this was not a minor incident, not a mere blip on the old "luck o' the Jackson" screen.

Man, you really wracked yourself up this time. This is gonna hurt for a few days.

Little did I know.

I rubbed my hand across my aching neck, a gesture I would come to perfect over the years. I could feel everything starting to stiffen up as I gave in to queasiness and exhaustion. But my sleep was fitful at best. I couldn't open my mouth, couldn't rest my head comfortably against the pillow, and couldn't sleep on my side without feeling as though my jaw was going to slide off my face. The next day I headed over to the base dentist, who fit me in for a quick once-over between appointments.

"What happened, Captain?" He eyed the bruises and cuts on my face as he carefully manipulated my aching jaw.

"Uh, I think I may have broken my jaw." I was deliberately evasive. If I claimed to be injured, I might get grounded. If I got grounded, I wasn't doing my job. If I wasn't doing my job, I was just wasting space. Jacksonian Philosophy 101. Medical disaster 304.

The dentist probably attributed my condition to a good old-fashioned bar fight or a spirited wrestling match with one of the "steam and cream" gals. That was fine. The Jackson luck had failed me; I figured that if I pretended it didn't happen, well, then it didn't happen.

The dentist twisted my jaw a bit and pronounced it unbroken.

"It may have been dislocated, but it's back in place now. You're going to have some pretty sore muscles in your face, but everything should heal fine. If you want to make an appointment, we can get some x-rays just to be safe. It'd probably be a good idea."

I nodded, or tried to. Despite the desire to minimize my condition, I did go back for x-rays after several days of waiting for the pain to subside. The x-rays offered nothing conclusive, and I gradually adjusted to the jaw-popping.

I did confide to Ed, Jim Crookston, and another Bilk named John Downs that I had been temporarily sidelined by the North Vietnamese. Ed generously took my flight for the day so I could grab some much-needed rest. But by the next day, it was business as usual. At least that was what I told myself. I had no way of knowing that I had just spent the last painless day I'd ever know. I never pondered such things, then or now. All I really knew was that I hurt, but there was work to be done, so I did it. What I didn't realize was that the simple act of cramming my head into a heavy helmet and flying around the skies pulling G's would seriously hinder the healing of my battered bones and muscles.

OTHER VOICES: Colonel Arthur C. Evans, USAF (Ret.)

A FAC's life in Nam was a life of alien sounds, unnatural sights, and unaccustomed emotions. The day was filled with engine noise; incessant radio conversations, often more than one at a time and often frantic; the pop of your own rockets; the smoke, fire, death, and destruction created by your own words; the din of whatever watering hole you crawled into in the evening.

The night was jaundiced by the eerie light of the artillery flares around the perimeter, and the irregular thumps of outgoing howitzer rounds, made surreal by the sounds of Sonny and Cher broadcast from Monkey Mountain, and made hellish by the sounds of the rocket sirens and incoming 122mm rockets marching toward you—gifts from Charlie, carried on Charlie's back down the Ho Chi Minh Trail, and fired from bamboo launchers in the surrounding jungle.

BANG!!! It was after midnight and I had just turned out the reading light. The earth shook. I rolled off the bed and under it where my .45, AK and flak jackets were. I hadn't heard the siren and I didn't hear another blast. ONE rocket? MY personal rocket? I got up and exited the building where I was joined by other FACs contemplating, in sleepy confusion, a smoking hole right next to the wall against which I slept—and the outer wall was peppered with shrapnel pits. Across the small path by my building, a second building had taken the reflected shock wave and its own share of shrapnel. Standing in the door was a live (thank God) FAC—dazed, nose bleeding, unsure of what planet he was on, but Jackson had cheated death again. Cats had nothing on him!

When Mike visited me recently, I showed him pictures of the crater and the two damaged buildings, then handed him some of the pieces of that 122mm rocket. It all came home to both of us once again.

With only a few weeks left in my tour, I managed to ignore the discomfort. Once I got back to the States and started flying much longer missions in much heavier helmets—complete with a bulky oxygen mask—I would discover that, for the first time in my life, I could not think, talk, or otherwise weasel my way out of discomfort and inconvenience. In fact, I would end up at the Wright-Patterson Air Force Base hospital in traction as doctors poked, prodded, and examined me inside and out, hoping to somehow repair both my neck and my stomach. Neither would ever be the same again.

Still, for the remainder of my tour in Vietnam, I didn't have time to think about my neck. My stomach flared up on its own perverse schedule and I was forced to accommodate it, but I managed to do my job and fly my missions.

Things never quieted back down after the Easter Offensive got under way. There were days when it looked as though we might even get pushed out of Da Nang. And nights when I drifted off to sleep wondering whether I'd wake up with Charlie standing over me cradling a Russian rifle murmuring "rise and shine, flyboy."

By mid-May I still didn't know for certain when or if I was heading home. I wasn't especially afraid that I would die during these final weeks. Although the Jackson luck had deserted me briefly, I tried to look at the glass as half full and counted on the fact that I had successfully stared down my own worst-case scenario. Dying probably wasn't in the cards, but having my tour indefinitely extended was a distinct and disturbing possibility.

Although officially drawing down the troop counts, the U.S. government was playing a cagey shell game to combat the invading NVA. FACs were being rounded up from Shaw, Bergstrom, and Hawaii and sent TDY to Southeast Asia for up to ninety days. It was a nifty way to scrounge the additional manpower we needed without counting the extra warm bodies as actual incoming troops. Government statistics showed that these guys were still lazing by the pool or hanging out in the officers' club at some stateside paradise. (Any base in the continental United States—Laughlin and Laredo included—was a paradise compared to Vietnam.) As a result, we had a constant flow of new faces through our hooch. I roomed with an endless parade of people, never getting to know any of them well before they were shuttled off to do battle with the red menace in some other locale.

The threat level was constant and the pace was hectic, but May allowed for some brief return to normalcy. My South Vietnamese FAC training program resumed after being unceremoniously shelved as the VNAF guys scrambled to repel the invading army. The restored program was never as robust as the first phase, but I managed to get a few more FACs trained and into the sky. As for my previous students, I never saw any of them again. I hoped that they had proven to be so skilled and versatile that the VNAF had them dispersed throughout the country. I worried that the opposite was true.

Operating out of Da Nang did have a few advantages. The military structure of Da Nang was much more defined than that at Camp Eagle or Phu Bai. In those remote locales we rarely received a pre-mission briefing; if we did, it came in the form of a quick heads-up at the TOC as we drew our weapons. Hardly formal and rarely specific.

Da Nang was more "by the book." We had our own squadron building with a whole room devoted to pre-flight briefings and post-flight debriefings. We even had an intelligence officer who gave us the straight skinny on what was up, and where and when. This was especially important as we struggled to keep abreast of rapidly changing situations in our AOs.

On one especially memorable day almost two months after the Easter Offensive of 1972, our intel officer spoke in unusually vague terms as he briefed me on my upcoming mission.

"Captain Jackson, one of the old firebases in the 101st AO has been overrun by NVA. ARVN troops are taking heavy losses trying to get them out, and we're going to see if we can help convince Charlie to leave," he explained. "You'll be getting a flight of two VNAF A-37s; each carrying two special ordnance loads, for a total of four weapons. Are you clear on that?"

I shook my head in mild exasperation.

Sure. Why wouldn't I be? After eleven months in-country, I'm an old hand by now. If you need someone to direct an air strike that delivers some magical mystery ordnance, I'm your man. But my ears perked up when the intel officer identified the location of the NVA squatters as Firebase Bastogne. Located along Route 547 west of Hue, it had been one of "my" firebases, one of the places where I had conducted on-the-job training for the guys on the ground.

For all my early efforts to avoid being drafted by the Army, I had somehow managed to spend about 75 percent of my time with them. When I wasn't putting in air strikes, sucking down rusty orange soda, or honing my foosball skills, I was coaching my ground-pounder pals on the fine points of calling in an air strike and talking to FACs.

On a clear November day in 1971, I had climbed aboard a Loach and headed out from Camp Eagle to experience yet another step down on the SEA evolutionary ladder. In the course of my combat career, I'd gone from the States to the Philippines to Cam Ranh Bay to Da Nang to Camp Eagle, each destination a little more disheartening, a little more primitive. But the guys camped out on firebases would have gladly traded places with the lowest grunt at Eagle. The hooch that Tom O'Neill had viewed with a jaundiced eye would have looked like a little slice of heaven to one of my firebase associates. Then again, no one in SEA had a lower standard of living than the poor grunts on patrol in the bush. It was all relative, and I never lost sight of the fact that my living conditions, although not always comfortable, could have been much worse.

I had eagerly accepted the firebase training assignment. Not that it mattered; I'd have had to do it eventually regardless, but I genuinely wanted to see how these guys lived. Like my previous adventures with pink teams, I felt a certain obligation to experience a variety of perspectives. Perhaps I also wanted to combat the old "privileged pilot" stereotype. I knew it wasn't accurate, but I also knew that pilots were perceived as "the chosen ones." In fact, thirty-two years after the war, I still run into other Vietnam vets who, when I identify myself as an Air Force pilot, say something to the effect of, "Ah, you had the cushy job." Not exactly, but better than some.

Firebase Bastogne stood on the crest of a mountain, or, more accurately, a ragged ridgeline. It was a desolate location flanked by jungle on all sides. If I was uneasy falling asleep at Camp Eagle each night, I couldn't imagine trying to drift into slumber on this desolate mountaintop knowing that Charlie could be crouched on his haunches in the undergrowth, waiting to creep into the bunker and slit my throat.

The bunkers themselves were crude but effective. Ammo boxes filled with dirt were stacked atop each other and anchored against the hillside. Typical of the Army, the mountaintop had been cleared of all vegetation, leaving only a fine layer of dirt and pebbles. At the center of the complex, a large wooden boat resting on a reinforced platform served as a reservoir for water. It looked ridiculously out of place in the middle of the jungle, but it was typical of the military's make-do approach.

Packed with anywhere from twenty-five to fifty men or more at any given time, the firebase acted as a listening post, a base of operations in the 101st Airborne's western AO.

My dealings were with the firebase officer, a lieutenant. If there was a captain in residence, he didn't show his face; he probably didn't have time for some low-level Air Force puke.

As we initiated the training exercise, Ed O'Connor flew over on cue to serve as my simulated fighter and FAC. Fortunately, we were working with artillery guys who had some knowledge of munitions. We covered a broad spectrum of exercises, from communications to helping the FAC identify targets, describe landmarks, and use points of reference to establish distance. I coached them on instructing the FAC to fire a smoke rocket, then walking the rockets toward the target as they would with artillery. Then I slapped the radio into the lieutenant's hand and said, "There's the FAC. Pick out a target and talk him to it."

It was a good session. Although it wasn't rocket science, we knew it could pay dividends down the road. The more people who understood who we were and what we did, the more likely it was they would ask for our help—and know how to use it—when the situation warranted.

I remembered my day at Bastogne as I listened to the 20th TASS intel officer explain my mission to oust the firebase's current residents. They had holed up there on the heels of the Easter Offensive and were loathe to abandon such a strategic site. Who could blame them? Bastogne had been designed with efficiency and access in mind. Charlie set up housekeeping there, knowing it was tough to pry some-one out of a firebase. He also realized that he was now within a stone's throw of a large number of American soldiers and supplies.

Over the years, the dinks had become plenty savvy at using American tactics and materials against us. Firebase Bastogne was a prime example. ARVN troops had repeatedly tried to evict the intruders and had succeeded only in racking up a substantial body count on the "good guy" side.

Now it was my turn to give it a shot. I took off from Da Nang, still curious about the nature of my mission. It wasn't simply the "special ord-nance" that puzzled me but the fact that it was being delivered by VNAF aircraft. Most of my interdiction missions had been with American fighters.

What exactly are we going to drop on Charlie? Is it something brand new? Is it being delivered by VNAF pilots because it violates the Geneva Convention? Does it really matter?

I set up a low orbit over Firebase Bastogne. It all looked eerily familiar, and it was hard to believe that those weren't our guys down there. However, the sudden sparkle of automatic weapons fire coming at me from the jungle below reinforced the seriousness of the situation.

Okay, Charlie. You just can't play nice, can ya?

I changed the frequency on my UHF radio and waited for my VNAF fighters to check in.

"Firebird One Seven, flight check-in. Two."

"Bilk Two Four, this is Firebird One Seven with a flight of two A-37s."

I recognized the distinctive Vietnamese accent, but it was much clearer than that of many VNAF officers I had dealt with. I wondered in passing how much time this guy had spent in the United States.

The radio crackled again. "Firebird One Seven is with you at ninety-five hundred feet, ten miles north of Da Nang. We should be in the target area in about five minutes."

"Roger, Firebird One Seven. Bilk Two Four is fifteen nautical miles west of Hue, slightly south of Route 547 at three thousand feet. I understand that you know where the target is."

"Affirmative, Bilk. We on the way."

'Kay. I'm starting to wonder what you need me for, but, hey, here I am anyway.

I rolled into a turn, careful to stay south of the gunfire that still glittered against the tree line.

The firebase below was oddly calm, like some abandoned stronghold from a conflict long past. The occasional flash of a red tracer reminded me that it wasn't quite as quiet down there as I wanted to think, or hope. Someone among the stacks of ammo boxes was on high alert, but they had thus far managed to stay well hidden. I cracked my foul weather window, praying for a refreshing shot of cool air. Instead a blast of wet heat smothered me in its sweaty embrace. Same old, same old, I sighed.

My FM radio crackled. I was startled that my VNAF fighters had made it to the target area so quickly. But why were they coming up on the FM frequency instead of UHF?

"Beelk Two Four, come in?"

Huh? And who the heck is that? He was obviously Vietnamese, but the accent was much thicker than I was accustomed to. Something wasn't right. I spoke slowly and cautiously.

"uh . . . Bilk Two Four here. Are you ARVN? What's your unit?"

He ignored me. *Big surprise.*

"Beelk. What you doing up there?"

"Uhm, flying. What are you doing down there?" I answered, now reasonably certain I wasn't talking to one of the good guys.

"You up there all alone, Beelk," the taunting voice shot back. "You know why you up there alone?"

"No, Charlie, but I bet you're gonna tell me."

He chuckled. *Great. No one else thinks I'm funny, just the enemy.*

"You must be lieutenant or captain, Beelk Two Four."

"And why's that, Charlie?"

"Because majors and colonels never up there alone. They back at officer club with your wife or girlfriend," he chided.

Now it was my turn to laugh. I was pretty sure that Karen had better things to do than travel halfway around the world to drink warm beer, eat soggy crackers, and play foosball at the DOOM club. It'd have to be a pretty impressive colonel.

"You're probably right, and that kind of thing really ticks me off. But since I can't blow up the majors and the colonels, guess I'll just have to take it out on you. Keep talking, Charlie. I'm homing in on you."

Silence.

Well, that was interesting. It wasn't the first time I'd found myself chatting with the enemy. I never liked to connect the dots on those exchanges, because it inevitably led to the realization that Charlie's radio had been lifted off the body of a dead GI. *All the more reason to blow your ass back to Uncle Ho.*

I decided to check on my VNAF flight. It wasn't necessary to get a line-up; I already knew what they were carrying. Or, rather, I *didn't* know what they were carrying, but *they* did and that was all that mattered.

"Firebird lead," I radioed, "how do you want to handle dropping the special ordnance?"

"You go ahead and mark the target, Bilk. We plan to do a low-angle, low-release delivery, operating below two thousand feet."

"Roger, Firebird. Since it's a low-angle delivery, I'll hold over the target. Go ahead and set up your wheel. I'll mark the target."

I planted two Willie Petes at either end of the firebase complex.

"Firebird lead, do you have the smoke in sight?"

"Smoke is in sight, Bilk."

"Okay, you'll want to drop your ordnance between the two plumes of smoke. Be advised, I've been taking heavy ground fire from just south of the easternmost smoke plume."

"Roger, Bilk. We'll keep our eyes open."

I made sure I was well above the target and clearly visible. They probably could have completed the air strike without a FAC, especially considering the altitude of their delivery, but I orbited above them and tried to sound useful.

"Okay, Firebird, you're cleared hot. Hit my smoke."

Lead rolled in as something fell off his aircraft and tumbled through the air. It hit the ground, disturbing only the dusty turf surrounding the firebase.

"Lead, that's some special ordnance you've got there. That one was a dud." I suppressed a chuckle, but there was no mistaking the edge of sarcastic humor in my voice.

"Roger, Bilk."

That's it? No cursing, no laughing, no "what's up with that?" Maybe these guys' weapons are so primitive, they're used to duds.

Two rolled in and yet another gray cylinder plummeted toward earth, striking the firebase about midway between the white phosphorus plumes. Once again there was no explosion.

"Number Two, that one would also be a dud."

"Roger, Bilk."

Man, these guys are a couple of cool cookies. So what's the deal? Are we hoping that Charlie will get bonked on the head by one of these things? Based on what I've seen so far, that's about the only way that any of this "special ordnance" is gonna hurt him.

The process began anew as lead peeled out of the wheel and made his low pass over the firebase. Another cylinder smashed into the western edge of the facility. Again, nothing.

"Lead—another dud."

By now I'd figured out that whatever these things were, they probably weren't duds. Either that or I was dealing with the two most laid-back fighter pilots in the history of modern warfare.

Lead was silent as Two rolled in and dropped his final load. Once again, nothing. "Number Two, you've got a dud."

"Roger, Bilk."

Okay, now what? Do we just pretend we obliterated the base and head home? What's the deal, guys? I couldn't resist one more jab before we called it a day.

"Lead, I don't know what your special weapons are, but they're no good." *Didja check first to see if "Made in Japan" was stamped across the base?*

"Bilk Two Four, you should move away from the target area, right now."

Huh?

"Uh, roger, lead."

The tone in his voice told me that my efforts to lighten the situation were either unappreciated or unnecessary. I pushed the throttles forward and twisted the O-2 back to the east. I came around in time to watch one of the A-37s make a final pass over the firebase and shoot a high-explosive rocket squarely into the fortress.

At that point it became glaringly obvious that no duds had been dropped that day. In fact, I wondered briefly whether the stoic VNAFs had been toting nukes. The explosion, when it finally happened, was like an atomic blast; the air surrounding the firebase seemed to compress and expand in a violent hiccup. Shock waves rolled across the mountaintop like the ripples on a pond, and I could see trees and grasses being wildly buffeted by the force of the blast. Even as I urged my O-2 up and out of the vicinity, I could feel the massive concussion sweep over my airplane, whumping into it like the gust from a speeding truck on the interstate. The firebase itself wasn't consumed in some hellish nightmare of smoke and fire; rather, it was trampled by the rolling concussion, like being run over by a kettledrum.

As the violence below me subsided, I brought my O-2 around and surveyed the damage. This BDA would be simple.

"Firebird lead, this is Bilk Two Four. BDA will have to wait until ground troops can access the firebase. But you had 100 percent of ordnance on target, 100 percent of target covered, and . . ." I paused and chuckled, ". . . no duds."

"Roger, Bilk. Thanks for your help."

Several hours later, during my intelligence debriefing, I learned that the ARVN troops had walked right into Bastogne "standing up" and reclaimed it for the good guys. Not a shot was fired. Inside the bunkers, South Vietnamese soldiers were greeted by the grizzly sight of dozens of NVA hunkered against the ammo box walls, frozen with surreal detail in their final death throes. The doomed dinks were bleeding from their noses and ears, a testament to the implosive power of the special ordnance.

I never did learn specifically what we had dropped. I figured that it was some kind of gas bomb. By delaying the ignition process, the VNAF pilots gave the gas a chance to seep into the cracks and crevices of the firebase. When the explosive rocket hit, it literally ignited the fumes that hung in the air. I was oddly reminded of the mechanics of a gas stove and the sudden, explosive *whumpf* that jarred you backward and often singed your eyebrows if you made the mistake of allowing too much gas to escape before touching a match to the pilot light. *Multiply that by about a thousand times, Jackson. Actually, not a bad way to go. They probably never knew what hit them.*

The incident would prove to be my only mystery air strike. It left me with a renewed respect for the combustion properties of gasoline and its derivatives, and much more cautious when lighting a stove.

Throughout May, as I had done for my entire tenure in Southeast Asia, I continued to mark a giant red X across each day as it drew to a close. But now each X seemed to have a greater significance; I was weaving my own lifeline, and every new X was one more link, one step closer to my last flight out of Southeast Asia.

May brought another sign of better days ahead. I was called into the personnel office for my initial outprocessing. It was kind of like getting pre-engaged; it didn't mean anything, but it established a certain commitment to the process and an intention to follow through. Unfortunately, like most pre-engagements, it was subject to a complete reversal if a more tempting prospect came along.

Still, it felt good to be that close to the end of my tour. I was briefed by the transportation troops about my hold baggage, the stuff that would be held for me in the States until I reported to my next assignment. I was handed a not-so-subtle summary of what I could and couldn't take back, and what would happen to me if I so much as thought about shipping contraband back to the United States. Contraband meant everything from AK-47s to poncho liners, anything that technically belonged to any branch of the military. All the weapons I had traded back and forth with the Army guys were strictly prohibited from making the trip home.

Despite my advanced weasel skills, I tend to follow the rules that are laid in front of me. I dutifully gave away everything that couldn't pass the Jackson ownership test—that is, I had arrived with it or paid currency for it. I found out later that I may have been the only guy in Vietnam who did so. The hold baggage was being packed by Vietnamese, who couldn't have cared less what you took home. If a bazooka and two ARVN generals fit into your bags, they were happy to ship them.

The next phase of initial outprocessing included a mandatory "golden flow" drug test.

Nothing was more enjoyable than taking a leak while a big, burly security policeman (SP) scrutinized the process to make sure that whatever went into the cup actually came out of your body. For guys with bashful kidneys, it was an excruciating exercise. They'd suck down quarts of water and stand in line squirming uncomfortably, ready to burst. But the minute they aimed for that little cup under the watchful eye of the potty patrol, everything would snap shut and dry up. After a few minutes of undignified coaxing, the impatient SP would send them back to the end of the line, where they would stand squirming, ready to burst, only to repeat the same painful process several more times before eventually—sometimes hours later—relaxing long enough to provide the appropriate sample.

I was briefed on everything I needed to know about how to complete my final outprocessing: where to pick up my medical records, where to find my personnel records, how to set up a time for final outprocessing, how to get out of Da Nang—*great!* and how to get out of Tan Son Nhut—*better!* My tentative DEROS was June 25, but there was still a tightlipped response to my requests for confirmation.

Then came June 14, 1972, my last mission, commonly referred to as a fini flight. It was supposed to be a moment of celebration, remembrance, and sheer, white-knuckle terror. You didn't take off on your fini flight without thinking at least once, boy, if I get killed today, I'm gonna be really pissed.

The celebration could begin once you landed. For now, you just hoped that your emotions and anticipation didn't dull your edge or color your judgment. Charlie was still down there, still hoping to blast your ass into a thousand pieces, and he didn't give a damn if it was your first mission or your 450th.

It was, thankfully, a routine mission. People shot at me; I fired rockets and directed bombs at the guys doing the shooting. Everyone went home happy. Well, at least I did.

Landing at Da Nang, I got an odd twinge, and for once it wasn't in my stomach. As I climbed out of the cockpit, I hesitated beside the little sky pig for a few moments. She was funny looking, a little gawky, a little insect-like. But she was like a plain girl who suddenly appears beautiful once you get to know her strengths and qualities.

The O-2 and I had been through a lot in the past year. She'd saved my bacon more than once, and she'd met every demand I'd placed on her. Heading into this thing, I wasn't at all sure she was up to the challenge; heck, I wasn't sure I was! Somehow, we'd created a pretty effective partnership. She'd never failed to bring me home in one piece, even when Charlie was launching multimillion-dollar missiles the size of telephone poles at us.

I patted the engine cowling, feeling vaguely silly for treating the airplane as though it was capable of responding and comprehending. But I needed to say good-bye somehow.

"Here's to both of us making it home in one piece." I took a deep breath and walked away forever.

On June 16, I wrote Karen my last letter from Southeast Asia. It was filled with instructions and details about my homecoming. It was a rather mechanical summary, not oozing with anticipation as much as reeking of order and structure, something I'd been painfully denied for 366 days. Celebration and relaxation would happen once my feet were firmly planted on Tipp City soil. Now I just wanted to make certain that everything fell into place as required.

I drafted the letter with my trusty ballpoint pen, purchased at the Cam Ranh Bay BX on my first day in Vietnam. Suddenly, in what seemed to me—both then and now—an odd twist of fate, my pen ran out of ink. Right in the middle of my last letter home, it just died. I grinned and tossed it in the trash (I wish now I had saved it) and went in search of another writing utensil. The irony was not lost on me. That pen, like my O-2, had seen me through twelve grueling months in a very strange place. Apparently it decided that if my tour was up, so was its.

It had been one heck of a ride, sometimes literally. Despite everything, as I lugged my bags out to the C-130 transport plane at Da Nang, I couldn't help but feel an odd nostalgia. I think when you survive an event or a situation—when you beat something that seems determined to wear you down—you develop a grudging respect for it during the process. Somehow you and it are forever linked.

As far as I was concerned, Southeast Asia would never be a stop on any of my future travel itineraries. I had no desire—then or now—to obsess over my Vietnam experiences. But it was part of my history, and I couldn't deny that it had added a certain unique color and texture to my life story. For that, I am strangely grateful.

As I watched the I Corps region disappear against the horizon, I couldn't say I was going to miss it. In fact, I was beginning to feel almost giddy about the trip home. But I could acknowledge that this place, and everything I'd learned here, would be with me for the rest of my life. How I used the experience and whether it changed me for better or worse would be my decision, and mine alone.

I leaned my head against the web seat of the airplane and peered through the small porthole window as the ground slid by beneath me. I didn't know anyone else on the plane. I was completely alone, lost in a rapid-fire succession of thoughts. I knew there would be no marching bands or ticker tape parades to greet me. It wasn't like World War II. It wasn't like any war America had ever fought.

Yet at that moment, none of those things mattered. I'd done it. I'd made it through. I'd performed well, and with honor. And I was going home. Finally.

". . . Lieutenant Colonel Mike Jackson, United States Air Force, Retired. Colonel Jackson?"

The over-amplified voice startled me and I looked around, confused for a moment about where I was and feeling a little stupid for zoning out. *Did you fall asleep, Jackson? Were you drooling on the guy next to you? Cripes.*

I stared at the darkened auditorium of Veterans Hall in Columbus. It was 1997 again.

My neck was killing me. Parts of my rear end had gone numb. But I became suddenly aware that my name was being called. I pressed my hands against the orange plastic chair and rose to my feet, moving toward center stage to accept my award.

My body was tight and stiff. Apparently during my trip down memory lane, I had managed to tense every muscle I owned, and a few I hadn't heard from in thirty years. Still, I had an odd sense of accomplishment, based not just on today's events but on my impromptu rewind through "This Is Your Life, Scoop."

Standing at center stage, I stood crisply erect as a representative from the governor's office placed a medal around my neck and read through my achievements. I wasn't any more comfortable than I'd been sitting down, but at least I'd been granted the luxury of changing positions. Life was good. I could probably make it to the end of the ceremony.

As the speaker concluded his remarks, I paused so that friends and family could record the moment on film, not that anyone would probably give a darn in ten years—or, for that matter, in ten days. The silence was broken by the audible hiss of a woman in the front row. "But he's so young," she said, her voice hinting disapproval. I held my stone photo face, but the corner of my mouth twitched as I repressed a grin.

Young, eh? I sure didn't feel that way much of the time. Sometimes I felt downright ancient. But her words, even with their slight disapproving edge, were oddly reassuring. Yeah, I was young. I'd packed a lot of living into those years, and had a heckuva good time doing it. My life had never been boring. My problems had never consumed me. And my sense of humor had stayed firmly intact even when other, more tangible parts of my person were aching and grinding.

Turning away from the audience and heading back to my seat, I finally broke into a grin. *Not bad for a little guy from Tipp City,* I congratulated myself. *Not bad at all.*

EPILOGUE

"WE NEVER GOT OUR PARADE"

OBVIOUSLY my life didn't end with Vietnam. In fact, I made up my mind to get back to normal as quickly as possible. Did it always work? No. The physical side effects of my tour of duty sometimes complicated my ability to live a completely "normal" life. But what I couldn't control physically I was determined to conquer mentally. I had left a good life behind when I headed into combat; now I was returning to that same good life. I intended to savor it and never take too much too seriously.

My homecoming itself had a bittersweet edge, as had my departure from Vietnam. My family and friends were glad to see me again, and I was tickled to return to a yard full of hand-lettered "welcome home" signs. But the rest of the world not only didn't care, it seemed almost ashamed for me. I didn't care for that at all, because I felt no shame whatsoever. In fact, I was proud of my service to my country, proud that I had fought the good fight and lived to tell the tale. Problem was, nobody much wanted to hear it.

I returned from Vietnam bubbling over with stories from my 366 days in-country. It had been a year of excitement, fear, comedy, and tragedy. I wanted to share my incredible journey. But, by and large, America just wanted me to shut up and blend in.

I sensed a creeping exhaustion with all things Vietnam-related. For more than a decade, Americans had been getting their daily dose of war—and growing ever more polarized in the process. The media had jumped eagerly into the fray, painting lurid portraits of battle-scarred, emotionally unstable veterans who experienced horrific flashbacks, prompting them to rob liquor stores and kill people. No wonder nobody wanted to hear my stories; they were probably afraid I'd yank out a machete and whittle off a few body parts, theirs or mine!

If you polled every Vietnam vet in America, you'd probably hear a similar lament. It's one of those things that unites us, gives us empathy for one another, regardless of which branch of the armed forces we served or what point in the lengthy Vietnam conflict we did our tour.

But I've always found the efforts to sweep us under the rug as troubling as they are understandable. The majority of us went to Southeast Asia, did our time, and came back to meaningful, productive lives. Like those who served in conflicts before and after Vietnam, we left the United States apprehensive and uncertain yet proud and honored to serve the cause of freedom. But there were no parades for Vietnam vets, no heartfelt gestures of "welcome home" from a grateful nation.

Over time, we found ourselves essentially conditioned to minimize our service in Southeast Asia or, in my case at least, to talk only about those aspects that people could handle—the funny stuff. And there was plenty of funny stuff. But, like all experiences in life, my tour of duty was a blend of good and bad that acquired more shape and definition with the passage of time. A few years back, while I was having breakfast at Sam and Ethel's, a little diner in my hometown, I happened to overhear a couple of guys I'd gone to high school with discussing their football glory days. I eavesdropped for a bit—first in amusement, then with growing irritation—as the ex-jocks traded tales of gridiron bravery, liberally peppered with near-religious fervor and combat analogies.

"Man, I remember that championship game between Tipp and West Milton. We were so outmanned, it wasn't funny! I got the ball and looked down the middle and nearly shit myself," one of the jocks recalled, speaking a little louder than his normal conversational tone. "There was no way I was gonna make it through in one piece. Those guys were massive, and just waiting to kill me. This was going to take some real strategy on my part, and a whole lot of 'nads!"

I laid down my newspaper and stared in the direction of my schoolmate. I wanted desperately to say something, to ask a pointed question or two, but I bit my tongue. I've been told that I invite—even savor—confrontation. I don't really see it that way; I just don't back down from a fight, and I have a soft spot in my heart for lost causes and people who can't defend themselves. Although I didn't begrudge these guys their glory days, something inside me resented anyone comparing a sports event to a life and death struggle.

It's a frigging football game, guys. If you lose, you go home, soak your leg or your arm and start all over again. Try rolling in on a target with guys on the ground who are armed to the teeth and throwing every ounce of fire-power right at your young ass. Try leading a platoon through a jungle, knowing that there's a VC behind every tree and a booby trap every twenty yards. Pardon me if I don't stand and applaud you and your pigskin.

I was right to keep my thoughts to myself. If I'd "gone off" on them, they'd probably have shook their heads and said, "Poor Mike. He's a Vietnam vet, you know." It was a lose-lose situation, at least at that time and in that place. But the whole episode grated on my sense of balance and fair play, and I filed it away in my mind for future reference. In fact, I recalled it yet again when former Arizona Cardinal Pat Tillman was killed serving his country in Afghanistan. The ex-safety had given up everything—fame, money and comfort—to protect and defend our nation as an Army ranger. It was one of the very few times I found it wholly acceptable to use the words "football" and "hero" in the same sentence.

As the years slipped by after Vietnam, my life continued its forward momentum. Karen and I had two beautiful, smart, and well-adjusted daughters, Lori and Katie. My Air Force career accelerated, thanks to a bit of Jacksonian weaseling—and a little help from my old ALO, by then Lt. Col. Dale Ullrich, who got me out of SAC after only two and half years! I earned my master's degree in business administration, and, in 1992—after retiring from the Air Force as a lieutenant colonel—I accepted a position as executive director of the National Aviation Hall of Fame (NAHF), located in Dayton, Ohio.

It has been a dream job for me—full of challenge and excitement, endlessly frustrating yet always fulfilling. Through my position at the

NAHF, I have met some of America's most accomplished military and civilian pilots. In fact, I vividly recall a phone conversation that occurred during my first month on the job.

"Hi, Mike, this is Al. Hey, I'd like to talk to you about a couple of possibilities for this year's enshrinement ceremony."

Al? I searched my memory banks and tried to recall anyone I knew who was named Al. I drew a blank.

I shrugged and managed to fake it. It wasn't until about halfway through the conversation that I realized I was chatting with Alan Shepard—the first American in space, the first guy to play golf on the moon. Wow.

In the ensuing years, I have been proud to get to know men such as Neil Armstrong, Joe Kittinger, Frank Borman, Joe Engle, Robin Olds, Gene Cernan, Scott Crossfield, Jim Lovell, and Wally Schirra. I consider these men friends, and I remain incredulous at the twists of fate that brought me to this place.

But that was, and is, my life: charmed, at least by my measurements—always interesting, always unpredictable. I'd managed to see some of the worst that life had to offer, yet I could still look at this world overall as a pretty good place to be.

It's been a great ride so far, and I expect it will only get better. I've tried to do good work, have a lot of fun, and manage to cram in a few adventures along the way. Well, maybe more than a few. But that's another story. . . .

COAUTHOR'S NOTE

IN PREPARING and editing this book, Mike consistently resisted my efforts to paint him as a war hero or anything other than a regular guy who did the best he could with the hand he was dealt. In truth, he was—and is—so much more. He earned not only a Purple Heart during his tour in Vietnam (awarded to him belatedly in 1992) but also a Distinguished Flying Cross, and an Air Medal with eight Oak Leaf Clusters, in addition to several medals bestowed on him by the grateful South Vietnamese.

Had Mike not been stationed with the 101st Airborne, had he served his entire tour at an Air Force base with the requisite awards and decorations officer, he would certainly have received more medals and commendations. But then, as now, he simply wasn't concerned with recognition and rewards; he just wanted to do a good job and get home in one piece.

He managed to do the former; the latter was more problematic.

In 2000, Lieutenant Colonel Mike Jackson, USAF (Ret.), was declared 100 percent disabled by the Veterans Administration based on his combat injuries and the related complications that have developed over the years. What impact did that designation have on Colonel Jackson's enthusiasm and boundless energy? Absolutely none.

In 2003, Mike was the recipient of the Ohio Museums Association's Distinguished Museum Professional of the Year Award. The award paid tribute to Mike's abiding commitment to the National Aviation Hall of Fame throughout the twelve years he served as the facility's executive director. The letter nominating him for the honor noted that the efforts to build the organization's permanent facility, to create a dramatic array of exhibits and interactives, and to promote America's air and space pioneers had been successfully executed through his enduring energy and optimism, with no concessions to his pain or discomfort.

As one who worked with him for five of those twelve years, I learned the subtle signals that indicated an increase in his pain level—his jaw clenching a little tighter than normal, one pupil dilated slightly more than the other, his hand shaking as he stirred his coffee or held a pencil. Occasionally, in the midst of a meeting, I would notice him twisting his neck or running his hand across his shoulder. But his pain is not something he ever announces or discusses in detail, and I have never heard him complain. Ever.

Mike Jackson would be the first to admit that he has flaws, but he would argue that they are as much a part of who he is as are his strengths. He encourages people to celebrate their assets and their liabilities in equal portions because no human being is fully formed without both.

Mike is an entertainer at heart. He likes to leave people laughing and, if at all possible, scratching their heads slightly. He has the soul of an imp and a twinkle in his eye that captivates all but the most stubbornly sullen curmudgeon. There is nothing about him that screams "Vietnam veteran," at least not as the media popularly portrays such individuals. His pride in having served the United States Air Force for twenty-three years is tangible. His determination never to be defined by his combat experiences is endearing.

Did Vietnam change Mike? Certainly—and he would have it no other way. For in Mike Jackson's world, if you don't learn and grow from your experiences, you are simply wasting time and taking up space.

I signed on to this book project because of my love for the military, my gratitude to and abiding respect for veterans, and my simple desire to hear every story that Mike Jackson had to tell. I heard a lot of them—many more, in fact, than made it into this book, each consistent in its unique blend of humor and humanity.

Over the course of writing this book, Mike has become a dear friend, an inspiration, and a constant source of laughter and joy. I have had no greater honor in my life than the opportunity to share his story, one that is as motivational as it is simple, one that needs to be told. Thanks, Mike, and welcome home.

ACKNOWLEDGMENTS

Arthur C. Evans, Ph.D., Col., USAF (Ret.) | Bilk 21, Covey 03
Ed O'Connor, Lt. Col., USAF (Ret.) | Bilk 15, Bilk 25
Bob Gilday | Bilk 16

*(Thank you Art, Ed, and Bob for continuity
checks and proofreading.)*

Fred Barlow | Bilk 29
Lynn Damron, Lt. Col., USAF (Ret.) | Bilk 17
Pete Dunn | Lover 23
Clyde Elmgren, Lt. Col., USAF (Ret.) | Bilk 13
Kraig Lofquist | Snoopy 12
Tom McGrath, Lt. Col., USAF (Ret.) | Covey 247, Mike 88
David Napoli, Col., USAF (Ret.) | Covey 02
Bill Orellana, Col., USAF (Ret.) | UPT Class 70-05
Tom O'Neill, Col., USAF (Ret.) | Sundog 27
Dale Ullrich, Col., USAF (Ret.) | Trail 01, Bilk 01 and 10

Karen Jackson, whose tour of duty was tougher than mine
and who saved the letters that confirmed a timeline
Mikey Engel, whose patience and enthusiasm know no
limits
Lori and Katie Jackson, who are my greatest gifts
Ed and Winnie Jackson, who provided the tools for
survival and success
Roy and Barbara Dixon, who proofread and discussed
Debbie Jackson Becher, for her encouragement and
conviction
Joe Catey, for advice, friendship, and laughter
Chris Perkins, for believing
Paul Cotter, former Loach combat pilot, our resident
helicopter expert
Mitch Carley, for his artistic talent
Dan Patterson, for his photographic skills
Our editors, Richard Kane, Bob Kane and Barbara
Feller-Roth, for wisdom and guidance
Tom Rench, for supplying an O-2 for historical accuracy
and a great flight
Donald K. "Deke" Slayton, for posthumous life lessons in
tenacity, excellence, and never admitting defeat
Howard Benedict, for encouragement, motivation, and
Moonshots
The gang at Bob Evans restaurant, for an office away from
the office

To *all* our friends and acquaintances who offered input, followed
our progress, and provided support and encouragement, we thank you.
We have worked hard to be certain there are no factual errors contained
herein, but if there are, they are ours and ours alone.

GLOSSARY

A-4—Skyhawk, single-engine jet attack bomber flown by Navy and Marines off carriers in the South China Sea.

aileron—moveable surface on an aircraft wing that controls roll.

AK-47—standard NVA-issue 7.62-millimeter automatic rifle also used by the Viet Cong, Pathet Lao, Khmer Rouge, and the NVA.

AO—area of operation, the place where military operations are conducted pursuant to an assigned mission.

AR-15—version of the M-16 with a collapsible stock and shortened barrel.

arc light mission—code name for a high-altitude bombing raid conducted by B-52s.

ARVN—Army of the Republic of Vietnam.

A Shau Valley—25-mile-long valley in Thua Thien province near Laos; key entry point for the Ho Chi Minh trail.

B-52—eight-engine air force bomber whose large size and wingspan enabled it to drop enormous bomb loads from altitudes well above 30,000 feet.

BDA—bomb damage assessment, a review and report of the damage and casualties caused by a bombing mission.

Bilk—call sign of FACs assigned to support the 101st Airborne Division at Camp Eagle, Camp Evans, and Hue Phu Bai.

BOQ—bachelor officers' quarters, living area for officers not accompanied by their spouses.

BUFF—crude nickname for B-52, "Big Ugly Fat F—-er."

call sign—tactical code name of a person or unit, usually containing a word and numbers—for example, Bilk 12.

Cambodia—Southeast Asian country lying west of South Vietnam, east of Thailand, and south of Laos.

Cam Ranh Bay—seaport city built by U.S. forces and opened in 1965, located 200 miles north of Saigon in Khanh Hoa province.

Charlie—slang term for enemy soldiers, derived from the term Viet Cong and referred to as VC or, phonetically, Victor Charlie.

chopper—generic term for any type of helicopter.

claymore mine—antipersonnel mine that shoots a fan-shaped spray of fragments when activated.

close air support—air strikes against the enemy in which friendly forces are close by, thus requiring extreme precision.

Covey—Call sign for O-2 and OV-10 FACs stationed in Da Nang and Pleiku.

Da Nang—port city in South Vietnam and capital of Quang Nam province; located in I Corps.

delayed enlistment program—plan that permitted someone to join a particular branch of the military while not going on active duty until weeks or months later.

DEROS—date eligible to return from overseas, expected date when military personnel would complete their tour of duty and return home.

dink—derogatory nickname used by American troops for a Vietnamese.

Distinguished Flying Cross—medal awarded for extraordinary achievement while participating in aerial flight.

DMZ—demilitarized zone, 10-kilometer-wide buffer zone between North and South Vietnam from which both sides agreed to withhold military forces.

dustoff—radio call sign for medevac helicopter.

E&E—escape and evasion, fleeing the enemy on the ground, usually following parachuting into hostile territory.

Easter Offensive—also known as the 1972 Spring Offensive, Spring Invasion or Easter Invasion, a massive three-pronged North Vietnamese assault that poured across the demilitarized zone to the north and through Laos on the west with more than 120,000 men, artillery, and armor.

elevator—moveable control surface on an aircraft's horizontal stabilizer that adjusts the pitch of the plane.

F-4—also known as a Phantom II, a twin-engine jet fighter used by the U.S. Air Force, Navy, and Marines during the Vietnam War.

1505s—short-sleeved tan uniform worn by the U.S. Air Force during the Vietnam era.

FAC—forward air controller, pronounced "fak."

FEBA—forward edge of the battle area, where forward elements of two opposing forces engage in direct combat.

firebase—artillery firing position usually secured by an infantry unit.

FNG—f—-ing new guy, slang for a new arrival in-country.

FOL—forward operating location.

free fire zone—area under enemy control where no friendly personnel are located; hence, anything or anyone is fair game for bombing and/or strafing.

friendly fire incident—casualties inadvertently caused by friendly forces.

Gunfighter—call sign for F-4 Phantoms of the 366th Tactical Fighter Wing at Da Nang Air Base.

Hanoi—capital of North Vietnam.

high drag ordnance—parachute-like device on a bomb that slows its forward speed, allowing fighters to release closer to the ground for more accuracy and ensuring that the bomb will go off behind, not under, the delivery aircraft.

Ho Chi Minh—founder of the Vietnamese Communist Party and first president of the Democratic Republic of Vietnam.

Ho Chi Minh trail—North Vietnamese supply route into South Vietnam via Laos and Cambodia. The trail consisted of a winding network of paths difficult to see from the air.

hooch—dwelling in Vietnam, especially a crude wooden huts where military personnel typically lived.

hooch maid—Vietnamese woman paid to clean a hooch and do household chores such as laundry.

howitzer—cannon that combines characteristics of guns and mortars; capable of delivering projectiles with medium velocities and either low or high trajectories.

Hue—Vietnam's third-largest city, located 45 miles south of the demilitarized zone and just north of Phu Bai, the location of a joint American/Vietnamese Air Force air base. Often referred to as Hue Phu Bai.

Huey—generic name for Bell UH-1 Iroquois helicopter.

I Corps—northernmost of four military regions in South Vietnam, adjacent to North Vietnam; pronounced "eye corps."

IFR—instrument flights rules, the flight procedures necessary when weather is poor or visibility is low; flying by reference to aircraft instruments.

in-country—military reference to anything or anyone within the borders of Vietnam.

intervalometer—device in an AT-33 that selects ordnance to be used and the rate or intervals at which it is dropped.

jinking—maneuvering an aircraft erratically so movement is unpredictable, making the aircraft more difficult to hit with ground fire or missiles.

KBA—killed by air, designation for enemy personnel killed during an air strike.

Lackland AFB—U.S. Air Force base on the west side of San Antonio, Texas, used for all basic and OTS training during the Vietnam era.

Laos—mountainous country west of Vietnam.

Laredo AFB—U.S. Air Force base on the Mexican border near Laredo, Texas, used for undergraduate pilot training.

Laughlin AFB—U.S. Air Force base near the Mexican border, near Del Rio, Texas, used for undergraduate pilot training.

lead—commander of an airborne formation.

LOH—light observation helicopter (pronounced "Loach"). The LOH OH-6 was used for scouting and surveillance.

Lurps—freeze-dried food items named for long-range reconnaissance patrols (LRRPs); easily carried and consumed by patrols traveling on lengthy intelligence-gathering missions in enemy territory.

M-16—5.56-millimeter automatic rifle used by the American infantry beginning in 1967.

MARS—Military Amateur Radio Service, a network of volunteer ham radio operators in the United States and around the world that relayed two-way radiotelephone calls internationally and, during the Vietnam War, to and from the war zone.

mike-mike—spoken reference to millimeters.

Mk-82—Mark 82, a 500-pound bomb.

MPC—military payment certificate, scrip provided to American military personnel in Vietnam to be used in place of U.S. currency, to prevent American dollars from being sold on the South Vietnamese black market.

nape—napalm, jellied gasoline that burns at about 2,000 degrees Fahrenheit and was dropped in canisters as a bomb to burn and asphyxiate enemy personnel and defoliate terrain.

NVA—North Vietnamese Army.

O-1—early single-engine FAC aircraft, nicknamed Birddog.

O-2A—alias sky pig, Oscar Deuce, Oscar Duck, Suck and Blow, the flying speed brake, and the subsonic savior of Southeast Asia; a second-generation FAC aircraft, a militarized Cessna 337 Skymaster, not as basic as the early O-1 Birddog but cruder than the OV-10 Bronco, which offered genuine offensive capabilities.

O-2B—"Bullshit bomber," O-2 used for propaganda purposes rather than air strikes.

OTS—Officer Training School, 12-week program to train future U.S. Air Force officers.

OV-10 Bronco—twin-engine observation and light-attack aircraft used by forward air controllers in the U.S. Air Force.

pink team—hunter-killer team usually made up of a LOH (Loach), two gunships, and a command and control helicopter.

POW—prisoner of war, someone captured and held by the enemy in a combat situation.

Purple Heart—medal awarded to American military personnel wounded or killed in combat.

Quang Tri—Army of the Republic of Vietnam base north of Hue near the demilitarized zone.

relief tube—rubber hose and funnel device installed in some aircraft to allow the pilot to urinate in flight.

REMF—rear echelon mother f—-er (pronounced "remph"), derogatory term for military personnel who stayed as far from the action as possible, usually while simultaneously issuing orders that complicated and sometimes endangered the lives of those nearest the front.

Rocket City—nickname for Da Nang, a popular target for enemy rocket attacks.

ROEs—rules of engagement, the "Hoyle" of combat, which laid down territorial limits on U.S. military action and provided an array of complex and ever-changing restrictions on the conduct of air and surface battles.

SAC—Strategic Air Command, U.S. Air Force major air command that oversaw strategic bombers, tanker/refueling operations, strategic reconnaissance, and intercontinental ballistic missiles.

Saigon—capital of South Vietnam.

SAM—Soviet-built SA-2 surface-to-air missile.

sapper—soldier trained in infiltration and demolition.

SEA—Southeast Asia.

shit burner—Vietnamese base worker hired to burn tubs of bodily waste from outhouses/latrines.

short-round incident—also called friendly fire incident, occurring when U.S. artillery or bombs missed their mark (fell short) and injured or killed friendly troops.

SIE—self-initiated elimination, procedure to quit any U.S. Air Force training program.

snake school—nickname for U.S. Air Force Jungle Survival School at Clark Air Base, Philippines.

Strela—SA-7, Russian-supplied portable shoulder-fired, heat-seeking surface-to-air missile.

T-37—twin-engine turbojet trainer; nicknamed Tweet for its loud, high-pitched engine.

T-38—supersonic twin-engine jet trainer used in the final phase of undergraduate pilot training; nicknamed Talon.

T-41—military version of a Cessna 172; nicknamed "the attrition machine."

TAC—Tactical Air Command, U.S. Air Force major air command that oversaw tactical fighters, fighter-bombers and tactical reconnaissance.

tallyho—radio call indicating you have sighted something that has just been described, such as a ground target or another aircraft.

Tan Son Nhut—major U.S. headquarters and military facility near Saigon.

TASG—Tactical Air Support Group, which oversaw Tactical Air Support Squadrons.

TASS—Tactical Air Support Squadron, assigned to one of the four corps in Vietnam and Thailand to provide direct air support of combat operations. The 20th TASS supported I Corps.

TDY—temporary duty, a temporary assignment that could last for days or months.

Tet—lunar New Year, one of the most important holidays in Vietnam, marked by parties, fireworks, and decorations.

Tet Offensive—surprise attack by North Vietnamese troops on the south during the Tet holiday in 1968.

TOC—Tactical Operations Center, which coordinated air-ground operations.

TOT—time on target.

tracer—round of ammunition chemically treated to glow or give off smoke so its path can be followed.

UPT—undergraduate pilot training, 53-week U.S. Air Force pilot training program.

VC—Viet Cong (phonetically "Victor Charlie," hence the nickname Charlie), Communist guerrillas in South Vietnam.

Vietnamization—President Richard Nixon's policy from 1968 to 1973 of training South Vietnamese forces to defend their own country in preparation for American withdrawal.

VNAF—Vietnamese Air Force.

wheel—fighter attack pattern over a target that permitted fighters to approach the target from random headings.

Willie Pete—slang for white phosphorus, the type of smoke rockets used by forward air controllers to mark targets.

winchester—slang for out of bombs or ammunition.